WATER AN

MW01075912

MARCUS DUBOIS KING

(*Editor*)

Water and Conflict in the Middle East

جامعة جورجتاون قطر
GEORGETOWN UNIVERSITY QATAR

Center *for* International *and* Regional Studies

OXFORD
UNIVERSITY PRESS

OXFORD
UNIVERSITY PRESS

Oxford University Press is a department of the
University of Oxford. It furthers the University's objective
of excellence in research, scholarship, and education
by publishing worldwide.

Oxford   New York

Auckland   Cape Town   Dar es Salaam   Hong Kong   Karachi
Kuala Lumpur   Madrid   Melbourne   Mexico City   Nairobi
New Delhi   Shanghai   Taipei   Toronto

With offices in

Argentina   Austria   Brazil   Chile   Czech Republic   France   Greece
Guatemala   Hungary   Italy   Japan   Poland   Portugal   Singapore
South Korea   Switzerland   Thailand   Turkey   Ukraine   Vietnam

Oxford is a registered trade mark of Oxford University Press
in the UK and certain other countries.

Published in the United States of America by
Oxford University Press
198 Madison Avenue, New York, NY 10016

Copyright © DuBois King 2020

Library of Congress Cataloging-in-Publication Data is available
DuBois King.
Water and Conflict in the Middle East.
ISBN: 9780197552636

Printed in India on acid-free paper

CONTENTS

CONTENTS

LIST OF TABLES

LIST OF FIGURES

ACKNOWLEDGMENTS

This volume is the product of two working group meetings held under the auspices of the Center for International and Regional Studies (CIRS) at Georgetown University in Qatar. We would like to thank Mehran Kamrava, Director of CIRS, and Zahra Babar, Associate Director for Research, for initiating and guiding this project. We would like to also thank Suzi Mirgani, Managing Editor at CIRS, whose support and advice in the editing process was essential. We also benefited from the assistance of the staff at CIRS: Elizabeth Wanucha, Jackie Starbird, Misba Bhatti, Sabika Shaban and Maram Al-Qershi. In addition to the authors of the chapters in this volume, we would like to acknowledge the contribution of the Lama El Hatow to this project. Finally, grateful acknowledgment goes also to the Qatar Foundation for its support of research and other scholarly endeavors.

ABOUT THE CONTRIBUTORS

Hussein A. Amery is Professor of International and Middle East Studies at the Colorado School of Mines. He is Director of the Division of Humanities, Arts, and Social Sciences, and served as Associate Provost of the University. Amery's expertise covers water and food security in the Gulf Cooperation Council states, as well as threats to critical infrastructure in the Middle East. He published *Arab Water Security: Threats and Opportunities in the Gulf States* (Cambridge University Press 2015), and coedited Water in the Middle East: A Geography of Peace (Texas University Press 2000). Amery has written papers on themes such as the potential for water war, Islamic perspectives on the natural environment, and conflict resolution along the Tigris and Euphrates rivers. His academic contributions led to his selection as Fellow by the International Water Association. Amery has consulted for US and Canadian government agencies and US engineering firms.

Mark Giordano is Professor of Geography and Cinco Hermanos Chair in Environment and International Affairs in Georgetown University's Walsh School of Foreign Service. His research focuses primarily on the international political dimensions of water, agriculture, and the environment. Giordano is a founding member of Georgetown's India Initiative and serves on the

Institute for the Study of Diplomacy's Working Group on the Global Commons. As part of his interest in using objects such as maps and art in international education, he sits is on the Board of Directors of the Kentler International Drawing Center and the Mokuhanga Project Space. Prior to joining Georgetown in 2013, Giordano held multiple roles at the Sri Lanka based International Water Management Institute and earlier served as a trade economist with the US Department of Agriculture. He has spent a substantial part of his professional life in Asia and Africa and is from the other Washington.

Islam Hassan is a PhD Candidate at the School of Government and International Affairs, Durham University. His research interests include comparative politics and international relations of the Persian Gulf. Hassan is author of "The Ruling Family Hegemony: Inclusion and Exclusion in Qatari Society," in *Sites of Pluralism: Community Politics in the Middle East* (2019); and "The Ruling Family Security: Inclusion and Exclusion in Qatari Society," *HAWWA: Journal of Women of the Middle East and the Islamic World* (2018).

Marcus DuBois King is John O. Rankin Associate Professor of International Affairs and Director of the M.A. Program in International Affairs at George Washington University's Elliott School. His research focuses on environmental security, climate change and security, and water stress in fragile states. Previously, he served as a research analyst at CNA Corporation's Center for Naval Analyses where he directed studies on climate security, resilience, and adaptation for US Government clients. King serves as Senior Fellow at the Center for Climate and Security and the Vice-Chair of the Council on Strategic Risks. His publications include "Dying for a Drink," *American Scientist* (2019); "Water Stress, Instability, and Violent Extremism in Nigeria," in *Water Security and U.S. Foreign Policy* (Routledge 2018); "Water

Security," in *An Introduction to Non-Traditional Security Studies: A Transnational Approach* (Sage 2016); and "The Weaponization of Water in Iraq and Syria," *The Washington Quarterly* (2015). King's current book project focuses on linkages between water stress and violent extremist groups.

Helen Lackner is a visiting fellow at the European Council for Foreign Relations. She is the author of *Yemen in Crisis: Autocracy, Neo-Liberalism and the Disintegration of a State* (Saqi Books 2017). The book was published in the US by Verso in 2019, and an Arabic translation was published in January 2020. Lackner is the editor of the annual *Journal of the British-Yemeni Society*; *Why Yemen Matters: A Society in Transition* (Saqi Books 2014); among other publications, and has contributed chapters to many books on Yemen and the Arabian Peninsula. She is a regular contributor to *Open Democracy, Arab Digest, and Oxford Analytica*. She also speaks on the Yemen crisis in many public events, including in the UK House of Commons.

Nael Shama is an independent political researcher and writer based in Cairo, Egypt. His research focuses on the international relations and comparative politics of the Middle East. Shama is author of *Egyptian Foreign Policy from Mubarak to Morsi: Against the National Interest* (2013), *Egypt before Tahrir: Reflections on Politics, Culture and Society* (2014) and *The Stagnant River: The State, Society and Ikhwan in Egypt* (In Arabic, 2016). He has written papers on foreign policy making in Egypt, civil-military relations in the Middle East, and Islamist politics. Shama's writings have appeared in *Le Monde Diplomatique, Reuters Opinion, Jadaliyya, Al-Ahram, Al-Hayat*, and have been published by POMED, Al-Jazeera, the Atlantic Council, the Middle East Institute, among others.

Signe Stroming is a graduate from Georgetown University's Edmund A. Walsh School of Foreign Service, and a former

ABOUT THE CONTRIBUTORS

Undergraduate Research Fellow at Georgetown's Mortara Center for International Studies. She holds a Bachelor of Science in Science, Technology, and International Affairs, with a concentration in energy and the environment, and she was awarded the Carol J. Lancaster Award for outstanding academic achievement in the International Development Certificate Program and for displaying a commitment to improving the lives of the world's most vulnerable. While a student, Stroming worked with the International Water Management Institute in Gujarat, India; Resources for the Future in Washington, DC; and Georgetown University's Office of Sustainability. Stroming currently works for IDinsight in Delhi, India, monitoring and evaluating international development programs.

Tobias von Lossow is Research Fellow at Clingendael—Netherlands Institute of International Relations. He is also a lecturer at the Freie Universität Berlin. Von Lossow regularly holds guest lectures at other universities and gives diplomatic training courses and briefings for government agencies. His recent publications include: "Nile Conflict: Compensation Rather than Mediation" (SWP, 2020, co-authored with L. Miehe and S. Roll); "The Role of Water in the Syrian and Iraqi Civil Wars" ('MENA's Fertile Crescent in the Time of Dry Geopolitics', ISPI, 2020); "From Risks to Opportunities—Climate Security and Water in the MENA Region" (IEPN, 2019); "More than Infrastructures: Water Challenges in Iraq" (Clingendael & PSI, 2018); "Africa's Sleeping Giant: Regional Integration and Intersectoral Conflicts in the Congo Basin" (SWP, 2017); "The Multiple Crisis: Perspectives on Water Scarcity in the Euphrates and Tigris Basin" (Orient, 2017); "The Rebirth of Water as a Weapon: IS in Syria and Iraq" (*The International Spectator*, 2016); "Gender in Inter-State Water Conflicts" (*Peace Review*, 2015); "Egypt's Nile Water Policy under Sisi" (SWP, 2015, co-authored with S. Roll).

ABOUT THE CONTRIBUTORS

Katalyn Voss is an Adjunct Professor in the School of Foreign Service at Georgetown University. She is a hydrologist who utilizes field-based geochemical/isotopic tools, remote-sensing datasets, and stakeholder engagement to inform water management strategies. Her previous work and research include: water supply and hazard assessments in the Himalayas; water risk mapping for the private sector; and, science-driven diplomacy in the Middle East and California.

Paul A. Williams is a Washington, D.C. area-based academic who has taught International Political Economy at American University's School of International Service and US Government in affiliation with Northern Virginia Community College. His research focuses on energy and water politics as well as American and Turkish foreign policies, with publications including: "Energy and Trans-European Networks-Energy (TEN-E)," in *Europeanization of Turkish Public Policies: A Scorecard* (Routledge 2016); "Climate Change, its Effects, and the Political Economy of Adaptation and Mitigation: Turkey and the Eastern Mediterranean Region," in *Climate Change, Sustainable Development, and Human Security: A Comparative Analysis* (Lexington Books 2013); "Euphrates and Tigris Waters—Turkish-Syrian and Iraqi Relations," in *Water Resource Conflicts and International Security: A Global Perspective* (Lexington Books 2012); and "Turkey's Water Diplomacy: A Theoretical Discussion," in *Turkey's Water Policy: National Frameworks and International Cooperation* (Springer 2011).

INTRODUCTION

NEW POWER DYNAMICS AND HYDROPOLITICS IN THE MIDDLE EAST

Marcus DuBois King

Introduction

Global security challenges surrounding control of water supplies and access to strategic waterways are considerable and will continue to grow in the coming years. Despite this fact, the topic of water and conflict is understudied in political science and international relations. This timely volume on water and conflict in the Middle East addresses an issue that is receiving growing attention in this region in the context of rapid economic, political, social, and environmental transformations.

Water has always been intrinsic to civilization in the Middle East. As Hussein Amery notes in his contribution to this volume, shariʿa, the Arabic word for Islamic law, literally translates as "pathway to a water source." Water scarcity has also long influenced relations between different communities in the Middle East. For instance, Peter Gleick writes, "no region has seen more water-related conflicts than the Middle East, and some of these go back more than 5,000 years to the earliest civilizations in Mesopotamia."[1] Terje Tvedt further emphasizes this notion by studying the historical trends of British colonization of river basins such as the Nile all the way to their headwaters purely for the control of water for cotton production in Egypt and Sudan. Tvedt explains that, if history has shown us anything, it is that colonizers have invaded other states largely for the control of water.[2]

There are profound physical challenges to water supply. The World Resources Institute estimates that by 2040, fourteen of the thirty-three countries likely to be the most water-stressed will be in the Middle East, including nine considered extremely highly stressed: Bahrain, Kuwait, Palestine, Qatar, United Arab Emirates, Israel, Saudi Arabia, Oman, and Lebanon.[3] The Intergovernmental Panel on Climate Change (IPCC) estimates that climate change is likely to put ever-greater pressure on water resources in the Mediterranean and North African region over the next decades.[4] These bleak projections are especially troublesome considering the foundational role that water serves for socioeconomic needs, such as food, energy, sanitation, and industry. The effects of increased consumption, climate change, and agricultural practices, as well as poor water governance, have exacerbated regional concerns.

The following chapters explore water security and conflict in the Middle East from an international and subnational perspective. Evidence has shown that on an international level, between states,[5] cooperation over water resources is more likely than conflict. On a national and sub-national level, however, conflict over water has existed in various regions across the globe.[6] Conflict is rarely, if ever, caused by one factor. The contributors to this volume shed new light on the role that water scarcity and manipulation of water resources play in ongoing internal conflicts, and as an underlying factor driving historical political instability and social stratification. As Mirumachi has elaborated through the TWINS concept, conflict and cooperation are not linear opposites, but in fact co-exist in a dynamic process that is constantly changing over time.[7] Equitable access to scarce water resources is a requirement if Middle Eastern nations are to maintain political stability and sustain healthy populations. Recent scholarship has attributed political unrest in the Middle East and the Arab uprisings of 2011 to environmental resource scarcity and changes in both Syria and Egypt.[8] However, this linkage has been challenged due to lack of evidence to support causation.[9] It is important to clearly understand the linkages between water, conflict, cooperation, and resource scarcity within this region, and hence any claims about causation must be carefully evidenced. It is essential to mitigate marginalization for different communities within many of these states suffering from chronic instability.

The Middle East also features conflicts between nations over allocation of waters in shared rivers systems such as the Tigris and Euphrates. States often place blame for monopolizing water resources at the feet of the upper riparians—those nations that possess upstream water resources—but hydropolitics are often complicated. In chapter three, "Turkish Hydro-Hegemony and the Impact of Dams," Paul Williams builds on the notion of Hydro-Hegemony coined by Mark Zeitoun, which asserts that on transboundary river basins, there is often a dominant power actor, or hegemon, that positively or negatively influences negotiations and water allocations based on the hegemon's upstream, midstream, or downstream position.[10] For example, the ever-shifting state of regional politics and the construction of new dams and other water infrastructure further complicates international hydropolitical relationships, as seen in both the Nile River Basin with the construction of the Grand Ethiopian Renaissance Dam on the Nile River, and on the Euphrates River Basin with the Ilisu Dam. The record shows that changes in the availability of water can either spark conflict or create opportunities for increased cooperation among nations even when other mutual hostilities exist. The dominant argument advanced by influential scholars asserts that water is a highly complex resource that mostly creates cooperative relations,[11] and at times can serve to mend even the most dysfunctional of interstate relationships. On the other hand, many analysts agree that the popular discontent that fueled the Arab Spring in 2011 had some roots in water-driven food insecurity.[12] More research on the topic is needed, but what is certain is that issues related to water resources have greatly influenced political relations in the region.

This Volume

This volume utilizes an analytical framework that proceeds from the assumption that the intrinsic linkages between water and security are upheld by both scholarly and policy-focused work. The authors recognize that there is no conclusive evidence that sharing scarce water resources drives conflict at a significant scale. However, these findings are challenged by an emerging body of evidence presented in this volume and elsewhere, indicating that increased water stress and competition over scarce water resources will create more severe impacts on fragile states and societies in the region and, in turn, may precipitate conflict. The Water, Peace and Security Partnership is one group that explores this relationship.[13] The authors herein examine poor water governance as another factor driving water stress in the Middle East. In some cases, national governments and subnational actors have weaponized water to achieve tactical or political objectives, including the legitimization of authority.[14] This behavior should not be surprising because, as González-Hidalgo explains, "environmental conflicts are essentially social conflicts produced by asymmetrical access and distribution of environmental benefits and costs."[15]

The authors in this volume use a case-study approach to reconceptualize ways that water-related factors can contribute to conflict in the Middle East. The cases are written by experts on various facets of water governance who possess vast experience in the relevant countries. The authors analyze newly emerging trends, recognize rising threats and, in almost all cases, identify the need for urgent actions due to changing power dynamics in the fields of transboundary river basins, groundwater, weaponization of water, hydro-hegemony, and securitization of waterways. Recent wars or political shocks are a common theme woven through the chosen cases, including the Eastern Nile Basin, Iraq, Iraqi Kurdistan, Turkey, and Yemen. Political shocks present new opportunities, as for example in the Eastern Nile River Basin. Here, new regimes have come to power: in Sudan after the overthrow of Omar al-Bashir; in Egypt with the January 2011 Revolution and the ouster of Mubarak; with the independence of South Sudan from Sudan in 2013; and in Ethiopia with the death of Meles Zenawi. In all cases, new leadership and political turbulence has changed the face of discussions and hence the power relations of the actors across this sub-basin. Another example is seen with the government of Iraqi Kurdistan, which has the opportunity to exercise emerging political agency by leveraging water resources. War-torn and fragile states such as Yemen can improve the prospects for political stability through better approaches to water management.

The volume comprises seven chapters in which the authors survey political and hydrological conditions unique to the region, as well as national and subnational complexities related to water.

This information leads to a consideration of how these conditions are changing power dynamics in specific cases, providing the reader with good working knowledge of the water conditions, but also encouraging a reconceptualization of some basic assumptions underlying hydropolitics. Ultimately, the authors demonstrate that these changing dynamics are creating greater urgency for actions to avoid or mitigate conflict.

Hussein A. Amery sets the political stage in chapter two, "Malthus in the Middle East: Scarcity-Induced Water Conflicts." He addresses the politics surrounding the Southeast Anatolian (Güneydoğu Anadolu Projesi or GAP) project in Turkey and the Grand Ethiopian Renaissance Dam (GERD) under construction on the Blue Nile in Ethiopia, and finds them to be illustrative case studies of the potential for a significant deterioration in relations between upstream and downstream riparian states. He argues that risk of conflict between Egypt and Ethiopia over the flow rate of the Nile is at an all-time high. In addition to the reduced flow in the Nile and Tigris rivers due to new dam constructions, the riparian states in question have long histories of tension and distrust over many issues. Amery documents how rapid population growth, infrastructure development, climate change, and geophysical conditions are factors that have adverse cumulative effects on water supplies and water management. These effects are, in turn, creating unprecedented pressure on the demand for freshwater and an increase in competition over water. He concludes that the convergence of these factors points to a likely future of more scarcity-induced conflicts in these river basins.

Similar to Amery's exploration of the water conflicts on the Nile and Euphrates from a power relations perspective, Williams explores Zeitoun's concept of hydro-hegemony on the Euphrates and Tigris river basin with regard to Turkey's geopolitical position on these waters. He asserts that Turkey, situated at the headwaters of the Euphrates and Tigris rivers, is now in a position as the upstream state to achieve full "hydro-hegemony" on these basins. This means physical control over the total flow of water from these river basins, which also cross into Syria and Iraq, where they meet much of the latter countries' water requirements.

Williams' analysis is premised on the realization that the last three main dams of the massive GAP project—all in the Tigris Basin—are going ahead, albeit far behind the original schedule. The controversial Ilisu Dam, begun in 2006, was already nearing completion in 2018. The Silvan Dam, centerpiece of GAP's second-largest irrigation scheme, may be completed at any time, thus bringing Turkey's long march towards completing the entire scheme close to finish, and cementing its role as the regional hydro-hegemon. There is evidence that the Turkish government has used its ability to control water flow to pressure Syria, the downstream nation, to drop its support of the Kurdistan Workers' Party (PKK), a separatist militia. Williams concludes with the interesting argument that Turkey now has the power to exploit its position as a hydro-hegemon to create both positive and negative outcomes for the other riparian states: Syria, Iraq, and the Kurdish enclaves. Turkish motivations are based on evolving regional politics.

Allocation of the Euphrates and Tigris waters has been a source of tension between Iraq and its neighbors for generations. Relationships among the riparian states have been thoroughly examined in the water and conflict literature. A recent development is Iraqi Kurdistan's emergence as a proto-state. The role of Iraqi Kurdistan as a de-facto riparian actor, particularly within the Tigris River system, has received little attention to date. Within its boundaries, Iraqi Kurdistan is blessed with regionally abundant water resources. In chapter four, "A Watershed Moment: Assessing the Hydropolitics of Iraqi Kurdistan," I assert that water stress has now reached a tipping point due to several converging issues. First, water quality is a problem, distinct from the sheer volumetric availability. Second, the needs for potable water for the large number of internally displaced people and other refugees displaced to Iraqi Kurdistan as a result of the regional conflict is another significant factor. Third, there is concern about the future effects of water impounded by the new construction of Turkish and Iranian dams.

The water situation in Iraqi Kurdistan presents both challenges and opportunities. Despite emerging water supply issues and its disadvantaged status as a proto-state, Iraqi Kurdistan is still in a position to use its relative water assets as a coercive tool to support political objectives. Iraqi Kurdistan has access to the waters of the Tigris River before they pass through the rest of Iraq, a situation increasingly viewed as untenable in Baghdad. Iraqi Kurdistan's lack of nationhood status is problematic from an operational perspective, in that it may preclude full participation in water-sharing regimes among the riparian states of the Tigris-Euphrates river system.

If current trends continue, increasing water stress carries internal political risks for the Kurdistan Regional Government (KRG). The KRG must recognize these risks, and use this understanding to develop a comprehensive water strategy. If successful, a comprehensive strategy will guarantee sufficient water for Kurdistan's people while maintaining the ability to use water as political leverage in support of their designs toward autonomy or, more altruistically, to improve the quality of life for *all* Iraqis. If the KRG fails to seize the opportunity of this "watershed moment," water stress will erode food security in this agriculturally reliant region. Iraqi Kurdistan will also become more susceptible to conflicts over water across a spectrum, ranging from localized violence between local water users to the strategic coercive manipulation of water resources by neighboring states. This insecurity is one factor that could preclude future realization of political autonomy.

Academic research on water and conflict in the Middle East and elsewhere is focused on surface waters in shared river basins.

INTRODUCTION

As Abuzeid points out, when looking at transboundary shared resources, it is necessary to explore all the forms of water, including green water (atmospheric water and soil moisture), blue water (surface water), and white water (groundwater).[16] In support of this wider argument, Mark Giordano, Katalyn Voss, and Signe Stroming's chapter, "Groundwater in the Middle East and North Africa: Supply, Use, and Security Implications," focuses instead on the implications of the distribution of groundwater in the Middle East and North Africa. The situation is critical because the region is now highly dependent on groundwater for domestic and agricultural supplies, which has led to overuse and declining water tables in many areas across the region. The chapter presents a comprehensive picture of the location of shared groundwater aquifers that will underlie future transboundary water disputes.

Giordano, Voss, and Stroming not only recognize the domestic political implications of groundwater overuse, but also address the additional challenges created when aquifers, or the rivers that feed them, transcend state boundaries. Having established a foundational understanding of the physical shortage of groundwater resources, the authors probe broader social, political, and economic contexts driving groundwater use across the region. Finally, the authors explore the rapid transformation in the technology used to collect and share groundwater data. While advanced technology provides new data and information for groundwater decision-making, the basic politics behind groundwater governance and management remain problematic. The chapter concludes with an overview of considerations from both within and beyond the water sector toward reducing the negative impacts of continued over-abstraction of groundwater. Increased vigilance in managing the overuse of groundwater will improve regional food security and political stability.

In chapter six, "Revitalization of Community-Based Water Practices in Yemen," Helen Lackner observes that internal and localized conflict may intensify in Yemen. As Wolf and others indicate, water conflicts are less likely when transboundaries are international,[17] and water conflicts may in fact be more prevalent on a national or even sub-national level.[18] In Yemen, conflict over water began several decades before the current civil war. Today, this is one of the most extreme examples of water stress globally and despite the many other prominent facets of the current war, it is attracting attention. Some analysts have claimed that Sana'a will be the first capital city in the world to run out of water, possibly as soon as 2025.[19] Lackner's chapter on water management in Yemen also demonstrates that water is often a casualty of war. The 2016–2017 horrors of the cholera epidemic in Yemen have largely been attributed to improper sanitation and inaccessibility to clean water, and have placed the far-reaching consequences of water scarcity in the midst of conflict on full display.

Lackner notes that the mismanagement of Yemen's water resources was a major contributing factor to the social tensions that exploded in the uprisings of 2011, and marked the descent into civil war since 2015. Millions of Yemeni citizens were contending with consequences of significant water stress, particularly in the agricultural sector, where 90 percent of water is used. Water management policies exacerbated societal cleavages and became a major element in the emergence of acute social differentiation between small groups of beneficiaries who, thanks to their financial ability to access deep aquifers, enriched themselves while the vast majority of Yemenis were impoverished. Ill-conceived water policy on the part of international funding agencies also contributed to the deterioration of conditions. Lackner argues that, given this history, the inequities have been magnified by the ongoing conflict, and war has elevated water scarcity to a heightened critical level.

Yemen's plight should serve as a warning for other nations in the Middle East. In a post-conflict Yemen, a government that is capable of addressing the people's basic needs for water will be necessary. Understanding the complex details of Yemen's water situation is essential to identifying and promoting viable water policies. Other governments should be aware that Yemen's water crisis could cascade into mass environmental migration that could further destabilize the entire region.

Water scarcity sometimes functions as a factor leading to conflict. It can be viewed as a causal mechanism. However, the ways that belligerents control water resources during armed conflict itself is an underexplored and evolving topic in the Middle East. In chapter seven, "Weaponizing Water in the Middle East: 'Lessons Learned' from IS," Tobias von Lossow fills this gap with a presentation of a closed case study of the conflict in Syria and Iraq, arguing that the use of water as a weapon is a newly emergent practice that warrants attention from both scholars and policymakers. Von Lossow defines weaponization of water as a direct abuse of water resources, as an instrument of war during armed conflict, and as a tool to achieve strategic political and/or tactical military goals.[20] The author argues that while weaponization of water is by no means a new phenomenon, it has gained momentum in Syria and Iraq with implications for other Middle East conflicts. The Water, Peace and Security Initiative has been exploring the securitization of water,[21] and how it is being represented in different ways, with potential for military action.[22]

Von Lossow illustrates how the so-called Islamic State (IS) can be seen as a frontrunner in using water as a weapon in Syria and Iraq, since the militia applied it systematically, frequently, and openly. Arguably, the use of water was a key factor for IS to gain legitimacy in its struggle for recognition in the conquered territories and its consolidation of the proclaimed caliphate. In fact, his central argument is that while IS was among the first actors weaponizing water in this case, nearly all of the conflict parties in the region adopted this practice over the course of the conflict. Some of these actions eventually exceeded IS practices in scale and scope. Over the course of the conflict in Syria, the Syrian army and pro-government forces loyal to the regime, Russian forces, the Free Syrian Army, and other rebel groups, all proved at least as rigorous in weaponizing water as IS.

Historically, nation-states are hesitant to deploy the water weapon and tend—at least officially—to shun the practices, in part because weaponizing water is proscribed by international humanitarian law and banned by the 1977 additional protocols to the Geneva Conventions of 1949. On the contrary, the actions of the Syrian army and pro-government forces may have set a new precedent. Universal employment of the water weapon by all parties in this case study has raised broader awareness and fore-grounded it on the agenda of water and security discourses, including in the Middle East.

Finally, Nael Shama and Islam Hassan add a fresh perspective on power dynamics in another conflict-prone corner of the Middle East. Writing in the final chapter, "In Pursuit of Security and Influence: The UAE and the Red Sea," the authors focus on the United Arab Emirates (UAE) and its newly assertive power projection strategy. This strategy employs the waterspace of the Red Sea, including the chokepoints of the Bab al-Mandab, and the Gulf of Aden and its littoral territory—the arid nations of Djibouti, Eritrea, and Somalia.

The architect of this strategy, based on dual geopolitical and economic considerations, is Mohamed bin Zayed, the UAE's de facto ruler since 2014. The economic component of the strategy consists of the acquisition of operational and management rights over ports and economic zones along the Red Sea, one of the most important global shipping lanes.

Given that states and non-state actors have vied for control over the Red Sea waterspace, the UAE has established naval and military bases in and around the Red Sea to protect its geopolitical and economic interests in the region. This insightful chapter adds to the literature on international relations and the Middle East in two distinct ways. First, it addresses understudied theoretical questions concerning foreign policy change in small states. Second, by exploring the nature and motivations of Emirati activism in the Red Sea, the chapter addresses the unexplored trend of securitizing waterspace and shipping lanes in the Middle East.

Collectively, the chapters of this volume present compelling evidence that alters our conceptualization of physical and political realities in the Middle East. The regional power structure, always in flux, is changing significantly today. Considering this, the authors offer critical insights into the future of water allocation, often in the context of growing water inequalities both between nations and within the nations themselves. These inequalities were a critical factor in the incitement of wide-scale unrest across the region, including the Arab Spring uprisings of 2011[23] and the Syrian civil war. Generally, the authors' arguments conclude that, without decisive international agreements over water sharing, dam construction, and improvements in national water governance policy, the world will face a future of dangerous growth in inequalities across the Middle East, and their attendant consequences in the form of more conflict.

2

MALTHUS IN THE MIDDLE EAST

SCARCITY-INDUCED WATER CONFLICTS

Hussein A. Amery

Introduction

Water is so vital to life that sometimes it is described as being life-giving or even life itself, which explains why water has always been narrated in intense terms. In many cultures, certain waters are believed to be holy or to possess healing qualities. *Shari'a*, the Arabic word for Islamic law, means "pathway to a water source," suggesting that, in a desert environment, the path to water was a metaphor for the path to life. Water is so imperative that its scarcity has long influenced relations between different communities in the Middle East. For instance, Peter Gleick writes that, "no region has seen more water-related conflicts than the Middle East, and some of these go back more than 5,000 years to the earliest civilizations in Mesopotamia."[1]

In the last four decades, the narrative of "water war" has been pervasive. While only a small fraction of conflicts over water deteriorate into outright violent confrontations, people are inclined to believe that it is far more prevalent; the media often obliges this perception. This popular perception may relate to primordial and political facts. Water is critical to human survival, fixed in volume, and is without substitute. In addition, the growing demand for water is fueling competition between different users and interests, which increases political and social volatility during periods of drought. Competition over scarce resources happens between urban and rural residents, between upstream and downstream users, and between stakeholders from different sectors of the economy. Such competitions sometimes lead to conflicts that are often resolved by mediation or through courts of law; a small minority of them spiral into violent confrontations.

Because freshwater is important for economic development, and for a certain quality of life, countries often view it through a political prism, one that can either enhance or weaken the power of a riparian state. For countries that are politically unstable or have an economy that is heavily dependent on the agricultural sector, like Syria, Sudan, and Yemen, water is often associated with national security. Conflict between stakeholders over water quality or quantity is affected by economic policy, political considerations, and geo-climatic conditions.[2] Furthermore, climate change, the growing water demands of upstream states, as well as the cumulative effects of mismanagement of water and land resources contribute to conflict between riparian states,[3] or to civil war as in the case of Syria.[4] The likely impacts of climate change on the farming systems of the Middle East and North Africa (MENA) are captured in Table 1.

Table 2.1: Climate change impacts on farming systems of the Arab region

Farming system	Exposure: What climate change-related events will occur	Sensitivity: Likely impacts on farming systems
Irrigated	– Increased temperatures – Reduced supply of surface irrigation water – Dwindling groundwater recharge – Loss of production in low-lying coastal areas	– More water stress – Increased demand for irrigation and water transfer – Reduced yields when temperatures are too high – More difficulty in agricultural planning – Salinization due to reduced leaching – Reduction in cropping intensity
Highland mixed	– Increase in aridity – Greater risk of drought – Possible lengthening of the growing period – Reduced supply of irrigation water	– Reduction in yields – Reduction in cropping intensity – Increased demand for irrigation
Rainfed mixed	– Increase aridity – Greater risk of drought – Reduced supply of irrigation water – Loss of production in low-lying coastal areas	– Reduction in yields – Reduction in cropping intensity – Increased demand for irrigation – More difficulty in agricultural planning
Dryland mixed	– Increase in aridity – Greater risk of drought – Reduced supply of irrigation water	– System very vulnerable to declining rainfall; some lands may revert to rangeland – Increased demand for irrigation
Pastoral	– Increase in aridity – Greater risk of drought – Reduced water for livestock and fodder	– A very vulnerable system, where desertification may reduce carrying capacity significantly – Increase in nonfarm activities, exit from farming, migration

Source: World Bank, "Adaptation to a Changing Climate in the Arab Countries," (2013), p. 170.

WATER AND CONFLICT IN THE MIDDLE EAST

Most countries in the Middle East fail to treat water as an economic resource, and the state often subsidizes water, especially for irrigation. Market economics teaches that under conditions of scarcity, when supply declines, prices rise. This is not the case in the Middle East. Governments subsidize utilities and other services in order to earn the acquiescence of the population, which has been the case in the oil- and gas-rich Gulf states. However, the precipitous drop in oil prices in 2014 forced Gulf governments to gradually lift subsidies on water supply.

Conceptually, the Malthusian perspective views human consumption as overshooting available resources, creating conditions of scarcity that will induce economic decline and social and political instability. Conflict over water is more likely in countries that do not have strong national institutions or international agreements to resolve disputes between riparian states. In these cases, countries resort to the unilateral development of water resources, regardless of its impacts on other riparians. Countries with well-established institutions and strong economies will be better situated to adapt to resource scarcity, but countries that are less endowed will suffer the adverse consequences of this new reality.[5] Alternative conceptualizations, however, foresee optimistic outcomes. This "cornucopian" perspective posits that technological innovations will help human society overcome resource shortages. It also views water through an economic lens in which market mechanisms and economic tools will help society find policy fixes for shortages (Table 2).[6]

This study reviews water management along the Tigris and Euphrates rivers systems, and along the Nile River. It argues that prevailing geophysical scarcities have been aggravated by poor water governance. This and the rising demand for water, are pushing riparian states towards conflict. This appears to support the Malthusian perspective of scarcity-induced conflict.

MALTHUS IN THE MIDDLE EAST

Water and Food as Weapons

The vast majority of freshwater used by people goes to the production of food, with beef being the most water intensive commodity. Globally, 70 percent of the world's water is used for farming; this share could reach 90 percent in some arid regions like the Sahara and the Middle East and North Africa. In times of war and instability, some countries manipulate access to water and food supply in order to advance their political or military goals. Food has been and continues to be used as a weapon of warfare,[7] as demonstrated by the United States of America, Israel, and Russia in recent history.[8]

In the current war on Yemen, while residents were facing deep food insecurities, the Saudi-led armed forces targeted agricultural infrastructure destroying "cattle farms, food factories, water wells and marketplaces, along with the ports, airports, roads and bridges on which effective supplies of food aid depend."[9] Furthermore, airstrikes by Saudi-led coalition forces against Houthi rebels damaged the preserved northern conduit of the ancient Great Marib Dam, which was first built in 1700 BC.[10] On the other hand, some argue that Houthi rebels in Yemen have destroyed seaports and other infrastructures, which have aggravated food insecurity.[11]

Syrian government forces similarly used water and food as weapons to subdue its own rebellious population. A UN independent International Commission of Inquiry reported that government forces "purposely targeted" a spring in Wadi Barada valley near Damascus in December 2016, which halted water supply for 5.5 million people living in the area.[12] A survivor of the Assad government's gas attack in 2013 wrote about how the regime laid siege to a suburb of Damascus, hoping to starve its residents into submission. Consequently, some people were forced into eating weeds, tree leaves, and food remains in heaps

Table 2.2: Theoretical Approaches to Conflict Natural Resources

Approach	Contours of Theory	Main ideas
Malthusian Theory	Rising resource consumption due to population growth will ultimately exceed the availability of natural resources creating adverse effects like war, disease, and famine	– Population growth – Natural resource scarcity – Socio-political breakdown
Cornucopian (Classical Theory, Adam Smith)	A system based on supply and demand will effectively address resource scarcity. Market mechanism deters over-consumption and spurs technological developments and substitutions. This sustains economic growth minimizing conflict over resources	– Economic development – Trade – Innovation
Scarcity-induced Conflict (Neo-Malthusian, T. Homer-Dixon)	Natural resource scarcity can cause conflict due to economic slowdown, weakening of political authority, human migration, and overall socio-political collapse	– Scarcity of natural resources – Socio-economic breakdown – Conflict more likely

Source: Adapted from Thomas Bernauer, Tobias Bohmelt, and Vally Koubi, "Environmental Changes and Violent Conflict," *Environmental Research Letters 7*, no. 1 (2012): 015601; Alex de Sherbinin et al., "Population and Environment," *Annual Review of Environment and Resources* 32 (2007): 345–73.

of garbage.[13] These political and military uses of natural resources in the Middle East occur despite the fact that Islamic law forbids the withholding of water or food from humans or domestic animals.[14]

Conflict over the Tigris and Euphrates Rivers

In 1975, the Turkish government initiated a long-term, multi-phased scheme to develop the water resources of the Tigris and Euphrates rivers, resulting in the Southeast Anatolia Project (GAP). The vision was to build twenty-two dams and nineteen hydropower plants across the two rivers. When completed, GAP will reduce the flow of water into Iraq by about 80 percent and into Syria by 40 percent. When Syria began building its Tabqa Dam on the Euphrates, relations with Iraq deteriorated and almost resulted in open warfare. While Syria and Iraq have built dams on these rivers, the dams that Turkey built tend to be much larger in size and have greater storage capacity.

For decades, the downstream states of Syria and Iraq have been agonizing as a result of the multi-dam projects in upstream Turkey. In 1990, Turkey began filling its massive Atatürk Dam, with its 27 billion cubic meter capacity, reducing the water flow of the mighty Euphrates down to a trickle for a period of one month. More recently, and despite strong objections by Iraq, Turkey completed the construction of the Ilisu Dam on the Tigris River in 2019, with a storage capacity of 11 billion cubic meters. Given that the flow of the Tigris is 15 billion cubic meters and that the normal operating capacity of the reservoir is 7.46 billion cubic meters, the filling of the reservoir will have devastating effects on riparians downstream. The Iraqi Minister of Water Resources, Hasan al-Janabi, quoted the Turkish Foreign Minister Mevlüt Çavuşoğlu as saying: "Turkey is committed to postponing the filling of the Ilisu Dam and that the Turkish president is committed [to not harming] Iraq."[15] It has been estimated that the Ilisu Dam could desiccate and shrivel 670,000 hectares of arable land inside Iraq.[16] The many dams on the Euphrates and Tigris Rivers have reduced flow and adversely affected water quality downstream. For example, in the Euphrates river, the total dissolved salts (TDS) went from 457 parts per million (ppm) in the 1980s to 1200 ppm in 1999,[17] which is significantly over the safe, acceptable 500 ppm limit defined by the World Health Organization. According to a 2018 United Nations Environment Programme report, what aggravates Iraq's water security further is that 70 percent of its freshwater originates outside of its borders. Moreover, this war-torn country is unable to prevent household and toxic waste generated by oil refineries, hospitals, and urban centers from being discharged directly into the Tigris.[18] For instance, between 2016 and 2017, the UN estimates that up to two million barrels of oil were either burned or spilled, and it is feared that much of the oil may have reached local aquifers and the nearby Tigris River.[19]

Iraq blames Turkey's excessive control measures over the Tigris and Euphrates rivers for the drought affecting it, which is creating thousands of "water refugees" annually, primarily from rural areas that are heavily dependent on irrigated agriculture. An Iranian paper, the *Financial Tribune*, reported that "despite evidence to the contrary," the Turkish Ambassador in Tehran, Reza Hakan Tekin, has denied charges that excessive damming has severely reduced water flow to neighboring Iraq and Syria. The ambassador also said that his government "would never give up sovereignty over its water."[20] This perspective, aligning with the principle of absolute territorial sovereignty, posits that a riparian state may use water flowing through its territory regardless of the adverse effects it may have on other states; a position that is in conflict with the principles of international law.[21]

After decades of stormy affairs, Syria and Turkey normalized their relations from the late 1990s until 2011 when the war in

Syria erupted. During this period of détente, Syria and Turkey nurtured a relationship of friendship and cooperation, and Syria's policies towards Turkey became more pragmatic. Syria appeared to acknowledge Turkey as a regional power due to the size of its economy and military, and also due to its hydro-hegemonic status as an upstream state on the Tigris and Euphrates rivers. Furthermore, Syria cannot afford to be surrounded by enemies in the south (Israel) and the north (Turkey). Moreover, Syria is mindful that the United States has effectively been a neighboring power since it invaded Iraq in 2003.

In March 2010, Turkey and Syria signed fifty-one protocols on trade, development, and cultural exchanges, "shelving for now differences over their long-standing disputes over Hatay and sharing the Euphrates and Tigris rivers."[22] Historically, Syria has always laid claim to the province of Alexandretta, which Turkey calls Hatay. This was a colonial era territorial gift that France handed to Turkey a century ago, and remains a sore point in relations between the two countries. Despite these frictions, in February 2011, Turkey and Syria initiated construction of the "Friendship Dam" on the Assi (Orontes) River in the province of Hatay. The dam is located on the border between Al Allani village in northern Syria and the Turkish village of Ziyaret. It is estimated to cost $28.5 million, has a storage capacity of 115m cubic meters, and is designed to irrigate 13,000 hectares and to generate 16 million kilowatt hours of electricity annually.

Intrinsic Advantage of Upstream States

Prior to the Syrian civil war, Turkey had a "zero problems with neighboring states" policy. Despite this, in 2010, there had been an "absence of progress toward a Turkish-Syrian-Iraqi water-sharing agreement regarding the Euphrates, where a multilateral cooperation mechanism [was] urgently needed."[23] The riparian states have a fundamental, long-standing, and seemingly unbridgeable ideological divide: while Turkey considers the waters of the Tigris and Euphrates as transboundary, Iraq and Syria consider them international. The former implies no legal requirement to share surface water, while the latter implies a hydrological commitment to downstream states.

The 1997 UN Convention on the Law of Non-navigational Uses of International Watercourses codified the principles of equitable and reasonable utilization and no harm done to riparian states.[24] The Turkish government has approached this water-sharing requirement as sharing services and benefits of the resource, having joint projects, and sharing scientific and technical expertise.[25] Turkey regards the Tigris and Euphrates as a single river system because these converge in southern Iraq where they form the Shatt al-Arab waterway, and because the Tharthar Canal in Iraq links the Tigris with the Euphrates through the Tharthar depression. This position excludes co-sovereignty of the rivers. On the other hand, Syria states that the water infra-structures in the basin are discrete, and Iraq views the varying topography, geography, and hydrology are evidence that the basins are in fact separate.[26] Furthermore, if a development project were to cause qualitative or quantitative harm to another riparian state, multiple decisions by the International Court of Justice (ICJ) have made it clear that the upstream state is required to inform others in advance and to limit damages.[27]

The Arab press has long considered the multiple dams that are being built by Turkey on the Tigris and Euphrates as an act of "belligerence." Syria perceives Turkey's unwillingness to negotiate or sign a water allocation treaty as an assertion of the latter's unchecked hydro-hegemonic influence. While Turkey's reservoirs on the Tigris and Euphrates rivers are engineering tools that help regulate water flow throughout the year, they also serve as a hydro-political tool or "weapon" that can be deployed to regulate the "political behavior" of Arab riparians downstream.[28] The latter was the view of the site supervisor of the Atatürk dam, which brings to mind the Native American Proverb: "First of all, see to it that you are always positioned upstream and your enemies downstream."[29]

The upstream location of even a friendly state endows it with power that results from its ability to reduce or threaten to reduce water flow, a hydropolitical position that makes dependent downstream states insecure. This is particularly relevant today because the riparians on the Tigris and Euphrates rivers have not been able to reach a water-allocation agreement. Downstream states blame Turkey for the obstruction. The nascent Syrian-Turkish friendship of the 2000s ended with the start of the civil war in Syria. It is worth noting that the 1997 UN Convention has been approved by 103 countries, except for Turkey and two other states. Turkey's official position is that it has sovereignty over waters originating within its borders. This, Syria and Iraq argue, causes harm to them as downstream riparians and violates international law.

The goal of food security has always been high on the Syrian government's agenda, which explains its subsidy of all inputs into the production of wheat, a food staple in the local diet, and requires farmers to sell their produce through its outlets. From the early years of his reign in the 1970s, Hafez Al-Assad sought to boost wheat productivity by expanding and modernizing the irrigation infrastructure, investing in research and development, and by subsidizing inputs such as seeds, fuel, and fertilizers. The government largely succeeded in meeting its economic and food security goals, which were focused on self-sufficiency and the availability of food at cheap prices.[30]

In Syria, hand-dug wells were shallow, and muscle-power was used to draw small amounts of groundwater for people to meet their daily needs. Small-scale abstraction of water meant that precipitation routinely replenished the aquifers. All this changed with the unregulated introduction of diesel motor pumps in the 1960s, which spread across the country at a rapid pace; so much so that, between 1999 and 2010, the number of wells went from 135,089 to over 229,881. As recently as 2010, it was estimated that 57 percent of wells were unlicensed. Poor governance led to overexploitation, whereby groundwater levels in certain areas of the Damascus governorate dropped by more than six meters per year.[31] In 2010, Robert F. Worth of *The New York Times* filed a report from Raqqa, Syria, that painted a grim picture of environmental devastation and social collapse, and predicted dire political consequences. The story focused on the area north and east of the Euphrates River in Syria and northern Iraq, an area it called the "heartland of the Fertile Crescent."[32]

Once the breadbasket region of Syria, the area had been battered by four consecutive years of drought that decimated 85 percent of herders' livestock in the northeast, and pushed up to three million people into extreme poverty. In this region of Syria, "ancient irrigation systems have collapsed, underground water sources have run dry and hundreds of villages have been abandoned as farmlands turn to cracked desert and grazing animals die off. Sandstorms have become far more common, and vast tent cities of dispossessed farmers and their families have risen up around the larger towns and cities of Syria and Iraq."[33] The journalist quoted a local farmer-turned-water refugee saying: "I had 400 acres of wheat, and now it's all desert. ... Now we are at less than zero—no money, no job, no hope."[34] This farmer and his family, as well as many others, had left their homes and were living in burlap and plastic tents. Back in 2010, Worth warned that "the collapse of farmlands here—which is as much a matter of human mismanagement as of drought—has become a dire economic challenge and a rising security concern for the Syrian and Iraqi governments."[35] Similarly, a recent study concurred that "government agricultural policy is prominent among the many factors that shaped Syria's vulnerability to drought."[36]

Given the government's former focus on food self-sufficiency, between 1971 and 2000 it initiated policies to boost agricultural output and subsidies for "diesel fuel to garner the support of rural constituents. ...These policies endangered Syria's water security by exploiting limited land and water resources without regard for sustainability."[37] Furthermore, "three of the four most severe multiyear droughts have occurred in the last 25 years, the period during which external anthropogenic forcing has seen its largest increase."[38]

Syria's agricultural policies and mismanagement of resources aggravated water scarcity, which the government then framed as the country's geo-climatic developmental challenge, without any mention of human contributions to it.[39] The drought of 2006–2011 turned Syria into a wheat importer, and forced hundreds of thousands of people out of their villages, especially those living east of Raqqa in the northeast. By 2010, the drought made 17 percent of the Syrian population (or 3.7 million people) food insecure.[40] This, along with overgrazing, unsustainable management of ground water supplies, and weak governance structures contributed to the outbreak of civil war in 2011—a situation that has been described as the culmination of decades of mounting "mismanagement of water and land resources."[41]

In an effort to liberalize the economy, President Bashar Al-Assad decided to cut fuel and food subsidies, a policy that he maintained despite the drought, "further destabilizing the lives of those affected."[42] Farmers' reliance on agricultural production left them unable to outlast a prolonged drought, and a "mass migration of rural farming families to urban areas ensued."[43] The drought-induced harsh social and economic conditions and the people's desperation had set the stage for Raqqa to become the self-declared capital of the so-called Islamic State (IS), which stretched from northeast Syria into northern Iraq. On the Iraqi side, Zaid al Ali, a native-born academic studying at the Institut d'Études Politiques in Paris was conducting a field survey of water and farm conditions in Kirkuk and Salahuddin Provinces, and reported seeing desperate conditions where whole villages were buried in sand.

Sabbagh and Ismael of the *Syrian Arab News Agency* wrote in 2011 that the Syrian government had initiated a massive $2.1 billion irrigation project.[44] It planned to pump 1.25 billion cubic meters (330 billion gallons) of water from the Tigris River in order to irrigate around 200,000 hectares (770 square miles) of land in the province of Hassakeh, a fertile agricultural region near the Turkish-Iraq border. Furthermore, the project was to provide residents with 125 million cubic meters of potable water annually. Even though this project appears to have been a response to the drought that had started a few years earlier, the Hassakeh Province became the heartland of the Islamic State terrorist group.

In sum, water scarcity in Syria and Iraq was made worse by multiple factors: water mismanagement, uncoordinated development of water resources along the Tigris and Euphrates rivers, political and social instability, as well as ethnic difference and distrust (Arab versus Turk). This contributed to the rise of water conflict between the riparians. In Africa, similar issues are fueling water conflict between Egypt and Ethiopia on the Nile River Valley.

Damming the Nile

For Ethiopia, Sudan, and Egypt, the Nile River has always played an important role in their political economy and national identity. The mythology and popular culture around the Nile show that the people see the river as a "1) as source of identity,

2) as a healing power and source of life, 3) as unifier of societies along its course, and 4) as a source of physical destruction on the one hand and 5) as an enormous untapped potential for economic development along its course, on the other hand."[45] During the Pharaonic era, the people even worshiped the Nile River as a god, underscoring the immense importance that they associate with it.

Throughout history, communities and countries of the Nile basin have sought water-sharing agreements that would ensure access and water security in ways that would mitigate the effects of fluctuations of flow. The first agreement in 1929 was between Egypt and Great Britain, the latter representing Uganda, Kenya, Tanzania, and Sudan. Egypt was granted an annual water allocation of 48 billion cubic meters compared to Sudan's allocation of 4 billion cubic meters, out of an estimated total of 84 billion cubic meters.[46] The agreement also gave Cairo veto rights on projects higher up the Nile that negatively impacted its water share. The 1959 accord between Egypt and Sudan appended the previous agreement and increased the share of Egypt and Sudan to 55.5 and 18.5 billion cubic meters per year, respectively. It also reinforced the "natural and historic rights" of downstream states to Nile waters, which became Egypt's baseline in future negotiations with other basin states. The two agreements disregarded the water rights of upstream states like Ethiopia, despite the fact it is the source of the Blue Nile tributary.

Most recently, the Nile Basin Initiative, a cooperative institution whose members are the riparian states, sought "to achieve sustainable socio-economic development through the equitable utilization of, and benefit from, the common Nile Basin water resources."[47] It sought to quell water conflict through cooperative water management that would yield socioeconomic benefits for all. In 2009, all the Nile basin states, except Egypt, signed a Cooperative Framework Agreement. Egypt's objection was related to a clause that commits states "not to significantly affect the water security of any other Nile Basin State."[48]

Egyptians have always seen the Nile's water in existential terms because the river is the only source of sustenance in the country, providing 96 percent of renewable freshwater supplies. In this arid to hyper-arid country, some 95 percent of the population lives within a twelve mile strip of the Nile River valley, producing a high population density.[49] This leaves the vast majority of the country's territory virtually uninhabited.

Even as the volume of water flow in the Nile has been declining over the past century, overall quality of life has been improving,[50] and the population size (about 400 million) in the eleven riparian countries has been rising rapidly. When the government of Ethiopia established political stability, it was then able to start investing in its infrastructure, including the construction of the $4.5 billion Grand Ethiopian Renaissance Dam that would support the largest hydroelectric power plant in Africa containing sixteen turbines with the capacity of producing 6,000 megawatts of electricity.[51]

Egypt's overarching fear is that the dam will reduce the 55.5 billion cubic meters of water per year that the country has long received, which would hinder its development and prosperity. The reservoir behind the Ethiopian dam will retain about 63 billion cubic meters of water and will take five to fifteen years to fill.[52] Using a five to seven year scenario, the volume of water reaching Egypt could be cut by 25 percent, and electricity generated by the Aswan High Dam would be cut by one third.[53] This would adversely impact Egypt's economy, degrade resiliency of its agricultural sector, and cast doubt on the reliability of water supply from Egypt's lone source of freshwater. Egypt's strong objections to the Renaissance dam had blocked Ethiopia's efforts to get international funding for the project. Ethiopia then took the "bold decision to pay for" this mega dam by itself, which "overturned generations of Egyptian control over the Nile's waters."[54] Given this, it is likely that Ethiopia is under economic pressure to get quick returns on its investment, meaning it may be tempted to follow a quick-fill timeline of its reservoir. The political and economic impacts of that on Egypt would be dire.

Cornucopians would expect that the economic development and (hydrological) interdependence of riparians would induce upstream-downstream cooperation between them. This is not what happened when Ethiopia started building its mega-dam in 2011. The hydropolitical tension in the Nile basin originates from factors such as downstream insecurity about upstream actions; the absence of an institutional framework to manage water allocation; unilateral development of water resources; barely concealed military threats; and the Afro-Arab divide.[55]

Mubarak's Pyramid: A Hydro-Disaster

In addition to foreign challenges to Egypt's water supply, the country has faced domestic mismanagement that increases the likelihood of water conflict in the Nile Valley. Since the 1960s, Egyptians have been contemplating a massive agricultural project in the southern parts of the country, one that would siphon water from Lake Nasser to irrigate 500,000 acres of reclaimed desert farmland. This long proposed project was discredited, given its remote location (about 1,000 kilometers south of Cairo), far away from urban centers and services; the cost involved in lifting water for many meters before dropping it in the open-air Sheikh Zayed Canal that takes it to Toshka Lake; and the uncertainty regarding the continued availability of water supply. Despite these concerns, in 1998, the Egyptian President Hosni Mubarak inaugurated the New Valley Development Project and singed an initial contract worth $450 million. The project's goals are to double the area of arable land in the region, create 2.8 million new jobs, and entice over 16 million people to leave the crowded Nile Valley and live in towns that will be built in the New Valley. Upon its completion, originally scheduled for 2017, the project is expected to cost around $70 billion.[56]

The economic challenges and political turmoil that Egypt has been experiencing since the popular uprisings of 2011 are impacting the future of the Toshka project. For example, the position of the Muslim Brotherhood was against continuing the Toshka project. The current president, Abdel Fattah el-Sisi, appears to support it, but the economic contractions that the country has been experiencing renders the project a low priority, given that the project "failed to create even 10% of the arable land Mr. Mubarak planned."[57] Heads of state have long built massive water projects as monuments to their own leadership and legacy for future generations,[58] and this project is "symbolic of the misgovernance of the country more generally and the aggrandizement of power by the military."[59] Critics have referred to the Toshka project as being "an expensive disaster,"[60] and as "'Mubarak's pyramid' for its unprecedented scale as well as the slow pace of construction."[61] Supporters of the project argue that it may be "Hosni Mubarak's grandest legacy—an answer to Egypt's crowded cities, pollution, food shortages and unemployment problems all addressed in one mega-project."[62]

Unlike Egypt, Sudan is not solely dependent on one water source. Yet many of the country's hydroelectric power plans and mammoth irrigation schemes depend on water originating in Ethiopia. Although Sudan and Egypt, two Arab countries, have historically been on the same side when it comes to water conflict on the Nile, Sudan broke ranks with Egypt regarding the Renaissance Dam. Sudan would benefit from the year-round regulation of water flow, which minimizes flooding, and allows farmers to plant crops twice or three times a year.

Ethiopia has been considering the construction of major hydropower and irrigation schemes on the Blue Nile since the

1970s, which ushered an era of heightened tensions in the Nile Valley. At one point, the Ethiopian government favored founding a series of small, micro-dams instead of a mega-dam. The construction of micro-dams would neither require foreign financing nor be an attractive military target for Egypt. Ultimately, however, Ethiopia decided to build the Grand Ethiopian Renaissance Dam (GERD), a move that strained relations and spiked water conflict between Egypt and Ethiopia.[63] Some 85 percent of the Nile River's waters come from the Blue Nile, which starts in Ethiopia. Given Egypt's heavy reliance on the Nile for water security, it has been particularly critical of the Renaissance Dam, arguing that it will reduce its majority water rights of the Nile.[64] Despite Egypt's objections, Ethiopia has continued with the construction of the dam, which was around 62 percent complete in late 2017.[65] Egypt also claims that the dam has been planned and constructed in secrecy and that people affected by the dam (Egyptians) have not been given meaningful opportunity to critique the project.[66]

Egypt has even threatened military action against Ethiopia over what it perceives at its rightful share of Nile waters.[67] In discussing Egypt's possible response to the construction of the Renaissance Dam, former Egyptian President Mohammed Morsi said that Egyptians are dependent on the Nile water, so if its flow "diminishes by one drop then our blood is the alternative,"[68] adding that "all options are open" for how to respond to the project. Egypt has been continuously lobbying the international community for support against what it says is a violation of international law,[69] arguing that international watercourses are governed by a set of agreed legal rules and principles, such as the equitable and reasonable utilization of the river. Overall, Egypt is opposed to GERD because of its perceived historical right to the Nile and its reliance on its water, which the country feels will be severely impacted by the dam.

Recently, two different ministers of Irrigation and Water Resources in Egypt warned of dire consequences if water supply were to become scarce. In 2012, Minister Mohamed Nasr El Din Allam, said that Ethiopia's dam would cause water shortages and starvation, and "would lead to political, economic and social instability."[70] In 2018, Minister Ahmed Abdel Alti warned that Egypt's environmental challenges could make millions of Egyptians living in the Nile Delta "vulnerable to being resettled" and would put billions of dollars of investments "at high risk."[71] To be sure, the cumulative effects of decades in mismanagement are converging, and "rising sea levels in the Mediterranean have increased the salinity of underground water and the soil. Population growth has put more pressure on existing water resources, while the mass dumping of industrial waste in irrigation canals has polluted waterways."[72] This growing national vulnerability may encourage desperate decisions by the military-controlled government in Cairo.

In May 2010, the Sudanese President Omar al-Bashir agreed to allow Egyptian commandos to use Sudanese territory to launch an attack on Ethiopia's water facilities on the Blue Nile.[73] A leaked internal email from June 2010 quotes a high-level Egyptian intelligence officer arguing that Ethiopia was not yielding to diplomatic outreach by Egypt, and that "if it comes to a crisis, we [Egypt] will send a jet to bomb the dam and come back in one day, simple as that. Or we can send our special forces in to block/sabotage the dam."[74] In the same dispatch, he compared this to a little known operation in the 1970s, when Egypt blew up dam-related equipment "while it was being transported by sea to Ethiopia."[75] This high-level officer was in regular communication with President Mubarak and his chief of intelligence, Omar Suleiman. Mubarak's regime came to an abrupt end in February 2011, after which the country descended into instability and political turmoil. Egypt's preoccupation with domestic challenges worked in Ethiopia's favor at a critical juncture in the construction of its mega dam.

For Ethiopia, GERD will bring about a new era of domestic prosperity and economic growth and will attract foreign currency with the export of hydropower to neighboring states.[76] According to the World Bank, Ethiopia could earn $1 billion a year, making it the largest exporter of power in Africa.[77] The dam would reduce major flooding downstream, and would allow Sudan to buy electricity, hence its support for the project.[78] Ethiopia also states that Egyptian farmers use wasteful antiquated irrigation methods, such as controlled flooding of fields to irrigate crops,[79] but if they were to use modern ones, such as sprinkler or drip irrigation methods,[80] the post-dam reduced Nile flow would be sufficient for Egypt's needs. Egypt's irrigation network draws heavily from the Aswan High Dam through a vast network of canals that extends over 18,000 miles. This system is highly inefficient, losing as much as 3 billion cubic meters of Nile water per year through evaporation.[81] Ethiopia states that evaporation losses of the Nile could be greatly reduced with GERD because of the depth of the reservoir compared to the surface area, and the ability to use fewer canals. The annual evaporation from Lake Nasser, the reservoir behind the Aswan High Dam, is equivalent to a quarter (or 40 percent, in dry years) of the Nile's average flow.[82]

Egypt's persistent position is that it has a "historical" right to the Nile River, and relies on its 1959 water allocation treaty with Sudan, which gives it two thirds of the river's flow. Ethiopia, however, dismisses colonial-era agreements because they did not obtain the consent of upstream states.[83] In addition, GERD will provide increased storage in upstream Ethiopia, which can provide a greater buffer to shortages in Egypt during years of drought. Also, the dam will retain silt, which will increase the useful lifetime of the Aswan High Dam in Egypt. Overall, Ethiopia believes the dam will provide increased prosperity to the country and the region, and will not impact the water needs of Egypt.

As of late 2019, Ethiopia and Egypt were still far from an agreement on the Nile. The occasional airing of new allegations muddies the political water even more and fuels further distrust. In the fall of 2017, Egyptian media reports claimed that Qatar was funding the Renaissance Dam, allegations that were firmly denied by the Ethiopian government. In June 2017, Egypt, Saudi Arabia, the United Arab Emirates, and Bahrain initiated a political and economic boycott of Qatar. Since then, state media outlets have been critical of each other's foreign and domestic policies, sometimes fabricating baseless claims that foster distrust and harden attitudes. Nevertheless, it is an example of how unrelated regional geopolitical issues could cast a dark cloud on water negotiations.

Analyses and Conclusions

Throughout world history, water conflicts between riparian communities have been common. The vast majority of them are resolved peacefully. What is new, however, is that competition for water supplies is becoming more intense as demand has been rising at unprecedented levels. Rapid population growth, the improved quality of life, along with protein-rich diets, the drying effects of climate change, and the prevailing geophysical conditions have adverse cumulative effects on water demand in the Middle East. In addition to these natural conditions, distrust between different water stakeholders within a country, unilateral development along international water basins, and gross mismanagement accentuate the problems facing a country and raise the specter of water conflict. This chapter shows that the risk of water conflict between Ethiopia and Egypt is at an all-time high. The authoritarian, militarized government in Egypt is less predictable than Mubarak's government, and the media's coverage is fanning the flames of distrust and conflict, which pressures the government to act decisively.

Transboundary water conflicts rise and fall over time, and will dissipate only after countries have worked out their disagreements, which often include non-water issues. Conflicts often force countries to consider creative solutions to their problems, and to discuss options that they would not have taken seriously if not for the conflict at hand,[84] including scenarios for creating new institutional structures on an international river. However, while some cooperative agreements mark historical breakthroughs, like the Israel-Jordan agreement on the Jordan River, they have critical structural flaws. The Jordan River agreement did not include the Palestinian Authority, Lebanon, or Syria, so the potential for water conflict remains. Similarly, the historical agreements on the Nile River were crafted by colonial authorities without the consultation or agreement of national authorities,[85] and included only two of the eleven riparian states that share the river today. In short, "politics and powerful agendas" allow for "processes that appear procedurally fair to lead to highly asymmetric outcomes,"[86] ones that would nurse grievances that could grow over time, leading to conflict or cooperation over the river system. Just as upstream riparian states on the Jordan River disregard the bilateral water agreement, so does Ethiopia with respect to the historical Nile River agreement. Whereas the hydropolitics of the Jordan River see the hegemon (Israel) maintaining its position, Ethiopia is upending the balance of power in the Nile River basin by challenging Egypt's exclusive millennia-old hegemonic influence.

In 2009, Ethiopia initiated a twenty-five year Master Plan that envisioned the construction of hydroelectric dams on twelve of its rivers, with the goal of turning the country into a major energy producer and exporter to nearby countries. Ethiopia's development and hydrological ambitions were assisted by China's growing interest in Africa and its identification of Ethiopia as a rising regional power. Since the early 2000s, China has been deploying its dam-building capacity around the world and funding hydraulic infrastructures on the African continent. Chinese funding does not require "notification or consultation with downstream riparians,"[87] unlike funding from international institutions like the World Bank or the International Monetary Fund. As for the Renaissance Dam, it is estimated that China contributed $1.8 billion (25 percent) of its total cost.[88]

The challenges that hydro-climatic conditions present for Egypt are aggravated by poor planning and poor leadership. In 2015, President el-Sisi revived the El Salam Canal project, which would carry Nile water from the right bank of the Damietta branch to irrigate reclaimed desert lands in northern Sinai. Part of the 277 kilometer long canal is located west of the Suez Canal and another to the east. It would irrigate a total area of 620,000 feddans (260,400 hectares) in the underdeveloped periphery of this large country. The canal is planned to carry 2.2 billion cubic meters per year of fresh water from the Nile basin and about 2.25 cubic meter per year from Bahr Hadous and Lower Serw drains.[89] Water from the last two sources raises questions about water quality in the El Salam canal, because they reuse discharged agricultural drainage that is contaminated with residue from agricultural chemicals. Furthermore, climate change scenarios and the Renaissance Dam are projected to reduce water flow in the Nile River.[90] In short, el-Sisi's reauthorized irrigation canal is likely to become his Toshka of the north.

In many ways, the contemporary conflict between two key riparian states on the Nile River is similar to current tensions between riparian states along the Tigris and Euphrates rivers. In 2018, the Egyptian government issued directives that restrict the cultivation of water-thirsty crops, cutting the rice-growing area in half. Battered by transnational forces, Egypt's Delta farmers will likely have a bleak future.[91] Similarly, the filling of the Ilisu Dam has forced the government of Iraq to significantly reduce the area of wheat cultivation, hence turning the heart of the Fertile Crescent into the second largest wheat importer in the Middle East.[92]

In the case of Syria, the cumulative effects of decades of water mismanagement have wreaked havoc in the country. Looking forward, a reliable water infrastructure would be a key building block for reconstituting the conditions for community development in post-war Syria. The challenges are immense. For instance, by the summer of 2014, some 35 percent of all water treatment plants in Syria had been damaged by war. In 2015, an estimated 49 percent of pumped water was lost through gaps in the network due to damage caused by the conflict.[93] Providing safe drinking water would have to be the first step that the Syrian government would take to provide living conditions for its displaced citizens. A 2017 UN report found that, despite six years of war, the important role that agriculture plays in the Syrian economy has not diminished; it still makes up about 26 percent of gross domestic product and "represents a critical safety net for the 6.7 million Syrians—including those internally displaced—who still remain in rural areas."[94] Rebuilding of the infrastructure, especially irrigation systems, would be necessary for the eventual return of the refugees to their communities and fields, meaning that Syria's agricultural policies would need updating, human capital responsible for water-related institutions need upskilling, irrigation infrastructure need modernizing, and corruption need stamping out. This is a tall order for any government, and even more so for one emerging from one of the most destructive wars the world has seen since World War II.

Resource pressures and geopolitical realignments in the Nile, Tigris, and Euphrates river basin states are increasing the risk of water conflict. Without boosting irrigation efficiency and significantly improving water governance, hydropolitical tensions between upstream and downstream states will remain. In both regions, filling up a huge reservoir created by a new large dam project is the principal trigger of water conflict where riparian states' water demands are growing and rivers' flows are fixed or declining. The significant erosion of the geopolitical statures of Syria and Iraq does not give Turkey incentives to be hydrologically magnanimous. In East Africa, Ethiopia's geopolitical weight has been rising, aided by its political stability and hydro-development and by the distinct weakening of the political power of Egypt, the hydro-hegemon on the Nile throughout history. The convergence of historical distrust between governments, water mismanagement and corruption, as well as political instability appears to lend support to the Malthusian perspective on scarcity-induced conflict.

3

TURKISH HYDRO-HEGEMONY

THE IMPACT OF DAMS

Paul A. Williams

For over four decades, Turkey's physical mastery over its inland rivers has increased. This includes the Euphrates and Tigris basin, which also supplies much of Syria and Iraq's water needs. Together, Turkey's Keban dam and the Southeastern Anatolian Project's (Güneydoğu Anadolu Projesi or GAP) Karakaya and Atatürk dams—installations built in hydrological and temporal succession on the Euphrates—can store a usable volume of water nearly equal to the average annual flow of the river that reaches Syria. GAP's Birecik and Karkamiş dams further lift that amount to just above total flow. On the Tigris, GAP's Ilisu (now completed), Silvan, and Cizre dams will quintuple the active storage volume already contained in the Kralkizi, Dicle, and Batman dams, raising usable capacity to 70 percent of the mean annual flow of the river to Iraq.

In short, this has increased the salient material basis of upstream riparian Turkey's "hydro-hegemony"—a term coined by Mark Zeitoun and Jeroen Warner to signify a country's favorable power and riparian position as well as "resource exploitation potential"—giving it real technological capability to control the volume of vital freshwater supply reaching its downstream neighbors.[1] At the same time, however, this elevates neighbors' concerns over potential permanent water deprivation to a degree that compels Ankara to speak and act with greater care in terms of how it actually uses this lever. Turkey has concretized its "first-mover advantage,"[2] increasing the immediacy of the prediction made in the 1990s that Syria would lose 40 percent of this water and Iraq would lose 80 percent.[3] In a starker zero-sum setting, the fear is that the hydro-hegemon may be able to exclude most downstream users from access to water altogether.[4]

Turkish officials tend to downplay these fears, touting the ability of these dams to supply "public goods," especially intra- and inter-year flow regulation. This has some plausibility. Responding to the 1970s oil crises, Turkish state planners sought to address the country's vulnerability to imported-energy price swings—a weakness rooted in the unstable nature of Turkey's pre-2002 economic growth—by focusing on GAP's energy projects. As such, hydropower's extant economic returns might keep total water diversions for irrigation well below the uppermost goal, which would forestall deeper cuts in downstream flows and what could be up to 22 percent reductions in GAP's high-end energy output.[5] In June 2018, following a reported May 2018 agreement on Ilisu Dam's impending fill, Turkey's ambassador to Iraq voiced a similar logic, and reassured that "the dam was built for power generation rather than irrigation."[6]

Lasting water-centric peace remains elusive. First, Turkish politicians have undercut the "public goods" narrative themselves, as when Prime Minister (1991–1993) Suleyman Demirel remarked that "the more [dams] it [Turkey] builds, the fewer threats it will be faced with."[7] Second, dramatic economic growth following the Justice and Development Party's (Adalet ve Kalkinma Partisi or AKP) first election victory in 2002 boosted Turkey's self-confidence. This improved tripartite basin relations in line with Ankara's initiatives under Ahmet Davutoğlu—an advisor to then Prime Minister Recep Tayyip Erdoğan before becoming foreign minister in 2009—to enhance cooperation in general, but also increased Turkey's financial means to accelerate GAP's lagging irrigation and Tigris targets. This presaged renewed rifts between Turkey and its downstream neighbors. For example, Iraq's water minister, Latif Rashid, reportedly urged Veysel Eroğlu, now Turkey's minister of forestry and water works, to expedite the Ilisu Dam in 2008,[8] but objected a year later that Turkey had not increased Euphrates water flow as pledged, amid rising worries that Ilisu would "reduce the waters of the Tigris River by 47% and deprive the northern Iraqi city of Mosul of 50% of its summer water requirements."[9]

The GAP Action Plan 2008–2012 centered more on irrigation and reflected refocused attention on the need to repair *domestic* gaps in Turkey's hydro-hegemonic armor. By developing the local economy, irrigation could weave the GAP region's heavily Kurdish population more tightly into the Turkish social fabric and the AKP fold, and could dry up recruitment into the Kurdistan Workers' Party (Partiya Karkeren Kurdistan or PKK), which was closely linked to Syria's 1984–1998 hostility to Turkish dams.[10] On the other hand, related to at least 150,000 inhabitants' loss of homes to Euphrates and Tigris reservoirs since 1974,[11] Kurdish nationalist resentment of the eastern dams as military tools of "depopulation" and "political genocide" has run high. No alleviation of underlying discontent came from the 2008 tendering of a dozen "border dams" in Turkey's far south-eastern provinces of Şirnak and Hakkari, which have been associated with a strategic goal of submerging PKK hideouts, depots, and passages.[12] Turkish armed forces' post-July 2015 crackdown in the southeast, and interventions against the PKK in Syria and Iraq since August 2016, have dominated regional security measures, but any real or perceived enlistment of dams for this purpose will ensure perpetuation of a conflict that feeds back on Turkey's hydro-hegemony as well.

The first two sections of this chapter survey Turkey's Euphrates and Tigris river basins and GAP's place in that hydro-economic setting before examining how GAP and Ankara's hydro-hegemony evolved in relation to Turkey's political economy. The third section addresses challenges to GAP and hydro-hegemony, while the fourth section focuses on a PKK-related security dilemma that has implicated GAP and forced Turkey's defensive perimeter outward.

The Euphrates and Tigris Rivers and GAP

The watercourses of the Euphrates and Tigris rivers are long, and their drainage basins vast. While Turkey's territory covers one-third of the Euphrates's 444,000 km²—greater than Syria's 19 percent, but less than Iraq's 46 percent share—it generates most of the water.[13] Karasu and Tuzla tributaries emerge in Turkey's northeastern province of Erzurum and flow west to join in Erzincan province to form the Euphrates River, which travels through Sivas, picking up the Çalti Suyu stream on its way south to a northwestern pool of Keban dam reservoir in Elazığ. Keban dam also receives the Kozluk creek flowing from Malatya in the west, the conjoined Munzur and Peri Suyu tributaries from the northeast, and Murat river, which flows from Ağri province (north of Lake Van) and through Muş and Bingöl provinces. Flowing for half of its 2700 kilometer length in Turkey, the Euphrates later receives the Kuruçay, Tohma, and Mamikan streams above Karakaya dam, the Göksu and Birimşe tributaries north of Atatürk dam, and, finally, the Nizip between Birecik and Karkamiş, where cumulative annual natural flow once averaged 28 km³ (cubic kilometers, or billion cubic meters), about 90 percent of the total flow that reaches Syria.

Turkey contributes a smaller, but still substantial, volume of Tigris river water. Near Akçayurt in Diyarbakir province, the 1,840 kilometer Tigris unites the Kara and Aktoprak tributaries that rise in Bingöl—the former just south of the Euphrates's Murat—and flows south into Dicle dam before receiving outflow from Kralkizi dam, which stores water from the Maden, Inci, and Koşkar streams, and then from Batman river, a collection of the Zori, Kulp, and Hani streams that reach Batman dam. The Tigris gathers more tributaries, including the Botan and Cehennem, on its way past Hasankeyf and Ilisu to Cizre, where mean annual flow reaches 21–22 km³ (about 40 percent of the total). It then demarcates a thirty kilometer section of the Turkey-Syria border before merging with the Hezil river that runs along the boundary between Turkey and Iraq, which also receives the Turkey-origin Greater Zab River further downstream. Turkey makes up 15 percent of the Tigris's 387,000 km² basin area, larger than Syria's respective 0.3 percent, but much smaller than Iraq's three quarters, with Iran accounting for the 9.5 percent that generates the Lesser Zab, which demarcates a segment of the Iran-Iraq border.[14]

Turkey's development, as manifest in the government's five-year plans (starting in 1963–1967), has featured increased energy and crop supplies via dams, hydro-electric power plants, and irrigation. According to official accounts, Turkish users cannot feasibly exploit more than 112 km³ of gross national annual water supply, total consumption of which increased from 40 km³ in 2006 to 54 km³ in 2016, with 10 km³ of this increase coming in the latter year alone, and four-fifths of that for irrigation—a jump disproportionately greater than that of area.[15] Irrigation consumption in 2016 matched nearly 80 percent of Turkey's contribution to the Euphrates and Tigris basins, which may have met 7–8 km^3 of Turkey's total 2009 water use.[16]

GAP per se was formed in 1977. In 1989, it acquired its own agency—the GAP Regional Development Administration (GAPRDA), which was created by decree-law and originally located under the prime ministry—to coordinate this integrated regional development project. Ahmet Davutoğlu called GAP the largest such scheme "ever in Turkey and also one of the largest throughout the world,"[17] since it initially spanned six provinces (Adiyaman, Diyarbakir, Gaziantep, Mardin, Siirt, and Şanliurfa) and later nine (including Batman, Kilis, and Şirnak, the latter pair respectively part of Gaziantep and Siirt until the 1990s). Its core infrastructure of twenty-two dams and nineteen HEPPs in thirteen main project groups (see Tables 1–2 for more comprehensive lists of GAP-affiliated facilities since the project's inception) aim to develop one-fifth—respectively, 1.6–1.8 million hectares and 26,000–27,000 gigawatt hours—of Turkey's maximum irrigable area and annual hydropower potential, foundations for boosting growth, trebling regional per-capita incomes, employing 3.8 million, curbing rural and regional out-migration, and expanding exports.[18]

The project centers on, but is not coterminous with, the Euphrates and Tigris basins. While its administrative boundaries span 10 percent of Turkey's 783,577 km^2 surface area, the basins in question comprise 28 percent of the country's surface water and 24 percent of its territory. The location of the Botan tributary's upper section in Van province leaves only one-fifth of the Tigris River's 38,295 km^2 catchment area in Turkey *outside* of GAP, but only one-fifth of the Euphrates River's 102,876 km^2 Turkish catchment area lies *inside* of GAP, between Karakaya Dam (GAP's uppermost Euphrates project) and the Syrian bor-

Table 3.1: GAP Dams and Hydroelectric Power Plants (HEPP): Euphrates

Project Units	Years Built	Storage (hm³)		Energy	
		Total	Active	MW	GWh/a
Karakaya Dam & HEPP	1976–1987	9,580	4,353	1,800	7,354
Atatürk Dam & HEPP	1983–1992 & 1993	48,700	11,000	2,400	8,900
Şanliurfa HEPP	1994–2006	0	0	51	124
Birecik Dam & HEPP	1985–2000	1,220	622	672	2,516
Karkamiş Dam & HEPP	1996–1999	157	0	189	652
Çamgazi [Sariçal] Dam	1990–1999	53	44	0	0
Gömikan Dam	2016–present	56	52	0	0
Koçali Dam & HEPP	2014–present	297	288	39	136
Sirimtaş Dam & EPP	2009–2013	32	29	30	84
Fatopaşa HEPP	not started	0	0	22	32
Büyükçay Dam & HEPP	not started	n/a	130	30	84
Bulam Regulator & HEPP*	2007–2010	0	0	7	33
Kahta Dam & HEPP	not started	7	41	75	71
Çataltepe/Çetintepe Dam	2012–2013	460	212	0	0
Erkenek HEPP	2003–2010	0	0	12	52
Hancağiz Dam	1985–1989	100	82	0	0
Kayacik Dam	1993–2005	104	122	0	0
Doğanpinar Dam**	2013–2016	153	144	0	0
Bayramli Regulator [& HEPP]***	n/a	0	0	1	3

47

Kemlin Dam	not started	n/a	32	0	0
Seve Dam****	1995–2005	19	18	0	0
Ungrouped Projects					
ÇağÇağ HEPP	finished 1968	0	0	14	42
Hacihidir Dam	1985–1989	68	46	0	0
[Derik-]Dumluca Dam	1985–1991	27	22	0	0
Besni Dam	not started	32	n/a	0	0
Ardil Dam	2012–2016	11	8	0	0
Çermik-Kale [Kale] Dam	2014–present	183	130	0	0
14 main dams (unshaded)		**60,766**	**17,008**		
All 21 dams	–	61,260	17,376	–	–
11 main HEPPs	–	–	–	**1,128**	**3,787**
All 14 HEPPs	–	–	–	1,142	3,829

Sources: GAPRDA "*Son Durum*" reports (Project Units); DSI website (Dams—Years Built & Storage); DSI "*Faaliyet Raporu*" reports (Çataltepe/Çetintepe, Doganpinar, Ardil, and Çermik-Kale—Years Built); GAPRDA *Son Durumu 2018*, 35 (HEPPs—End Dates, MW, and GWh/a).

Notes: *A later addition to the Adiyaman-Kahta Project, but more recently listed as "ungrouped".

**Listed in two DSI reports as "Doğanpinar-Kayacik" (under Gaziantep Project), but separate from Kayacik.

***The HEPP function never appeared in DSI or GAP reports, which no longer list the project at all.

****Listed initially under the Gaziantep Project and then as an "ungrouped" project, but no longer listed at all.

Table 3.2: GAP Dams and Hydroelectric Power Plants (HEPP): Tigris

Project Units	Years Built	Storage (hm³)		Energy	
		Total	Active	MW	GWh/a
Kralkizi Dam & HEPP	1985–1998	1,933	1,697	94	146
Dicle Dam & HEPP	1986–1997 &				
	1999	583	307	110	298
Batman Dam & HEPP	1986–1999 &				
	2003	1,244	816	198	483
Silvan Dam & HEPP	2011–present	7,013	4,067	160	623
Ambar Dam*	2011–2017	132	117	0	0
Pamukçay Dam*	2009–2012	33	24	0	0
Kuruçay Dam*	2013–2016	41	38	0	0
Başlar Dam*	2014–2016	29	21	0	0
Bulaklidere Dam*	not started	n/a	n/a	0	0
Kibris Dam*	not started	n/a	n/a	0	0
Karacalar Dam*	not started	n/a	n/a	0	0
Kayser Dam & HEPP**	not started	n/a	527	150	n/a
Garzan Dam & HEPP	2007–2013	156	145	43	158
Ilisu Dam & HEPP	2006–2018	10,625	7460	1,200	3,833
Cizre Dam & HEPP	not started	360	n/a	240	1,208
Ungrouped Projects					
Devegecidi Dam	1965–1972	219	194	0	0
Çinar-Göksu [Göksu]					
Dam	1987–1991	57	57	0	0
Ergani Dam	2013–present	15	13	0	0
8 main dams (unshaded)	–	**21,914**	**15,019**	–	–
All 18 dams	–	22,439	15,482	–	–
8 HEPPs	–	–	–	**1,798**	**6,147**

Sources: GAPRDA *"Son Durum"* reports (Project Units); DSI website (Dams—Years Built & Storage); DSI *"Faaliyet Raporu"* reports (Ambar, Pamukçay, Kuruçay, and Başlar—Years Built), GAPRDA *Son Durumu 2018*, 35 (HEPPs—End Dates, MW, and GWh/a).

Notes: *DSI and GAP reports list only the irrigation aspect of these seven projects (each of which nonetheless corresponds to a dam with the same respective name) falling within the scope of the Batman-Silvan Project, which is centered on the Silvan Dam & HEPP and separate from the Batman Project.

**Kayser Dam & HEPP originally fell within the scope of the Batman-Silvan Project, but was indicated as being "suspended" as far back as the original Master Plan report and is now no longer listed at all.

der.[19] The basins' potential generation capacity of 47,000 GWh per year came to 40 percent of the 1989 national total (but about 26 percent of the current 180,000-GWh estimate),[20] with a 1992 DSI report putting respective potential dam numbers and water storage volume in the Euphrates and Tigris basins at eighty-one and twenty-eight and 130 km^3 and 15 km^3, respectively.[21] By 2018, the Euphrates Basin was associated with an estimated eighty-three HEPPs (sixty-six operational) having maximum annual electricity generation potential of about 38,000 GWh and fifty-two dams (thirty-nine operational) to hold 107 km^3 of water in storage, whereas the Tigris accounted for another twenty-one HEPPs (twelve operational) with 11,229 GWh of per-year production potential and twenty-one dams (thirteen operational) with total storage capacity of 24 km^3.[22]

Political Economy of GAP and Turkey's Hydro-Hegemony

GAP took shape in the late 1970s, when Turkey was experiencing highly inflationary growth. The negative effect of the oil shocks on Turkey led to an IMF standby agreement and stabilization program in 1980,[23] indicating that prevailing financial conditions made GAP's projected cost of US$32 billion prohibitive for the state alone to cover. Thus, the expected involvement of domestic firms and foreign assistance was factored into GAP from the outset. Forecasting 4 percent annual growth, scenario "A," one of maximum irrigation, added foreign currency requirements of US$6.1 billion to total 1989–2005 public investment needs of TL28.8 trillion (US$21.3 billion in 1988); scenario "B," of maximum hydro-power, respectively required TL6.4 trillion and US$800 million less; and a recommended scenario "C" of "priority" projects (equivalent to 894,000 hectares and 5,300 MW) lowered respective financing needs by TL8.6 trillion and US$1.2 billion.[24] Steady IMF pressure to maintain deflationary policies and downstream-state objections to World Bank funding for GAP led to the passage of the Build-Operate-Transfer (BOT) law to attract FDI into Turkey's infrastructure sector in 1984 and a later privatization law in 1994, during the country's first financial crisis since the 1989 liberalization of capital accounts.[25]

In the interim, though, the GAP region relied on large transfers from the central budget and official non-budgetary support from state enterprises (SEEs) and the public-housing fund. During 1981–1985, the private sector comprised only one-third of fixed investment in this region—and *none* in its energy sector—and so the central government filled the breach, directing 52 percent of fixed public investment in the region (versus 20 percent in the nation) to energy, and bringing GAP to nearly 13 percent of the nation's sectoral total.[26] Two-fifths of GAP's installed capacity was already operational in 1992, when authorities expected Keban Dam HEPP on the Euphrates River upstream from Karakaya, plus six of GAP's dam-and-HEPP plants slated to finish by then, to supply one-fourth of the country's energy and 85 percent of its electricity.[27] For ten years of the 1995–2008 period, GAP's output, ranging from 11,500 GWh in 2001 to 21,500 GWh in 2006, actually generated 45–50 percent (and once, in 2007, nearly 52 percent) of Turkey's annual hydropower and 10–20 percent of Turkey's overall electricity—respective fractions that later fell to 25–35 percent and 5–10 percent.[28] GAP's cumulative electricity generation (and monetary value) rose from 57,800 GWh (US$3.47 billion) in 1993 to 443,800 GWh (US$26.63 billion) in 2017.[29] Bringing seven main GAP dam-and-HEPP facilities on line by 2003 (Table 2) transpired in a growing economy, albeit one marked by lower average annual rates and sharper standard deviations of growth in the 1990s than in the 1980s (respectively, 3.96 percent vs. 5.22 percent and 5.64 vs. 3.33), reflecting 6 percent contractions in 1994 and 1999 and 80 percent inflation and depreciation.[30]

The top-down nature of GAP proved costly in its own right. Parliament adopted a new expropriation law in 1983 "to allow for the smooth implementation of" GAP.[31] The Atatürk Dam required expropriation of 25,700 parcels across 43,300 hectares and resettlement of one hundred hamlets and villages as well as 55,000 people, but submarket values of cash packages and non-inflation-adjusted payouts triggered lawsuits that resulted in victory for 90 percent of plaintiffs, driving up DSI's expropriation costs (10 percent of construction) by 30 percent.[32] Militarization of the region compounded the problem. Clashes with the PKK inflicted massive property damage and raised costs of reinforcements, ammunition, and civil servant hazard pay,[33] helping to boost GAP-related expenses to TL1 billion per hour by late 1993.[34] At the start of the PKK's guerrilla warfare in 1984, the Turkish military emptied 3,800 southeastern villages of a million people and, by 1994, had amassed troops in the southeast at an annual cost of US$6–7 billion.[35] While work on Kralkizi Dam halted in 1991 due to the lead firm's financial problems, Batman Dam's construction stopped due to "terror," a factor that reportedly afflicted the Kralkizi-Dicle Irrigation Conveyance Canal as well. However, construction on all three resumed in early 1994.[36] Moreover, this restart occurred *during* a crisis that preceded the July IMF standby agreement, suggesting that these projects were of such significance as to override normal financial prudence.

Although three-quarters of GAP's hydropower target was met within GAP's overall deadline of 2005, in 1998, the Council of Ministers pushed the deadline back to 2010.[37]

In short, the government failed to finish even GAP's "priority" irrigation projects on time. Though GAPRDA estimated that irrigation might account for 53 percent of GAP's annual total benefits,[38] conveying water to 1.6 million hectares by 2002—about 100,000 per year—demanded enormous socioeconomic undertakings of "land consolidation" and "on-farm development," notably drainage, to minimize water-logging and salinization.[39] In the GAP region, 41 percent of 326,000 rural families owned one to five hectares (10,000–50,000 m^2) of land, while 38 percent share-cropped for another 8 percent of large landowners with 51 percent of the land, but who had an uncertain interest in "optimal" cropping and water management.[40] As land reform was circumscribed by a 1978 court decision overruling expropriation of 161,800 ha in Şanlıurfa and a 1984 law applying only to the Urfa-Harran project, "irregular shape and fragmentation of holdings" made irrigation more costly by hindering "rational canal lay-out."[41]

The government started with Urfa-Harran Plains Irrigation, 140,000 hectares in GAP's Lower Euphrates Project centered on the Atatürk Dam and its Urfa Tunnels, capable of diverting 328 m^3/second of the Euphrates River's mean flow—just under one-third. However, even this priority unit did not get underway until 1995, three years after its original deadline (Table 3). From 1995 to 2006, Urfa-Harran grew from 30,000 hectares (one-quarter of GAP irrigated area) to over 130,000 hectares (then half of GAP). It reached cumulative gross production value of US$2.34 billion (64 percent value added) and represented four-fifths of all consolidated GAP land and nine-tenths of related villages.[42] Two-thirds of Urfa-Harran was planted with cotton, which worsened salinization and ruined 15 percent of the Urfa

Table .33: Status of GAP 1989 Irrigation Schemes

Irrigation Schemes [Main numbered]	Target (ha)	Est. H₂O Use/a (km³)	Deadline	Start	Initial area (ha)	End	2017 (ha)
1. Urfa–Harran	**141,535**	1.527	1992	1995	30,000	2008	147,887
2. Mardin–Ceylanpinar 1st Stage	230,130	2.370	1996	–	–	–	**56,264**
Gravity	–	–	–	2006	6,065	no	43,164
Pumped	–	–	–	2016	500	no	13,100
3. Mardin–Ceylanpinar 2nd Stage	104,809	0.994	2000	2011	61,883	no	**61,883**
4. Siverek–Hilvan pumped	160,105	1.523	2002	none	0	no	**0**
5. Bozova Pumped	69,702	0.718	1995	2005	8,669	no	**28,637**
6. Suruç–Baziki [Suruç–Yaylak]	146,500	1.472	2000	–	–	–	**74,617**
Yaylak Plains (target of 18,322 ha)	–			2004–05	5,250	2006	18,322
Suruç Plains (initial 94,814 ha target lowered to 56,295 ha)				2013	16,500	2017	56,295
7. Adiyaman–Kahta	77,409	0.677	1994	–	–	–	**10,806**
Çamgazi Dam	–	–	–	1999–00	1,000	2009	8,000
Şamsat Pumped Irrigation	–	–	–	2007	960	2008	2,806
8. Adiyaman–Göksu–Araban	71,598	0.428	1997	none	0	no	**0**
9. Gaziantep	81,670	0.720	1997	–	–	–	**29,109**
Hancağiz Dam	–	–	–	1989	7,330	1989	6,945
Kayacik Dam (target of 20,000 ha)	–	–	–	2006	680	no	12,000

Belkis–Nizip Pumped	–	–	–	2009	2,100	2012	10,164
Total Euphrates River	*1,083,458*	*10.429*	*–*	*–*	*–*	*–*	*324,302*
10. Dicle right bank-gravity	52,033	0.506	1993	2013	1,336	no	**18,859**
11. Dicle right bank-pumped	74,047	0.750	1993	2003	4,758	no	**18,585**
12. Batman right bank	18,758	0.169	1993	2006	604	no	**6,000**
13. Batman left bank	18,986	0.163	1993	2006	855	no	**13,836**
14. Batman–Silvan	213,000	1.752	2001	–	–	–	**4,860**
Ambar Dam (target of 12,325 ha)	–	–	–	2017	1,600	no	1,600
Pamukçay Dam (target of 5,100 ha)	–	–	–	2017	3,260	no	3,260
15. Garzan	60,000	0.537	2002	none	0	no	**0**
16. Silopi	32,000	0.770	2002	none	0	no	**0**
17. Nusaybin–Cizre–Idil	89,000	0.209	2002	none	0	no	**0**
Total Tigris River	*557,824*	*5.195*	*–*	*–*	*–*	*–*	*62,140*
Grand Total	**1,641,282**	**15.624**	**–**	**–**	**–**	**–**	**442,706**

Sources:

Numbered Schemes, Targets, Water Requirements, and Deadlines:

SPO, Final Master Plan Study, Volume 2: Table 3.1: DSI Original Schedule for Completion of GAP Irrigation Projects & Table 5.3: Summary of Irrigation Water Requirements

Non-numbered Schemes, Start Dates, Areas at Start, End Dates, and 2017 Areas:

DSI "Faaliyet Raporu" reports (various, 2006–2017), GAPRDA "Son Durum" reports (various, 1992–2005).

Plains' irrigation.[43] GAP's irrigation inched up from 4 percent finished (70,000 hectares) in 1992 to only 15 percent (273,000 hectares) by 2007,[44] with the Euphrates area faring better, as 19 percent of projects had finished by the latter year, compared to 6 percent for the Tigris.[45]

No dramatic shifts in this regard occurred during Turkey's first AKP-led government (2002–2007). The 2001 economic crisis that helped bring the AKP to power had also forced Turkey to seek two successive three-year IMF standby loans, in the pre-AKP months of 2002 and later in 2005, on condition of reducing inflation, balancing budgets, and raising monetary reserves—anchors for fourteen consecutive quarters of growth by mid-2005.[46] Between the 1998–2002 and 2003–2007 periods, however, even as Turkey's average annual public investment outlays contracted by 4–5 percent, GAP's increased 5 percent, lifting regional period-average share from 6 to 7 percent of country total (Table 4). GAP's irrigated area, which grew by 74,894 hectares over 1995–2002, for an average of 9,362 hectares per year, expanded by 88,441 hectares over 2002–2008, averaging 12,634 hectares per year (Table 5). Buoyed by earlier, albeit slowing, growth, the second AKP-majority government (2007–2011) spurned another IMF loan and authorized a new GAP Action Plan (AP) in 2008. Unlike 1994 and 2001, when annual public investment outlays for Turkey and GAP contracted—by 31 percent and 54 percent, respectively, in the latter year—in line with GDP, GAP investment rose by 45 percent in 2008 and 51 percent in 2009, contrary to 2008's weak growth of 0.9 percent and a 4.7 percent contraction in 2009.[47] Between 2003–2007 and 2008–2012, average annual public investment in GAP jumped 144 percent, boosting GAP's period-average share from 7 percent to 13 percent of Turkey's total (Table 4).

Planners also sought to fix the irrigation "gap" in a more prosaic way. They lowered the entire near-term target to 1.058 mil-

Table 3.4: Public Investment: Turkey v. GAP Region

TOTAL

Period (No. Years)	Turkey (2018 TL billion)	% 1990–2017	GAP (2018 TL billion)	% 1990–2017	GAP/Turkey (%)
1990–2017 (28)	1,358.63	100.00	119.30	100.00	8.78
1990–2002 (13)	508.76	37.45	36.22	30.36	7.12
2003–2017 (15)	849.87	62.55	83.08	69.64	9.78
1993–1997 (5)	160.40	11.81	12.24	10.26	7.63
1998–2002 (5)	213.37	15.71	13.24	11.10	6.21
2003–2007 (5)	203.51	14.98	13.94	11.68	6.85
2008–2012 (5)	262.29	19.31	33.99	28.49	12.96
2013–2017 (5)	384.06	28.27	35.15	29.46	9.15

ANNUAL AVERAGES

Period (No. Years)	Turkey (2018 TL billion)	Inter–Period Change (%)	GAP (2018 TL billion)	Inter–Period Change (%)	GAP/Turkey (%)
1990–2017 (28)	48.52	4.26	–	–	–
1990–2002 (13)	39.14	–	2.79	–	–
2003–2017 (15)	56.66	44.77	5.54	98.77	–
1993–1997 (5)	32.08	–	2.45	–	–
1998–2002 (5)	42.67	33.02	2.65	8.18	–
2003–2007 (5)	40.70	–4.62	2.79	5.25	–
2008–2012 (5)	52.46	28.88	6.80	143.83	–
2013–2017 (5)	76.81	46.43	7.03	3.42	–

lion "priority" hectares, implicitly equal to storage in fifteen operational GAP dams and slightly below the stated land-consolidation goal of 1.18 million hectares.[48] The plan focused on finishing main canals and irrigation networks attached to the Batman, Kralkizi, and Dicle dams in the Tigris Basin and to the Atatürk, Birecik, Çamgazi, Koçali, and Kayacik dams in the Euphrates, as well as starting *and* finishing the former basin's Silvan Dam and the latter basin's Çetintepe Dam (Tables 1–2).[49] Finalizing 935 km of main canals in the 2008–2013 period, and another 541 km by 2017 during the 2014–2018 Action Plan,[50] also aided in raising average annual expansion in irrigation to 19,631 hectares during 2008–2014 and 30,656 hectares between 2014 and 2017, when irrigated area reached 547,333 hectares (52 percent of the lower target).[51] Over the 2008–2017 period, Euphrates and Tigris irrigated areas grew by 88 and 150 percent, respectively, to reach two-thirds and 25 percent of the new targets.[52] Trailing Urfa-Harran irrigation, which had commenced over twenty years earlier upon completion of its affiliated diversion tunnel and came fully online in 2009, the second largest irrigation expansion within GAP's Euphrates command area came from a one-year increment of 61,883 hectares in the Mardin-Ceylanpinar YAS (*Yeralti Suyu* or "Groundwater") subproject,[53] which involved digging 1,600 deep wells.[54]

Earlier development of GAP's electricity-generation sector thus provided for nearly full Euphrates River flow control by the early 1990s. Perceiving that this could permit Turkey to divert more water for "consumptive uses" like irrigation, despite the contrary possibility that higher current returns from hydropower might ultimately serve to cap the expansion of irrigation and thus water diversions, Syria worked to block *any* upstream project, in part by backing the PKK and thus fomenting a transnational security dilemma with recurring implications for Turkey's dams. Indeed, GAP's hydro-electricity did factor into Turkey's national growth trajectory, which provided the means for greater investment in GAP's remaining irrigation and large Tigris Basin dam projects. As Turkey's technical capacity to use Euphrates and Tigris water for more "first-in-line" uses has grown, conflict over dams will continue, especially as drought renders "mean" annual flow less meaningful.

Table 3.5: GAP Irrigation

Period	Increase (hectares)	
	Total	Annual Average
1995–2017*	423,373	18,408
1995–2002	74,894	9,362
2002–2017	348,479	21,780
2002–2008	88,441	12,634
2008–2017	260,038	26,004
2008–2014	137,415	19,631
2014–2017	122,623	30,656

Sources: Based on GAPRDA, *Son Durum 2018*, 18 (Investment) and 32 (2002–2017 Irrigation), and idem, *Son Durum (Eylül 1996)*, 4 (1995 Irrigation).
Note: *Irrigated area was 547,333 ha in 2017.

Challenge(r)s to Turkish Hydro-Hegemony

Ankara had to devote considerable resources to get Turkey's costly and contested eastern water projects off the blueprint sheet. Over fifty years ago, Syria and Iraq sought negotiations over Turkey's Keban Dam, even prior to the dam's 1965 ground-breaking ceremony.[55] Sometime between its initial filling in 1974 to installation of its last turbine in 1982, Syria and Iraq were cognizant that the Keban Dam, with its storage volume of 31 km^3 (45 percent of that active), could stop the Euphrates River for one year (or more) initially and thereafter for five to six months per year. Shortly after a crisis between Syria and Iraq over the concurrent fillings of Keban and Syria's Tabqa Dam during the 1974–1975 drought, work on Karakaya Dam got underway, and, in 1977, this dam and Urfa Tunnels came under GAP's aegis.

Ankara's willingness to negotiate reflected an exigent need for outside financing. Turkey obtained multilateral loans to cover Keban's US$85 million cost and half of Karakaya's US$1.16 billion expense. This was not just because their sole hydro-power function would not "consume" water, but also because Ankara agreed to maintain respective flows of at least 350 m^3/second (amounting to 35 percent of mean annual flow) and 500 m^3/second (i.e. half of average annual flow) from these dams.[56] These unilateral pledges did not vanquish downstream fears. Ankara's evident determination to build the Şanliurfa Tunnels and their parent Atatürk Dam without World Bank funding would have given Turkey the means to capture the river's entire mean annual flow and divert at least one third of it for irrigation. From 1985 to 1987, during Karakaya Dam's filling and Atatürk Dam's initial construction, Turkey started the Kralkizi, Dicle, and Batman dams, which would put 3 km^3 of Tigris River water into live storage and service irrigation of 167,510 hectares.

Talks devolved into recitation of relatively fixed stances. In a 1964 meeting with Baghdad, Ankara proposed a Joint Technical Committee (JTC), which, in addition to inspecting "each river to determine its average yearly discharge," would "determine the irrigation needs of the three countries through joint field studies."[57] As epitomized again later by Turkey's 1984 "Three Stage Plan for Optimum, Equitable and Reasonable Utilization of the Transboundary Watercourses of the Tigris-Euphrates Basin," emphasizing joint flow measurement, soil inventories, and studies of water needs,[58] further "joint study" emerged as a core mantra of Ankara's technocratic approach to "allocation." It rejected "sharing" water to which it had made sovereign claims that it mooted within the JTC between 1980, when this body first met at Baghdad's request, and its 1993 suspension. This stance implicitly questioned the viability of Syria's planned irrigation of 640,000 hectares in the Euphrates basin.[59] Underlining the relatively larger availability to Iraq of Tigris water, the two rivers' confluence at the Shatt al-Arab, and Iraq's 1988 construction of the Tharthar Canal to divert Tigris water into the Euphrates Basin, Ankara also depicted the two rivers as one basin, implying that Iraq could take more from the Tigris.[60] In the first tripartite negotiation in 1965, Damascus backed Turkey's arguments and creation of the JTC, but later agreed with Baghdad to treat the Euphrates as one "international" river and to divide its flow according to stated needs, or even to divide it into thirds.[61]

Syria's leader, Hafez Al-Assad, searched for more coercive tools, as neither his Soviet benefactors nor lack of World Bank monies could stop Turkey. He offered sanctuary and bases in Damascus and Lebanon's Bekaa Valley to Abdullah "Apo" Öcalan, who fled Turkey before the 1980 military coup with members of his Marxist-style PKK.[62] In March 1987, the PKK killed a soldier guarding the Kralkizi Dam worksite, leading the Turkish Armed Forces (TAF) to reinforce security there and at other dam sites and conduct a bombing campaign against PKK camps in northern Iraq. In June of the same year, the PKK raided the non-GAP Özlüce Dam (and HEPP) site on the Peri Suyu above Keban.[63] That July, Ankara consented, for the period during construction of the Atatürk Dam, "to release a yearly average of more than 500 m³/s at the Turkish-Syrian border" and make up any deficits below 500 m³/s in the following month, though the larger bilateral economic protocol of which this was part lacked any Syrian quid pro quo on security.[64] The PKK raided the Çat Dam construction site above Atatürk Dam in

August 1987,[65] three months before Turkish President Turgut Özal's first overt threat to cut water.[66]

Thus, budding Turkish hydro-hegemony also began assuming a dominative profile. In a tense political climate aggravated by the 1988–1989 drought, Baghdad and Damascus complained that Atatürk Dam, which began filling in January 1990, had damaged crops, degraded water quality, and decreased hydropower output. They viewed Ankara's claimed use of the Keban and Karakaya reservoirs to keep flow at 509 m³/s over November 1989 to February 1990 not as an act of generosity (as Turkey may have hoped),[67] but as a demonstration of the upstream actor's exploitative capacity. In 1990, Syria and Iraq demanded that Turkey supply 700 m³/s in order to underpin their own agreement that 42 percent of the Euphrates' flow reaching the Syrian border go to Syria and 58 percent to Iraq. Ironically, the 1989 Master Plan estimate that GAP's Euphrates irrigation would require 10.4 km³ of water (Table 3) undergirded this demand, but also fed into the image of a "water-rich" Turkey that its authorities have been trying to dispel ever since.[68]

Conflict dragged on. In November 1991, Prime Minister Demirel threatened to bomb Lebanon's Bekaa Valley, and alluded to the dams' putative deterrent powers.[69] One year later, the PKK detonated a dynamite stockpile at the Batman Dam site.[70] The start of Atatürk Dam's HEPP led Demirel and Al-Assad to sign an accord in January 1993 pledging "not to permit any activity on their respective territories detrimental to the security of each other" and "to reach before the end of 1993 a final solution determining the allocation...of the waters of the Euphrates River."[71] Nonetheless, late the following year, the PKK attacked a military unit guarding the Mercan Dam works in the Euphrates Basin.[72] In 1995, Damascus sponsored a new PKK incursion into Turkey's Hatay province, and, along with Baghdad, threatened legal action in 1996 against the consortium to which Turkey had awarded a BOT contract to build Birecik Dam and HEPP.[73] That year also saw the PKK kill three security guards at Kralkizi Dam following President Demirel's visit there.[74] Then, in 1998, a suspected Syrian-backed sabotage plot against the Birecik Dam emerged and the PKK attacked a road-construction crew near Özlüce Dam,[75] both events preceding a TAF mobilization on the Syrian border that finally forced Al-Assad to expel PKK head Öcalan.

The salient inter-state dimensions of conflict over Turkey's dams began ebbing, as the PKK's loss of Syrian patronage and Öcalan's subsequent capture mitigated the overt threat posed by this group. The Ilisu Dam marked an apparent transition in the primary methodology of opposition. As Ilisu Dam's entry into Turkish public investment plans, initial consortium formation, and early provisional approval from export credit agencies (ECAs) occurred in 1997, before the Turkey-Syria rapprochement, it incurred one of the last rebukes from Damascus, which pushed for compensation from, and threatened to blacklist, private-sector backers, and thus raised alarms as late as 1999 over the chances of a "water war" over Ilisu.[76] In December of that year, ECAs conditioned their support for this project on Turkey's maintenance of "adequate" downstream flows.[77]

However, other actors rushed into the anti-dam campaign with more post-Westphalian concerns. One centered on the 10.4 km³ reservoir's anticipated inundation of up to fifty-two villages and fifteen small towns and the displacement of at least 20,000 inhabitants, including those of the 12,000-year-old town of Hasankeyf.[78] Lead NGOs pushed ECAs to get Turkey to accept the need for a resettlement program, upstream water-treatment plants, and archaeological heritage preservation.[79] In Britain, where the government had initially championed the dam project, ambivalent public response to the main Environmental Impact Assessment (EIA) report prevented consortium member

Balfour Beatty from securing an export-credit guarantee, so it withdrew in 2001–2002, along with other firms.[80]

Relations with Syria and Iraq, EU membership prospects, and economic performance improved under the AKP government. In 2005, Ankara assembled a new consortium, not only reviving the NGO campaign, but also drawing in local civil-society activists from Diyarbakir, Batman, and Hasankeyf.[81] Turkish authorities launched construction in August 2006, greeted by a protest of 8,000 people and possibly large Turkish Armed Forces contingents as well.[82] That December, the Export Credit Agencies' mandated Committees of Experts, over the course of 2007–2009, reported gradual improvement in Turkey's compliance with the stipulated conditions on the environment and resettlement—contrary to NGO findings. However, Turkey's efforts on heritage preservation continued to fall short, prompting ECAs and banks to back out again in July 2009.[83] Ankara handed financing over to Turkish banks, but loss of foreign backing worsened Turkey-EU relations, and the laggard pace of expropriation left many Turks, especially Erdoğan and his supporters, convinced that protesters and opponents were tools of outside powers "linked to Kurdish separatism and nationalism," and detrimental to "the nation and its hydro-based modernization."[84]

Back to the Dam-Centric Security Dilemma

Abdullah Öcalan's capture in Kenya and life imprisonment in Turkey dealt a blow to the PKK, which ceased fire between 1999 and 2003. Coinciding with the commencement of the AKP's first government, however, the start of the Iraq War widened the group's room for maneuver and incentives to return to combat. Nonetheless, until sometime after 2009, when the second AKP-led government began engaging in the "Kurdish Opening," the PKK was relatively inactive on the anti-dam front.

Laws on expropriation and the environment predating 2002 offered some alternative venues for asserting grievances. Given the checkered resettlement records of the Atatürk Dam and the European Court of Human Rights' large expropriation-related caseload (354 out of Turkish nationals' 1357 total petitions), during the initial pre-AKP era of IMF reforms, accompanying Turkey's 1999 attainment of EU member candidacy, the Grand National Assembly strengthened civil and property rights.[85] The parliament, which had passed an Environmental Impact Assessment (EIA) "By-Law" in 1993 on the basis of the 1983 Environmental Law, also revised it four times until 2008 to align it with the EU's governing 1985 directive.[86] The 2008 version featured lower respective minimum thresholds at which dams and run-of-the-river hydroelectric power plants (HEPPs) required an EIA—from 100 hm^3 (cubic hectometers or million cubic meters of storage volume), or 15 km^2 of surface area, and 50 MW to 10 hm^3 and 25 MW—and required new screening for dams of at least 5 hm^3 and HEPPs of 0.5 MW (down from 10 hm^3 and 10 MW).[87] An EIA would bring the public into the "scoping" phase and, though much participation remained weak or motivated by concerns on expropriation, it represented Turkey's only mechanism to insert public input into dam-building decisions.[88]

Less helpfully, albeit with little fanfare, a "Border Dams" project emerged at this time. Most assumed it would flood craggy terrain used for passage, shelter, and storage by PKK fighters based in the Qandil Mountains,[89] functions that the Turkish Armed Forces and media sources also envisaged for Ilisu.[90] The project consists of several roller-compacted concrete dams in Şirnak and Hakkari provinces, all tendered in July–August 2008, and eight in pairs.[91] In Şirnak, besides Hezil River's Silopi Dam (built in 2011), the Hezil's Ortasu tributary will host, in successive upstream order, Şirnak Dam, built in 2010 near the Hezil itself, and the Uludere-Balli (a pair), Kavşaktepe, and Musatepe-

Çetintepe dams—each of the latter duo built in 2014 and 2013, respectively.[92] In Hakkari, the Gölgeliyamaç-Çocuktepe pair is slated for Greater Zab's Güzeldere tributary and Aslandağ-Beyyurdu brackets part of the Büyükçay. DSI put the latter at 95 percent completion in 2017, with Forestry and Water Minister Eroğlu blaming delays on "terror" attacks.[93]

After 2009, some recentralization of expropriation and EIA decisions also occurred. In December 2010, parliament amended the 2005 Renewable Energy Law to permit dams in or near protected areas and decrees ordering "urgent expropriation" of immovable property.[94] Ilisu Dam accounted for 92 percent of total HEPP-related expropriations of 9,986 hectares between 2013 and 2017.[95] In September 2016, during the first three months of emergency rule after the coup attempt of July 15, the Council of Ministers approved DSI's "urgent expropriation" of 990 parcels (in fifty villages) that this dam would inundate.[96] In May 2013, the parliament also made statutory the 1993 EIA By-Law's legally contested "provisional" Article 3, allowing exemptions from the by-law itself in certain cases, such as Birecik and Ilisu (ECA demands had once superseded this exemption for the latter).[97]

Ankara's halcyon years of basin-centered cooperation also seemed to peak in 2009. In Istanbul in February, the revived Joint Technical Committee agreed on meteorological and water-quality data sharing; Turkey and Syria assented to increase water flow to Iraq in June; and the three states approved new climate- and drought-related data sharing and improved gauging capacity in September, at which time Turkey agreed to supply 550 m³/s of Euphrates River to *Iraq* until October 20, 2009.[98] However, with Iraq's January 2010 election ahead, discontent with Turkish dams resurfaced again. In May 2009, Iraqi parliamentarians, citing national experts' claims of normal rainfall levels, contended that these projects had lowered the country's water supply by three-quarters, from 40 km³ to 11 km³. They conditioned their vote for any new bilateral agreement on guaranteed Iraqi water rights.[99] Iraq's Water Minister Latif Rashid carried a similar plaintive tone into the aforementioned September 2009 meeting, arguing that Turkey had reneged on promises to increase Euphrates' flow. This claim was refuted by Turkey's Energy and National Resources Minister Taner Yildiz, who also stressed that central and eastern Anatolia were receiving only 350 m³/s of water.[100] He even alluded, at the height of the Foreign Ministry's "zero problems with neighbors" policy, to Ankara's sovereign right to manage its "own" water and energy resources.[101] As observers noted, cooperation elided the real problem,[102] which was essentially zero conflict resolution "in terms of the quantity or quality of the waters reaching downstream borders."[103]

The Syrian civil war, which spread to Iraq in 2014, upended the entire relationship. It certainly prevented implementation of the 2009 agreements,[104] though this did not disadvantage the hydro-hegemon, with time on its side. However, the war confronted Ankara with new threats from violent non-state challengers, including the so-called Islamic State (IS or Daesh) and the anti-Daesh People's Protection Units (Yekîneyên Parastina Gel or YPG), PKK-linked combatants to which Bashar Al-Assad ceded de facto control of large swaths of northern Syria in 2012. Despite the ongoing Kurdish reconciliation, PKK activity was revived in Turkey—the two-year ceasefire commencing in May 2013 was finally brought to an end in July 2015.

The PKK returned to targeting dams and other infrastructure. In 2010–2017, there were nearly seventy-five incidents focusing on dams, HEPPs, and relevant assets like stone quarries or military stations, over twenty-five of which took place *during* the ceasefire, across the Euphrates Basin (e.g. Alparslan-2, Dinar—not attributed to the PKK—Kiği, Koçali, and Pembelik), Tigris Basin (chiefly Batman, Ilisu, and Silvan), and elsewhere (e.g.

Narinkale on the Aras).[105] Declaring the truce over in July 2015, PKK faction KCK (Koma Civakên Kurdistan or Kurdistan Communities Union) claimed that the ongoing building of "military" dams and roads already resembled a type of war preparation and thus constituted a *casus belli*.[106] This was a view consistent with nationalist Kurdish militants' palpable fear that GAP's transportation networks could allow "far easier monitoring and access throughout the borderlands, making it difficult for separatists to retreat to small villages or to flee across the border."[107] Resumption of hostilities intensified attacks, with twenty-two targeting the Silvan project in 2015 alone, half of these after the fighting started.[108] An estimated thirty-eight incidents made 2015 a big year for dam-related attacks, with the two dozen occurring that year after the war resumed being directed not just against Silvan, but also Kiği on the Euphrates's Peri Suyu tributary, and the Tigris Basin's Batman, Çetin (on the Botan River) and Ilisu dam sites, plus the Kulp HEPPs on the same-named tributary that flows to Silvan and Batman dams.

Turkish authorities have subtly credited the PKK with the capability of slowing down key projects and driving up their costs. For example, Minister Eroğlu admitted in August 2015 that PKK damage to access roads had choked off supplies, nearly halting construction on Silvan Dam.[109] However, whether ascribing the motivations behind PKK attacks to the need to preempt loss of logistical routes and/or a desire to prevent the state from serving people in the southeast, officials have not called GAP's basic feasibility or rationale into question, but have stressed a national need and resolve to finish them. Indeed, one prevailing discourse sees large dams as "mad projects" ("*çilgin projeler*")—symbolizing worthy undertakings against formidable odds—and "terror-resistant" ("*teröre inat barajlar*").[110] Thus, Ankara's ruling circles have reacted to attacks on dams by doubling down on them.

The Al-Assad regime's August 1998 decision to expel Öcalan and close PKK bases occurred under direct Turkish military pressure, not "water pressure." In 2017, the YPG's political affiliate PYD (Partiya Yekîtiya Demokrat or Democratic Union Party) did accuse Turkey of manipulating the flow of water to disrupt operations of Syria's Tishrin Dam after the YPG had wrested it from IS, which leveled the same charge against Turkey in 2015.[111] Nonetheless, the TAF again had to intervene directly to stop YPG advances in northern Syria via "Operation Euphrates Shield" (August 2016–March 2017) and "Operation Olive Branch" (January–March 2018). The filling of Ilisu Dam is far more likely to diminish the water supply reaching Baghdad, making the central government—which has already opposed Turkish intervention in Iraq—even less receptive to helping Ankara on the PKK issue, than to force a removal of the PKK's older presence in the far northern areas of Iraq, where the Greater Zab is a more significant water resource. For the latter purpose, the TAF has set up several outposts in preparation for a possible ground incursion against PKK camps and caves in the Qandil Mountains.[112] Reversing the prior scenario of soldiers securing dams, water authorities are also aiding the military. For example, the DSI had been deploying machinery to erect barriers to PKK fighters trying to cross the Orontes River from Hatay to Afrin during the period in which the TAF and proxy force the Free Syrian Army had been fighting to retake it from the YPG.[113]

Conclusion

Maximization of flow control creates an obvious flashpoint, but does not make conflict inevitable, as demonstrated in the substantive, rather than merely instrumental, cooperation among Iraq, Syria, and Turkey in the 2000s. Moreover, though the PKK gained from Syria's Ba'th Party patronage and their common interest in frustrating Turkey's damming of the rivers in question, the two actors may have had some divergent perspectives on GAP as well. GAP's relatively rapid progress on hydropower benefitted downstream states to the extent that it limited upstream irrigation, but the glacial pace of irrigation likely nurtured further resentment of some who already viewed the project as sucking wealth out of the southeast. Indeed, improved water-centric relations at one level might worsen them at other levels,[114] circumscribing consent for Turkey's basin hegemony. However, Turkey's past threats to halt flow, as well as any intended use of dammed water to flood out guerrillas, could reunite *both* the downstream states—quiescent during the Syrian civil war—*and* Kurdish nationalists. Ultimately, GAP's political functions represent a "construct rather than a given."[115] Nationalists on opposite sides worsened conflict over Turkey's dams, including Ilisu, by portraying these as "security" dams beneficial to Turks, or as "military" dams harmful to Kurds. How this impacts Ankara's efforts to complete GAP and consolidate hydro-hegemony remains to be seen.

4

A WATERSHED MOMENT

ASSESING THE HYDROPOLITICS OF IRAQI KURDISTAN

Marcus DuBois King

Introduction

Allocation of the Euphrates and Tigris waters has been a source
of tension between Iraq and its neighbors for generations.
Relationships among the riparian states have been thoroughly
examined in the water and conflict literature. However, the
emerging role of Iraqi Kurdistan as a riparian actor has received
little attention to date. Therefore, a current analysis of the
hydropolitics of Kurdistan is limited by a sparse academic literature. This challenge of assessing hydropolitics is augmented by
a dynamic security situation on the ground that has diminished
Iraqi Kurdistan's control of water resources. The Iraqi Army,
supported by pro-Iranian militia, took possession of the city of

Kirkuk and the area adjacent to the Tigris River following its independence referendum of September 2017. The Kurdistan Regional Government (KRG) lost control of substantial water reserves. It also lost the political leverage that accompanied physical control of the Tigris River. Time will tell if this shift is permanent. To keep pace with such rapid changes in the geopolitical landscape, this study relies on academic sources and media reports, as well as interviews conducted with journalists, a relief worker, and a regional scholar between October 2017 and July 2018.

At the outset, it is useful to describe the term "hydropolitics." It was defined by Elhance as "the systematic study of conflict and cooperation between states over water resources that transcend international borders."[1] For the purposes of this chapter, Iraqi Kurdistan's hydropolitics will encompass water conditions affecting all political relationships on the national and international levels. The range of actors that fall territorially within this hydropolitical complex include the KRG, the Iraqi national government, Turkey, Iran, and Syria. External actors, such as the United States, also wield influence.

Hydropolitics is also used here to characterize contention for water resources within Iraqi Kurdistan's boundaries, including, for example, between refugees fleeing the violence in the rest of Iraq and Syria, and indigenous Kurds. Likewise, the definition of water stress used here moves explicitly beyond notions of simple water scarcity in the hydropolitical complex to an understanding that considers both the quality and quantity of available water resources.

Lastly, the definitional issue most essential to the conceptual framework of this study is the geographical scope of "Kurdistan." Many scholars, not to mention politicians, will disagree. Greater Kurdistan is an almost universally ambiguous and contested concept. The widest common usage of the term encompasses all land predominantly settled by the Kurds across four countries: southeastern Turkey, northern Iraq, northwestern Iran, and northern Syria.[2] This analysis focuses primarily on Iraqi Kurdistan (Figure 1), understood here to coincide with the area administered by the KRG as of summer 2018. As a self-governing region, Iraqi Kurdistan has a distinct political and legal personality. An understanding of how these factors evolved will be necessary for further analysis.

Background

The Emergence of Iraqi Kurdistan

Iraqi Kurdistan's contemporary hydropolitical challenges were not inevitable. Consideration of Kurdish history explains how both external aggression and internal political divisions played key roles. Political conflict and skepticism toward the federal Iraqi government's motives, and a fractured, sometimes self-defeating internal political dynamic, present challenges to the development of Iraqi Kurdish water strategy. The persistent historical question of Kurdish autonomy, either within or external to the federal Iraqi state, also presents barriers to regional cooperation. There is precedence for a proper Kurdish state dating back to the end of the First World War, yet its development was quickly smothered by prevailing regional powers.

Denial of statehood is just one factor that has led to Kurdish skepticism of their neighbors. Iraq in particular, as demonstrated acutely under the regime of Saddam Hussein, systematically attacked Kurds and hampered their development as a functioning nation-state. Moreover, it is this diplomatic tension that creates a substantial obstacle to meaningful dialogue on water management today—not only between Iraqi Kurdistan and Baghdad, but between regional neighbors generally. Iraqi Kurdistan's conflict

WATER AND CONFLICT IN THE MIDDLE EAST

Figure 4.1: State of the Kurds

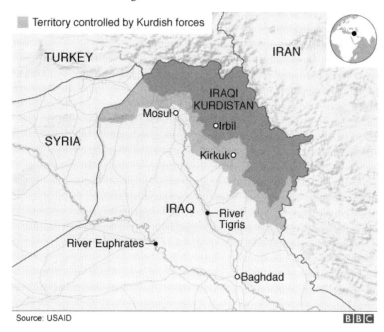

Territory controlled by Kurdish forces

TURKEY

IRAN

IRAQI KURDISTAN

Mosul○

○Irbil

SYRIA

Kirkuk○

IRAQ ◀—River Tigris

River Euphrates—▶

○Baghdad

Source: USAID

BBC

Source: "Iraqi Kurdistan Votes in Independence Referendum," *BBC News*, September 25, 2017, www.bbc.com/news/world-middle-east-41382494.

with its neighbors has driven cyclical gains and losses in territory, presenting serious barriers to development, particularly in infrastructure, where a stable internationally recognized state might have enjoyed external funding and investment. Nevertheless, it is not just external pressures that have led to a disjointed water management policy in Iraqi Kurdistan today. As the following section outlines, Iraqi Kurdistan's history explains failed attempts at internal political unification as well as the KRG's behavior and equities within a contested hydropolitical space.

While the Kurdish population is heterogeneous, they are a primarily mountain-dwelling people of Indo-European descent. By some estimates, thirty million people identify as Kurds, making them the fourth-largest ethnic group in the Middle East, despite never achieving statehood.[3] Iraqi Kurdistan is the geographical focus of this chapter. A Kurdish ethnic majority also exists in western Iran, southern Turkey, northeastern Syria, and pockets of the former Soviet Union. While their cultural self-identity is universally recognized, they share neither a single language nor religion. They speak a number of different dialects of Kurdish or Arabic, and practice several religions including Sunni Islam, Judaism, and Christianity.

The modern history of the Kurds is characterized by shared grievances brought about by substantial hardships and repression, including denial of statehood, military attacks, violations of human rights, and, by some accounts, outright genocide. Arguably, modern setbacks for the Kurds can be traced to the settlement of World War I. The Treaty of Sèvres of 1920 was ratified by the defeated Ottoman Empire upon that occasion, and provided for an independent Kurdistan.[4] But the successive Turkish Republic rejected Sèvres and its replacement, the 1923 Treaty of Lausanne, which designated the Kurds a minority in Turkey, Iraq, Iran, and Syria—a status that stands today. Iraq's independence from Britain in 1932 and its acceptance into the League of Nations was in small part contingent upon respecting the Kurdish minority, including provisions for limited Kurdish language use in elementary education.

After World War II, Mulla Mustafa Barzani founded the Kurdish Democratic Party (KDP) and established an Iraqi-Kurdish insurgent militia called the Peshmerga. The fall of the Iraqi monarchy in 1958 brought recognition of Kurdish nationality, but by 1961 the new Iraqi Republic soon moved to dissolve the KDP. Advances by the Peshmerga led the Iraqi government to grant limited Kurdish autonomy in 1974. Barzani rejected the so-called "self-rule" plan, however, as the Iraqi president would retain regional authority and the power to select Kurdish leaders or dissolve their legislative council.[5] In addition, the decree named Erbil the capital, a city of secondary importance to the oil-rich Kirkuk—a cultural center with a large Kurdish population. Around the same time, the more left-leaning of the Kurds under Jalal Talabani formed the Patriotic Union of Kurdistan (PUK), breaking away from the KDP. The PUK and KDP remain the dominant and contending Kurdish political parties today.

The ascendance of Saddam Hussein in 1979 and his espousal of strong pan-Arab nationalism were accompanied by a dramatic suppression of Iraqi Kurds. Saddam initially courted Kurdish factions throughout the early stages of the Iran-Iraq War (1980–1988), hoping to dissuade them from siding with Tehran. Nevertheless, the PUK supported Iranian operations, providing the rationale for Saddam to launch a series of scorched-earth attacks on Kurdish-controlled areas from February to September 1988. These operations incorporated the use of death camps and routine executions by firing squad. Iraqi forces used chemical weapons at least twice—including in the now infamous incident in the town of Halabja on March 16, 1988, in which 5,000 Kurds were killed. These operations, referred to as the al-Anfal campaign, killed as many as 100,000 Kurds, and have been declared as genocide by Human Rights Watch.[6] Kurdish mistrust of Baghdad was thus further forged in the crucible of suffering.

In 1991, the Kurds welcomed the US invasion of Iraq. The collapse of the Saddam Hussein regime enabled them to obtain significant autonomy in the north of the country. With US support and a no-fly zone for Iraqi aircraft, Kurdish authorities set up a 105-member parliamentary body in 1992. Rifts soon developed between the KDP and PUK—which effectively shared power—and a civil war ensued from 1994 to 1998. Washington brokered a peace between Kurdish political factions as the likelihood of another US invasion increased.

A WATERSHED MOMENT

After Saddam Hussein's regime was toppled in 2003, the relationship between the US and Iraqi Kurdistan became even stronger. With little direct combat in northern Iraq during Operation Iraqi Freedom (OIF), the Kurds formalized control over significant swaths of territory, including its vast water resources. Historian Michael Gunter recognized the relative prosperity of the Kurdish region at that time noting that, "a civil society is also emerging, with dozens of newspapers, magazines, and television and radio stations representing a broad spectrum of opinion. People have freedoms impossible to imagine in the rest of Iraq."[7]

After the 2003 invasion, Kurdish politics evolved rapidly. In 2005, a majority of Kurdish factions ratified a referendum that supported federalism, solidifying autonomous control of a Kurdish Region. In addition, PUK leader Jalal Talabani would soon be elected president of all Iraq, serving from 2006–2014. Around the same time, KDP leader Masoud Barzani, son of the party's now deceased founder, became President of Iraqi Kurdistan and the KRG. In the years after the invasion, the Iraqi Kurds solidified the autonomous aspects of their proto-state, including water governance.

In June 2017, KRG President Barzani set a referendum vote for Kurdish independence for September 25, 2017. Rejected by Baghdad via a November 20 Supreme Court ruling and discouraged by Washington, the vote yielded 92 percent in favor of independence.[8] Just weeks after the vote, in October 2017, the Iraqi national army and Popular Mobilization Front (PMF) militia retook control of Kirkuk and the surrounding region, which had been under Kurdish Peshmerga control since 2014 when it was captured from the so-called Islamic State (IS). Before IS, Iraq had control of Kirkuk. Currently, while IS has lost most of its significant territory in Iraq, it and other fluid militant groups may continue to present an enduring insurgent threat.

In the wake of the Iraqi assault, the PUK-controlled Peshmerga struck a deal with the Iraqis to retreat without a fight and without notifying the KDP forces; the latter group was overwhelmed. This illustrative episode contributes substantially to the rift between the parties that has characterized Kurdish politics since this incident.[9] The loss of Kirkuk was especially devastating because its rich oil fields were the KRG's chief source of revenue. The aftermath of the referendum has also proven negative, especially for Barzani's political fortunes. He announced his relinquishment of the KRG presidency amid military maneuvers by neighboring countries and a backlash from the vote.[10] The loss of Kirkuk also diminished the Kurds' direct hydropolitical advantage as they lost control of land adjacent to the Tigris River. The Kurds still control the Eastern bank of the Tigris as it enters Iraq from Turkey, which remains under Kurdish administration.

The Kurdistan Regional Government Today

The KRG is composed of a coalition government that consists of the Kurdistan Democratic Party, Patriotic Union of Kurdistan, Kurdistan Islamic Movement, the Chaldean Assyrian Syriac Council, Turkmen representatives, Communists, and Socialists. The KRG exercises authority over the provinces of Erbil, Duhok, Silemâni, and Halabja,[11] and, prior to October 2017, maintained de facto authority over parts of Diyala and Ninawa as well as Kirkuk province. The KRG is a democratically elected body that exercises executive power in accordance with regional laws, as stipulated by the Kurdish Parliament. Erbil serves as the capital of the Kurdistan Region, where the KRG's nineteen ministries operate despite historical claims to Kirkuk as the center of government.

The KRG's foreign affairs are conducted in a dualistic and ambiguous manner that occludes administration and negotiations over water resources. As a federated region of Iraq, the Government of Iraq (GOI) technically controls Iraqi Kurdistan's diplomatic relations as stipulated by the constitution. However, in practice, the KRG has established diplomatic and commercial relations with foreign capitals—including Washington, Ankara, and Tehran—with Baghdad largely turning a blind eye. The independence referendum now further occludes Baghdad's tolerance of Kurdistan's diplomatic activity.

The Iraqi Constitution is arguably ambiguous in the area of delineation of responsibility for governance of natural resources. Article 110 stipulates that Iraqi federal authorities have exclusive rights over the "planning processes connected to water resources from outside Iraq and guaranteeing levels of water flow into Iraq according to international law and custom."[12] This is obviously complicated by the fact that waters flowing into Iraq cross Kurdish territory in some areas. Article 114 of the Constitution further clouds this issue, assigning shared responsibility for "internal" water policy between the federal and regional authorities. Further, it notes that "internal water resources policy should be formulated and regulated in a way that guarantees their just distribution and this shall be regulated by law."[13] This body of law referenced in the second part of the provision does not exist.

In contrast to the prescriptions of the Constitution, the KRG has exercised de facto exclusive control of water resources within its political boundaries. Whether the shared jurisdiction over the water delineated in the Constitution can be operationalized to ensure benefits to the satisfaction of all the parties is an open question. It is a source of underlying tension that promises to become more immediate.

While largely beyond the scope of this chapter, it is worth noting that management of oil resources is a similar political flashpoint. The KRG depends very heavily on oil for revenue, producing some 650,000 barrels daily, which is exported mostly to Turkey, Iran, and other parts of Iraq—its immediate neighbors.[14] Oil production has fluctuated greatly in the face of factors such as IS militant offensives and, most recently, the Iraqi seizure of Kirkuk. Grievances are fed by the fact that, since early 2014, the KRG has not received its constitutionally guaranteed 17 percent share of the Iraqi federal budget apportioned according to Kurdistan's proportion of oil revenue. In response, Baghdad cites several political factors, including Kurdistan's autonomous decision to export oil to global markets.

Water Resources of Iraqi Kurdistan

Iraqi Kurdistan has been blessed with relatively abundant water resources, and enjoys substantial annual precipitation compared to regional neighbors. It is divided into three geologic zones: the northern range of the Zagros Mountains, the central transitional mountain range, and the southern plains along the Tigris River, with annual precipitation of above 500 millimeters (mm), 300–500mm, and below 300mm, respectively.[15] All of these ranges compare favorably to the national average for Iraq, which is 216 mm.[16] Iraqi Kurdistan has a Mediterranean climate (hot, dry summers and cool, wet winters), with approximately 80 percent of the region's precipitation falling between December and March.[17]

Surface water resources are profuse. The four major rivers in the Kurdish Region are the Tigris, Greater Zab, Little Zab, and the Diyala. The Tigris forms the border of the Dohuk governorate for 138 kilometers before leaving the region. In 2004, the flow of the Tigris as it entered Iraq was estimated at 21 billion cubic meters (BCM) and an additional 23 BCM is added through runoff within Iraq—nearly all of which comes from the Kurdistan Region.[18] The Greater Zab has its headwaters in Turkey, and the headwaters of the Little Zab and the Diyala are in Iran.[19] In sum, the rivers provide 75 percent of water for household and commercial use, drinking, and agriculture. The region's groundwater quenches the remaining 25 percent of the need.[20]

Despite relative water availability, mid- and long-term hydropolitical trends are emerging, including questions of water accessibility. Some of these movements are not apparent to hydrologists and the KRG because the distribution of water resources is not well documented, and there is also a lack of systematic collection of water data. There are few water-gauging stations and observational wells monitoring groundwater and aquifers, and so this aspect of the water inventory is little understood.[21] Water policymakers in Erbil are forced to regularly use unreliable hydrogeological data, hampering their ability to identify trends. However, some tools are available that allow for general conclusions about the severity of Iraqi Kurdistan's water situation. For example, the World Resources Institute's "Aqueduct Water Risk Atlas," a state-of-the-art web-based tool, assigns an ordinal level of water stress by weighing the ratio of total annual water withdrawals to total annual renewable supply, accounting for upstream consumptive use and incorporating regulatory positions, as well as media and public perceptions of water availability. Higher values and the resulting darker colorations on the interactive map indicate more competition among users.[22]

The Aqueduct Atlas demonstrates a baseline water stress of medium-to-high levels for Iraqi Kurdistan today, while territory south of Kirkuk under control of the GOI is classified as either high or extremely high. The Aqueduct Atlas finds that groundwater stress is especially low in the center of Iraqi Kurdistan. However, Kurdish territory suffers from increasingly significant seasonal and inter-annual variability of rainfall; and flood occurrence is dangerously high. Moreover, Erbil and much of Iraqi Kurdistan will likely encounter high or extremely high water stress and additional variability within the next two decades, while demand for the resource continues to climb. Water, the historical asset of the Kurdish people, is drying up, presenting new challenges to a government already under substantial internal and external political and economic pressures.[23] This development is consistent with predictions for general scarcity across the region. By 2040, the Aqueduct Atlas envisions that water stress will double from historical baselines in the Middle East.

Iraqi Kurdistan's large groundwater reserves are part of a foothills aquifer system fed by snowmelt from the Zagros Mountains. Groundwater quality here is sufficient for both potable and irrigation uses. However, the transmissive capacity, or flow rate, of the water in the regional aquifer is high, meaning that depletion of the aquifer can occur with relative ease, while recharge rates are not well understood.[24] Experts argue that more assessment needs to be done in this area to calculate the corresponding risks of depletion. Due to its relative percentage and connectivity of groundwater aquifers, systematic understanding and management of groundwater throughout Iraq is critically dependent on flows from Kurdistan.

In addition to natural forces, the water stress issue has also been exacerbated by bureaucratic mismanagement and governance issues. Despite the aforementioned vast groundwater reserves, Iraqi Kurdistan is suffering from localized water shortages. Failure to plan was evident in the case of Qaladze, a city of 80,000 in Iraqi Kurdistan, when Iran cut the flow of the Zei Bchuk River in the summer of 2017, leaving residents without water reserves.[25] Since the area is not suitable for groundwater extraction, a feasible long-term solution could have been the construction of dams, but no such plans were developed, even during the years that Iranian construction was clearly observed. Iraqi Kurdistan's water challenges were compounded by neglect and poor planning. Mohamed Amin Barzinji, dean of the Natural Resources Engineering and Management department at the University of Kurdistan-Hawler (UKH), stated the problem succinctly: "It is not that we don't have water, the problem is in our management."[26]

A WATERSHED MOMENT

Iraqi Kurdistan and Regional Hydropolitics

As part of a complex hydrological system, transboundary cooperation is essential to improving Kurdistan's water situation. This section considers a new approach toward understanding theoretical dynamics that govern the behavior of riparian actors in the Tigris and Euphrates Basin. Without a single political or legal unifying framework, hydropolitics in the Tigris and Euphrates Basin can be described using Keohane's construct as a "regime complex" or "a loosely coupled set of specific regimes."[27] Generally, it can be theorized that interactions between actors in this regime complex will lie somewhere between the extremes of genuine cooperation and cut-throat or violent competition.[28]

While the risk and consequences of conflict over water resources between riparian states has been debated, significant empirical evidence points to the historical prevalence of cooperation. A study by Wolf, Yoffe, and Giordano assessed over 1,800 events involving water conflict and cooperation from 1948–2000, and found that cooperative events were twice as common.[29] The Oregon State University's Transboundary Freshwater Dispute Database (TFDD) further demonstrates the extensive history of international water cooperation: over 650 treaties related to factors such as water quality, flow, and hydropower development have been signed since 1820. The TFDD data reveal that the large majority of conflictual incidents were purely rhetorical in the form of confrontational words among leaders and rarely lead to any sort of military or violent confrontation.[30]

There are, however, well-established hydropolitical disputes between riparians in the Tigris-Euphrates river basin system (Turkey, Syria, Iraq, and Iran). While these disputes have rarely resulted in violent conflict, they are contentious in very tangible political respects. For example, riparian disputants at the national level have sometimes resorted to covert action to achieve their ends. Until 1998, the Syrian government provided military support for the Kurdish Workers' Party (PKK), which conducted raids from Syrian territory into Turkey. This support was characterized as retaliation for continued Turkish development of the giant Southeastern Anatolian Project's (Güneydoğu Anadolu Projesi, or GAP) that threatened to withhold Euphrates River flow water to Syria.[31]

When attempting to characterize regional hydropolitical dynamics, it is essential to understand that water-conflict security analysis is overwhelmingly undertaken at the interstate level and relates to disputes over shared river-basin resources. Focusing entirely on the interstate level often leads one to ignore the real, complex relationships between water and security as a driver of instability in strategically important subnational regions. The risks of water-related violence and conflict are growing due to the impact of changing demographics and greater environmental pressures on water resources within states. These patterns are evident in so-called epicenters of water instability, such as Somalia and Nigeria.[32]

It is not surprising that while no water wars have broken out, historical hydropolitics in the Tigris-Euphrates region trend toward the conflictual end of the spectrum. Hydro-hegemonic behavior—monopolization of water resources—is a structurally aggressive action short of armed conflict. Zeitoun and Warner developed the "framework of water hydro-hegemony," under which hydro-hegemony is operationalized at the river-basin level through resource capture, integration, or containment.[33] Hegemonic actors are enabled by the exploitation of existing power asymmetries within a weak international water-governance regime.[34] Hegemonic maneuvers are then executed through instruments, including coercive political pressure, treaty development, and knowledge construction, which can be characterized as linguistic aggression. As essentially a non-state actor (for the purposes of the global internationalist system), the KRG lacks the standing and structural power to shape international conventions, but it can nonetheless exercise significant coercive hydro-hegemonic power through other instruments.

Hydro-hegemonic behavior is generally applied to state actors through the lens of classical realism. In this case, it is argued that hydro-hegemonic behavioral theory can still apply to Iraqi Kurdistan; a subnational or proto-national actor with a large degree of autonomous control over its water resources. A number of factors have normalized hydro-hegemonic behavior between riparians in the Tigris Euphrates hydropolitical regime. Some of these factors are examined below.

First, the riparian states have used water to achieve strategic objectives. As the upper riparian, this behavior can be easily attributed to Turkey. For example, Turkish officials have openly admitted their intent to disrupt Kurdish separatist militia operations in Turkey by denial of strategic territory. This is achieved by inundating areas through the construction of dams as part of the massive GAP project on the Tigris River.[35] Other examples abound. Likewise, as described in the previous section, Iran cut off the flow of Zei Bchuk River. The KRG believes, with credible justification as assessed by this author, that Iran's motivation was strategic and political. This behavior is thus a form of hydro-coercion. Although Iran is suffering from water stress accelerated by a drought, this action can also be read as a warning message in light of Iran's displeasure with the recent independence referendum.[36]

Second, the conflict in Syria and Iraq provides other examples of water being used for leverage, which can be characterized as "weaponization." A study conducted in 2015 found that water was used as a political or tactical weapon in this expanded theater of battle forty-four times from 2012 to 2016; more so by IS than other belligerents.[37] The political economy of water in Iraq is shaped by fears of a resurgent "IS 2.0" or a new al-Qa'ida affiliate dominated by Sunni Arabs.[38] If so, water weaponization by violent extremist organizations or other parties could also become a feature of future conflicts.

Third, the lack of a recognized framework for transboundary water management makes the Tigris-Euphrates hydropolitical regime a weak institution. As stated, hydro-hegemonic action is enabled by weak institutions, and conflicting understandings of "ownership" of the Tigris and Euphrates river waters are perpetuators of the weakness. Turkey holds a view of absolute sovereignty over these resources, whereas Iraq and Syria argue their right to equitable utilization of waters between the nations. Iraq and Syria are signatories of the UN Watercourse Convention of 1997, of which Article 7 requires signatory states to avoid causing significant harm to other co-watercourse states.[39] Turkey, however, is not a signatory of the convention. Remarks by former Turkish Prime Minister Suleyman Demirel referencing Iraq are telling: "Water resources are Turkey's and the oil is theirs. Since we do not tell them, 'look we have a right to half your oil,' they cannot lay claim to what is ours."[40] All indications are that Turkey views Kurdistan's claims to water flow as a downstream riparian through the same lens.

How then does Iraqi Kurdistan fit into the regional hydropolitical regime? The KRG has also been accused of using water to exercise leverage over other Iraqi contenders. These actions are supported by the historical narrative that the Kurds have been victimized by the Arab majority. In 2011, Arab farmers protested that the KRG was withholding waters from the Little Zab at the Dukan Dam before it entered Kirkuk in order to drive them from the area. In addition to their strategic value in the ethnic struggle for control of Kirkuk, these lands are some of the most fertile areas of Iraq.[41]

Water stored sitting behind two dams, the Darbandikhan and the Dukan, is a strategic asset for the Kurds. The Darbandikhan holds back three billion cubic-meters (BCM) and sits on the Diyala River in Sulaymaniyah Governorate.[42] The Dukan Dam impounds the Little Zab, thereby creating Lake Dukan that has a surface area of 259 square kilometers and holds nearly 7 BCM of water.[43] Currently, Iraqi Kurdistan has hegemonic opportunity to use water as leverage against Baghdad near these locations. For example, the KRG is able to impound the waters of the Little Zab River at the Dukan Dam, as water flows downstream before reaching the Tigris River.

As water stress grows elsewhere, the KRG continues to expand its own hydro-hegemonic capacity to store the resource. As of March 2017, Iraqi Kurdistan had seventeen small- and medium-sized operational dams, and twenty more were in various stages of construction.[44] However, the status of many of these projects is currently somewhat unclear as funds have dried up due to an economic recession.[45] Nevertheless, the increase in confirmed dam construction has expanded the KRG's overall capacity to act as a regional hydro-hegemon. Continued dam development within the footprint of Iraqi Kurdistan is bound to have a negative impact on the south. With 60.8 percent of its total renewable water resources originating outside of its borders, Iraq is the most vulnerable actor in the regime.[46]

The quality of water resources in Iraq is also in a general state of decline.[47] As water becomes more polluted and scarce, a concerning dynamic is emerging carrying implications for internal stability in Iraq. There is the perception in southern Iraq that the Kurds are overusing the waters in their territory—a perception that could further erode the tenuous working relationship that now exists between the capitals that are historically skeptical of the other's motives. In the most extreme circumstances, this situation could invite Iraqi military intervention. The United States would have to take sides on this issue and might find itself in the role of an indispensable if reluctant mediator due to its unique historical influence in the area.

Water Stress and Hydropolitics in Iraqi Kurdistan: Emerging Subnational Trends

Water Stress: Anthropogenic Factors

As identified in previous sections, water stress in Kurdistan is a growing trend caused in part by human actions, rendering these man-made water problems. The following section describes the interplay of anthropogenic and natural factors that are increasing water stress in Iraqi Kurdistan. Anthropogenic factors include demographic change, pollution, and limiting infrastructure development in neighboring countries, while natural factors include drought, climate change, and seismic activity.

Involuntary migration is one of the most important anthropogenic factors. Iraqi Kurdistan has a population of approximately 5.2 million permanent residents.[48] Since 2011, the region has hosted 2,250,000 internally displaced people (IDPs) and refugees fleeing conflict zones elsewhere in Iraq and in Syria.[49] The KRG receives support from the international donor community, but still struggles to meet basic human needs of IDPs in many cases. The limited coping capacity to address the impacts of this massive increase in population has been compounded by the economic crisis that hit Iraqi Kurdistan in early 2014 with the slump in prices of Kurdish oil exports.[50] These compound risks have negative implications for governability.

Developments within the agricultural sector add a new dimension to the problem. Kurdistan's economy has traditionally been agrarian and has the technical capacity to be self-sufficient in agricultural production. However, when world oil prices were high in the years after the US invasion in 2003, the windfall filled the coffers of the two political parties. The KDP and PUK established massive patronage networks that enticed farmers off their land and to migrate to the urban centers of Erbil and Sulaymaniyah. At one point, approximately 70 percent of working-age males were on the public-sector payroll.[51] Oil prices have not recovered, and so salaries are being slashed as the KRG's oil-backed patronage economy continues to collapse, forcing many Kurdish farmers to return to their land. While a return to agriculture as a major pillar of the Kurdish economy is a positive development from the perspective of food sufficiency, it will lead to even more pressure on the available water supply in the Tigris and Euphrates watersheds.

The large number of refugees and IDPs is depleting water supplies in some areas where refugee camps are located. On aggregate, according to the UNDP, the provision of humanitarian assistance to refugees and IDPs increased the water demand in the KRG by 15 percent in 2015, with the largest increases seen in Duhok and Erbil.[52] Likewise, a 2014 report by the UN High Commission for Refugees found that there was concerning variation in water availability for drinking between the major camps. Only 37 percent of households in Qushtapa camp near Erbil reported having enough drinking water, followed by 52 percent in Kawergosk and 59 percent in Akre. The Qushtapa camp also reported that only 25 percent of households had enough water for purposes other than drinking.[53] Finally, a French NGO that provides humanitarian assistance to the camps notes that water shortages there fluctuate seasonally, with the greatest scarcity of water for all uses occurring during the hotter and drier summer months.[54]

While around 90 percent of individuals in Kurdish areas have access to improved water sources, or systems designed to protect the delivery of water from outside contaminants, these systems are now grossly overused, especially in and around IDP camps. Even before the onset of IS and the chaos they created in the region, Kurdish residents lacked access to ample wastewater management systems. As large numbers of people relocated, existing systems became exponentially stressed. Currently, many camps are unable to properly dispose of wastewater, especially solid waste. Large open dumping areas have also developed, especially in areas like Erbil, which has more than seventy-five open dumping sites.

The IDPs and refugees in Iraqi Kurdistan are predominantly Sunni Arab agriculturalists from Syria or other regions of Iraq, although some are also Kurdish.[55] As of February 2018, when the battle against IS had essentially concluded, these populations had not begun to repatriate in significant numbers. The continued presence of the IDPs and refugees has led to inevitable irritation of ethnic tension, raising the possibility of civil unrest and localized violence.

The deep animosity that exists between the Kurds and Sunni Arab Iraqis can be traced to the legacies of horror enacted by successive Arabization policies and the aforementioned Al-Anfal campaigns launched by Saddam Hussein. When seen in this context, resettlement negotiations over the status of Iraqi IDPs could turn into a new source of tension between the Iraqi government and the KRG. The presence of a large number of Iraqi Arabs living in substandard conditions has been described as a time bomb by Kurdish observers.[56] Finally, overall population growth is another demographic trend putting at least some pressure on water supply. Birth rates in Iraqi Kurdistan average approximately 3.1 children for every mother—lower than the rest of Iraq at 4.5, but still well above the global average.

Lack of ecological awareness also contributes further to water stress. Across the country, untreated wastewater, untreated solid waste, and industrial waste contaminants are entering major rivers and tainting agricultural fields. The decline in water quality in Iraqi Kurdistan is epitomized by the plight of the Tanjaro River, which flows southwest of the city of Sulaimani. This historically large river was once fishable, swimmable, and drinkable, but has been depleted to a seasonally dry riverbed by overuse, waste disposal, and encroaching development.[57]

Over-abstraction of water resources has also been a major issue. Digging illegal boreholes has increased due to the lack of law enforcement or metering to measure consumption, which has had a negative effect on the groundwater quantity and quality in Kurdistan. As a result, there were more than 2,500 illegal boreholes in Erbil alone.[58] Finally, the quality of water resources in Iraqi-Kurdistan has declined significantly in recent years due to the compounding effects of ecological damage of warfare and a general lack of public ecological awareness.[59]

Iranian and Turkish Dam Construction

Turkey and Iran are generally hostile toward the project of Kurdish independence, and now have an opportunity to use withholding water as a political lever. Kurdish security is impacted by two dam construction projects that have culminated at roughly the same time, supporting the assertions of some conspiracy theorists. The Ilisu Dam, one of twenty-two dams that comprise Turkey's massive GAP project, is expected to impound a significant share of water and reduce the flow of the Tigris River as it enters Iraq.[60]

The Tigris River does not flow directly through Iraqi Kurdistan, though tributaries to it do, and some of the population of the Kurdish city of Dohok relies on water impounded by the Mosul Dam that also lies outside of Iraqi Kurdish territory.[61] The largest tributaries are the Greater Zab, Lesser Zab, and the Diyala Rivers. Turkey and Iraq held talks in January 2018 to reduce tensions, and Turkey delayed filling the Ilisu dam reservoir from March to June 1, 2018, to let Iraq store up more water for its summer needs—reducing tensions in the short run.[62]

From a Kurdish perspective, Ilisu's hydrological impacts are compounded by cultural damage. Although Iraqi Kurdistan is not physically threatened, the Ilisu Dam project carries other important sociopolitical impacts, including flooding the Kurdish cultural center of Hasankeyf, a city of 80,000 people. While located within the political boundaries of Turkey, the preservation of this city is culturally invaluable to local Kurdish communities in Turkey and Iraq.

Iranian completion of the Daryan Dam on the Diyala River poses a more direct threat to Kurdish water security. It is expected to reduce the flows of the Sirwan River—as it is called in Iran, or Diyala, as it is called in Iraq—by nearly 60 percent. This diversion takes place through underground irrigation tunnels that would desiccate the Diyala River completely, creating a large impact on both Iraqi Kurdistan and Iraq further downstream.[63] The full extent of the project's consequences could be water loss to the extent that the Darbandikhan Dam would no longer be able to produce electricity for Iraqi Kurdistan.[64] When confronted with this situation, the KRG has stated that it would be compelled to offtake more water from the Diyala, which would in turn reduce the water supply available to the rest of Iraq. Finally, in another action that suspiciously coincided with the Kurdish independence referendum, Iran built a dam on the Little Zab in Sardasht, temporarily holding back most of the Little Zab River. This situation led to a boiling point in the summer of 2018.[65]

Water Stress: Natural Factors

Drought, Climate Change, and Earthquakes

Iraq has been experiencing drought-like conditions in the north of the country, including Iraqi Kurdistan, threatening food security.[66] The snowpack coverage was depleted in the Zagros Mountains in Kurdistan's far northeast during the winter of 2018. Locals there say it has been the warmest and driest winter for at least a decade.[67] With reduced snowmelt in the spring of 2018, the water level in rivers will also be diminished.

Furthermore, precipitation patterns are increasingly erratic. In Kurdistan's Nineveh-Salahaddin-Kirkuk region, a so-called wheat belt, there has been so little rain that most farmers had not planted their fall 2018 wheat crop well into January 2018, jeopardizing the annual harvest. The increasingly erratic precipitation, where rain-fed agriculture had been sufficient in the past, has pushed many farmers there to tap into local irrigation networks, adding to the burden on the rivers.[68] In February 2018, a sharp drop in groundwater reserves coincided with these conditions. Artesian wells that could be tapped without pumps are running dry in some areas. Mohamed Aziz, the Deputy Head of Kurdistan's Department of Water Resources, cited underlying reasons for the decrease in water tables. He listed an increased number of legal and illegal wells, recent drought conditions in the mountainous areas, lack of reliance on available surface waters, and climate change.[69] The KRG has been constructing a series of more than 120 small dams to address this situation.[70]

Iraqi Kurdistan has been subject to the effects of climate change. In general, the Mediterranean littoral and the Middle East have warmed up considerably. The land area surrounding the Mediterranean Sea has experienced ten of the twelve driest winters since 1902 in just the last 20 years.[71] By the end of this century, the mean temperature in the region is projected to increase by three to five degrees Celsius, while precipitation will decrease by about 20 percent.[72] Likewise, water runoff, such as that from mountain snowpack, could be reduced by 20–30 percent by 2050.[73] Droughts are likely to become more frequent and intense. A recent study concluded that a reoccurrence of a three-year drought in Syria, as severe as that of 2007–2010, is two to three times more likely as a consequence of climate change.[74]

While climate change is difficult to predict with great precision due to the variances of regional climate models, the authoritative IPCC reports of both 2007 and 2014 agree on substantial climatic shifts in the Middle East. In fact, the 2014 IPCC report concludes that no other place in the world will be affected more severely than the Middle East and North Africa by climate change.[75] The lower ends of scientific estimates predict warming of between 0.8 and 2.1 degrees Celsius in the region by 2020, which will have profound impacts on water resources in particular.[76] As noted by the World Resources Institute Aqueduct interface, Iraqi Kurdistan already faces elevated risks from water stress.[77]

Average monthly precipitation could be in the range of 8–10mm by the end of the century, mainly in the Atlas Mountains and in the Upper Euphrates and Tigris basins.[78] Recall from the previous section of this chapter on Kurdistan's water resources that the current ranges of precipitation are 300–500mm/year, far greater than the predicted future range of 120mm, which is the high-end estimate. The Kurdish region's agricultural minister estimated that already fewer than 60 percent of farmers in northern Iraq receive sufficient water.[79] A decrease in rainfall and river-basin discharge will also see the amount of runoff decline. This is particularly concerning for a region already struggling to properly dispose of wastewater, and where natural river runoff assistance will diminish greatly.[80] Climate change will diminish precipitation and increase evaporation, and further damming of waterways will significantly diminish the capacity to withstand reductions in water levels.[81]

Seismic activity is another force of nature that has brought misfortune to Iraqi Kurdistan. The region lies on fault lines that are of critical concern not just for physical safety but for vulnerable local water infrastructure as well. Eastern Kurdish territory near the Iran-Iraq border sits atop an active fault line, which caused a major 7.3 magnitude earthquake on November 12, 2017.[82] This was the most severe local earthquake since the 1960s, injuring at least 500 Kurds and 7,000 others.[83] Both the Darbandikhan and Dukan Dams were threatened structurally, prompting the GOI to mobilize a World Bank technical-support mission to assess the damage, leading officials to call for lessening water weight on dam systems until a full assessment concluded.[84] Water levels in the reservoir were down by thirteen meters in June 2018, as engineers did not want to add more stress to the dam by attempting to store additional water.[85] Higher water levels will not be restored until these inspection teams finish their assessments. Darbandikhan Lake is the primary water source for the Kurdish Garmiyan Region where 95 percent of the farmland relies on irrigation infrastructure that feeds off of the river.

While the two aforementioned dams survived the earthquake, there is great uncertainty as to whether the Mosul Dam on the Tigris would prove as steadfast if hit by an earthquake of similar magnitude. The Mosul Dam is constructed on a foundation of unstable earth made of gypsum, which would likely be much more delicate in the face of seismic activity. Even during stable geological conditions, dam operators are required to work twenty-four hours a day to reinforce the dam with concrete. For these reasons, experts consider the Mosul Dam to be one of the most dangerously unstable in the world.[86] As touched upon in previous sections, water stress and uncertain political conditions are compelling officials to reserve as much water as possible today; an action that is testing the water-bearing limits of these structures. Should an earthquake of comparable size strike Mosul, the integrity of that dam would be tested drastically; and, in the event of a collapse, the surrounding area would face untold destruction. The threat of future seismic activity is a clear risk multiplier on this fragile system.

International and Internal Governance Challenges

Along with the challenges of a litany of natural impacts on water resources, Kurdistan also finds itself at a political watershed moment. The Kurdish independence project appears to be dead in the water, on the heels of the failed referendum. Just as the KRG has neglected the management of water resources, it has allowed lack of long-term thinking to dominate other facets of governance. Thus, the overall geopolitical health of the nation is mirrored in microcosm by conditions in the water sector. This will pose internal and multilateral water governance challenges for the KRG, precisely when the economy is shifting toward more dependence on water-intensive agriculture.

It is imperative that the KRG address water challenges within its borders. A report by the American University of Iraq in Sulaimani outlines a sound framework for taking steps toward improving water governance.[87] These interventions address many of the problems identified in this study. Key interventions include improving water-monitoring information systems; increased regulation of private groundwater withdrawals; and promoting greater ecological awareness among the Kurdish people.[88] The report also finds that efficiencies can be gained by consolidating water planning, currently handled by the Ministry of Agriculture and Water Resources, into a single water organization that is politically empowered. Previous ministers have been somewhat politically marginalized, since they were drawn from the ranks of a minor political party, the Kurdistan Islamic Union.

On the multilateral level, the KRG faces unique challenges as a proto- or non-state actor. Chief among these, from a political perspective, is the need to negotiate simultaneously with Baghdad, given historical animosities, as well as with the somewhat hostile riparian nations of Turkey, Syria, and Iran over issues governing the joint management of shared water courses and related resources. However, the Kurdish conundrum is made worse by the fact that there is no water-sharing agreement between all the riparian states of the Tigris and Euphrates River Basin, nor a framework or institution to implement such an agreement. The present Tigris and Euphrates water regime can be best characterized as "a chaotic regime of claim and counter-claim governed more by political than legal concerns."[89] To date, no Iraqi government has used the available legal means and negotiation tools to protect Iraq's right to water. The future prospects of Iraq doing so are unclear and the Kurds are likely to suffer alongside the rest of Iraq.

Instability stoked by Kurdish internal political fractures will have an indirect effect on the core interests of the US, which is the most powerful, long-standing, if fickle, Kurdish ally with a vital interest in Iraqi stability as a linchpin of its regional strategy. This stability arguably rests with a politically coherent Iraqi state. The findings of a US Intelligence Community Assessment on Global Water Security completed in 2012 seem prescient in this case. The study found that "during the next ten years, many countries important to the U.S. will experience water problems—shortages, poor quality or floods that will risk instability and state failure, increase regional tensions and distract them from working on important policy objectives."[90] The first part of the prediction has been realized, and the second may yet unfold.

In terms of internal politics, the Kurds of northern Iraq have long been more pro-US than the rest of Iraq due to their historical relationship. The continued support of the KRG is important to the US due to the apparent ascendancy of anti-US parties in Iraq's governing coalition, such as Muqtada al-Sadr and his Shi'i militias. On the military front, the Peshmerga served as a valiant and effective fighting force against IS, and their further assistance in combatting violent extremism could well be necessary. Therefore, US regional security strategy is dependent on the continued support from Kurdish Peshmerga forces in the battle against IS and any violent extremist organization that may emerge from the organization's ashes.

Iraqi Kurdistan's hydropolitical position is also dependent on the US to some extent. The US has sought to maintain a neutral stance in the post-referendum dispute between Baghdad and Erbil. However, Erbil would look to the US for protection, or at least mediation, if Iraq attempted to use force to prevent Kurdish manipulation of water.

In recognition of their role as the ultimate hydro-hegemon, any lasting solutions to regional water challenges involve, and arguably begin with, Turkish buy-in. A possible solution for easing water stress in Iraqi Kurdistan, and certainly for Baghdad, lies in cultivating better political and economic relations with Ankara. Such a strategy might lie at the intersection of hydropolitics and hydrocarbons, since commerce in oil resources has been a central factor in the equation for self-determination in Iraqi Kurdistan.

Turkey has relatively fewer oil and gas reserves than Iraqi Kurdistan, while its water reserves are considerable. Turkey's GAP dam project in the southeast is likely to hold back more water than is needed for domestic agricultural and hydro-electrical uses, which raises the possibility of an alignment of interests. In the face of growing water stress, the KRG and Baghdad could propose a bartering arrangement of swapping oil in exchange for a greater water allotment from Turkey, for example by reducing impoundment of the Tigris at the Ilisu.

There is some precedent for cooperation over energy resources. An arrangement for exporting oil was formalized in energy cooperation between Iraqi Kurdistan and Turkey in 2012. The KRG ignored a provision in the Federal Constitution calling for such deals to be regulated through Baghdad, and constructed a pipeline to pump 150,000 barrels per day of oil from the Taq Oilfield fifty-five kilometers north of Kirkuk to join the existing pipeline in Turkey. While Turkey opposes political independence for Iraqi Kurdistan, it must also reconcile its need for oil—a move that may require more open diplomatic considerations.[91]

As of January 2020, Turkey has not made good on threats to impose economic restrictions in response to the independence referendum, but fears it has emboldened Kurdish separatists in their own country. As such, the economic relation remains; Kurdistan already imports most of its food from Turkey, which amounts to a virtual water trade. Physically importing water from Turkey is a similar economic concept, but it would have the economic benefit of supplying additional water resources to Kurds returning to their occupations as farmers in response to prevailing economic conditions, while also contributing to additional flows toward Iraq.

Conclusion

This chapter has shown some of the many ways in which water stress is an increasing concern in Iraqi Kurdistan. It has considered both anthropogenic and natural drivers of this water stress. Evidence suggests that the KRG and international organizations have failed to grasp the severity of the water problem. On the geopolitical level, countries recognized that Kurdish participation was essential toward delivering a devastating blow to IS. With subsidence of that threat, the KRG has built a reservoir of international good will from which it may be able to draw. It has the opportunity to focus on two mutually reinforcing crises. First, the political complications with Baghdad posed by the independence referendum, and, second, the sudden economic downturn based on the collapse of oil prices and exports. As ever, the KRG must also exercise careful statesmanship in dealings with its more powerful Turkish and Iranian neighbors if it hopes to influence the hydro-hegemonic behavior these states have manifested. Continued rivalry within ruling political factions and electoral politics promise to bring new complexities to water management, but none of the shifting politics can alter the geophysical realities that are driving water stress.

The KRG must overcome political distractions and take action to quickly develop an integrated national water plan that responds to the water stress and supply issues identified in this study in time to forestall some of their worst consequences. If successful, the KRG will guarantee sufficient water for its people, while maintaining the ability to use water as political leverage in support of autonomy or to improve the quality of life in all of Iraq. If it fails to seize the opportunity at this watershed moment, water stress will increase food insecurity and economic hardships for the Kurds, which could lead to a political instability that mitigates against future realization of autonomy. It will also increase the chances of water conflict across a spectrum, ranging from localized violence between user groups in Iraqi Kurdistan to the strategic weaponization of water resources by neighboring states.

5

GROUNDWATER RESOURCES

SUPPLY, USE, AND SECURITY IMPLICATIONS IN THE MIDDLE EAST AND NORTH AFRICA

Mark Giordano, Katalyn Voss, and *Signe Stroming*

Seest thou not that Allah sends down from the sky, and causes it to penetrate the earth as water-springs, and afterward thereby produceth crops of diverse hues; then He makes it dry up and crumble away. Truly, in this, is a Message of remembrance to men of understanding.

Qur'an 39:21

Introduction

The Middle East and North Africa (MENA) is one of the most arid regions of the world,[1] with limited precipitation restricted primarily to the mountainous regions of Turkey, the Mediterranean, Yemen, and Iran. One outcome of scarce and variable surface-water supply is a heavy reliance on groundwater for both drinking and agricultural uses. This reliance has grown substantially in the last fifty years as abstraction technologies improved and allowed access to shallow aquifers renewed by rainfall and river flow, but also to deep "fossil" aquifers last recharged thousands or tens of thousands of years ago. While precise data on the supply and use of groundwater is lacking, it is well known that groundwater now provides virtually all water supply for many countries in the MENA region, and accounts for well over half of all use in many other countries.

The positive impacts of groundwater use in the region range from improved domestic water supplies to the increased agricultural income growth that facilitates the pursuit of higher paying urban employment and increased food security.[2] However, overuse and a declining groundwater resources base is now documented in every country in the region. As water tables fall, the economic costs of drilling and abstraction increase, as do environmental costs. When the interconnections between surface and groundwater systems are severed and streams and rivers dry, aquifer storage declines, land subsides, and, in coastal areas, salt water intrudes into aquifers. Equally important, overuse has implications for both short- and long-term food security. One of the key properties of groundwater is its value as a buffer to be used in times of drought. Drawing down the groundwater "bank" in years of normal water availability leaves no savings for use in water-short years, when food security and food price stability concerns are most critical. In the long term, abstraction of groundwater at rates greater than sustainable yield creates an explicit trade-off between current and future food production and food security. This is especially true in fossil aquifers where waters will not be recharged for hundreds or thousands of years, rendering the aquifer and investment in pumping wells obsolete.

GROUNDWATER RESOURCES

The goal of this chapter is to provide insights into some of the political dimensions of groundwater and its use and overuse in the MENA region. First, an overview is provided of current knowledge of groundwater resources, highlighting the rapid transformation in the way groundwater data and information is collected and shared outside of traditional, official channels. The domestic political implications of groundwater overuse for food security and food price stability, and the additional challenges created when aquifers, or the rivers which feed them, transcend state boundaries are then discussed. While the study recognizes the possibilities for technology to provide new data and information for groundwater decision making, it also acknowledges that groundwater governance and management is problematic worldwide. The chapter thus ends not with a vague call for "better" groundwater governance, policy, and management, but rather explores options for reducing the negative impacts of continued overuse.

Groundwater Supply and Use Data in the Middle East

A general idea of the major aquifers in the MENA is now known. As shown in Figure 1, these aquifers can be divided into three general types by their source of recharge. Aquifers in the mountainous regions of Turkey, the Mediterranean, Yemen, and Iran have relatively high levels of annual recharge supplied by orographic rainfall. Fluvial aquifers in the lower reaches of the Nile, the Tigris-Euphrates, and the Karkheh in Iran are recharged not by rainfall but rather by surface flows, sometimes originating at great distance and often transboundary in nature. Finally, the Arabian peninsula and eastern Sahara areas contain groundwater in the form of either nonrenewable deep fossil or minimally recharged shallow aquifers formed under previous hydrologic regimes.

103

While the general nature and extent of groundwater in the region is understood, it is difficult to derive reasonable approximations of aquifer volumes, recharge rates, and safe yields without extensive, detailed analysis of local conditions. Such analyses are necessarily limited and typically confined to relatively small areas and not easily extrapolated to regional or national levels. In addition, such groundwater assessments can only provide a baseline for understanding issues in groundwater use, since groundwater is in a state of constant flux from variation in precipitation,

Figure 5.1: Aquifers in the MENA Region

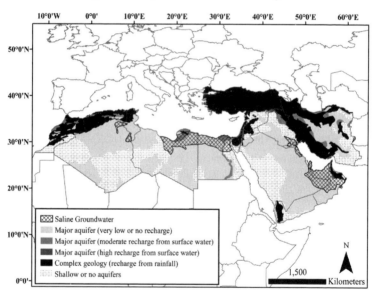

Source: The map is developed with data from the World-wide Hydrogeological Mapping and Assessment Programme (WHYMAP) coordinated by the German Institute for Geosciences and Natural Resources (BGR) and the United Nations Educational, Scientific, and Cultural Organization, "Groundwater Resources of the World—Transboundary Aquifer Systems," Special edition for the 4th World Water Forum, Mexico City, March 2006 (BRG, Hannover, and UNESCO, Paris, 2006). Aquifers in black are recharged by orographic rainfall; shades of grey indicate major aquifers recharged by surface flows; and, dotted regions indicates areas with no aquifers or shallow aquifers with little or no recharge.

surface water recharge (except in the case of fossil aquifers), and abstraction from wells.

Data on abstraction and use is also problematic because of its distributed nature—typically thousands of individual users within an aquifer, using unregulated wells and pumps paid for with personal funds—making systematic data collection difficult. Groundwater users are also often reluctant to allow data collection or even reveal well ownership out of fear that the information will later be used to regulate and reduce access. As Kuper et al. explained with reference to Algeria, Morocco, and Tunisia, well and use surveys are often out of date by the time they are published.[3]

Even when quality groundwater data exists, the politics of water can prevent its dissemination or result in obfuscation. For example, Elhadj and Keulertz et al. highlight how the politics of agricultural production subsidies in Saudi Arabia result in contested estimates of groundwater use and overuse.[4] Keulertz et al. describe how different interest groups pay for and promote varying estimates of availability to suit their individual interests: "in this political context, estimates of groundwater depletion are controversial and shrouded in strategic secrecy and interest politics."[5] In transboundary contexts, availability and use data may be considered strategic and therefore are not made public.

Despite these issues, most governments do supply official estimates of groundwater availability and use. The United Nations Food and Agriculture Organization provides the data of its member countries through the publicly available Aquastat database, though with no references to methodologies of collection. For some countries in the MENA region (Egypt, Iraq, and Israel) no data is available. For countries that do supply data, it is dated. The most recent groundwater use data at the time of this writing for any country in the region was 2006, for Saudi Arabia. Because of the inherent difficulty in measuring groundwater use combined with the rapid expansion of groundwater demand, Aquastat data probably substantially underestimate current use and can be used only as a general indicator of conditions. Nonetheless, the lack of alternative, accessible data sources and Aquastat's "official" characterization render it the most frequently cited source of country-level groundwater data.

Technology is rapidly changing the groundwater data land-scape. Modeling efforts are increasingly used to estimate variables such as saturated aquifer thickness and effective porosity, which can then derive estimated groundwater storage reserves. Most recently, Lezzaik and Milewski estimated groundwater reserves for a large area of the MENA region at approximately $1.28\text{x}10^6\text{km}^3$, with 74 percent of storage lying under the Sahara desert and the Arabian peninsula in Algeria, Libya, Saudi Arabia, and Egypt.[6] While such estimates have utility, as the authors point out, storage is always much greater than technically or economically utilizable groundwater resources, so such estimates have limited value in explaining current and potential future use, estimating sustainable use, or planning drawdown. Furthermore, as Allan points out,[7] even when groundwater exists and is of usable quality and at accessible depths, it can be located hundreds of miles from potential users (e.g. the Arabian peninsula), again highlighting the practical limitation of national and other large-scale availability assessments.

Other modeling efforts combine national and regional esti-mates of groundwater use with sustainability concepts. Wada, van Beek and Bierkens,[8] for example, used a gridded hydrologic model and large, international datasets of water balance components to estimate that, for year 2000, a number of countries in the MENA region (Iran, Saudi Arabia, Egypt, and Libya) were among the largest users of groundwater globally, and that the agricultural sectors of most countries in the region relied on unsustainable ("nonrenewable") groundwater abstraction to support agriculture.

They estimated that more than half of gross irrigation water demand was met by nonrenewable groundwater resources in Saudi Arabia, Qatar, Libya, and the United Arab Emirates (UAE). A major caveat of this and similar studies is that they rely in part on country-level Aquastat data in calibration.

Remotely sensed data, combined with modeling, has recently emerged as an alternative method for estimating groundwater storage and use at regional scales. The Gravity Recovery and Climate Experiment (GRACE) satellites measure monthly fluctuations in the earth's gravity field and can be used to derive total water storage,[9] including ground and surface water. To isolate changes in groundwater storage and estimate use, GRACE data is combined with global land-data assimilation models and observational data to estimate water budget components like precipitation and lake storage, and to partition the GRACE total water storage data into distinct components, including groundwater.[10]

Several recent studies use GRACE to quantify both groundwater resources and their relative stress/stability in the MENA region. Moore and Fisher used GRACE estimates to provide insights into rapidly declining groundwater tables in Yemen.[11] Voss combined GRACE data with altimetry measurements and hydrologic models to estimate groundwater depletion rates and the volume of nonrenewable groundwater extracted in Syria, Iraq, and western Iran from 2003 to 2009.[12] They found that 91 km³ of groundwater were consumed each year, as reliance on groundwater increased in response to a drought and diminished surface water availability due to dam construction in the upstream regions of the Tigris-Euphrates (see below). Richey developed stress metrics for the largest groundwater aquifers in the world based on GRACE results, modeled groundwater recharge estimates, and Aquastat use statistics.[13] In the MENA region, they found that the Arabian Aquifer System had a depletion rate of 29 mm/yr, predominantly driven by groundwater abstraction to support rapid agriculture expansion. Lezzaik and Milewski also coupled GRACE and other models to calculate groundwater use in the region.[14] They found that all countries except Morocco experienced a decline in groundwater resources from 2003 to 2015, with Algeria, Egypt, and Iraq extracting the greatest absolute volumes of groundwater. Over the twelve-year period, the region saw an average decline in groundwater reserves of 0.82 percent—negligible according to the authors. However, they also estimated larger declines in Syria (-1.5 percent), Iraq (-2.6 percent), Lebanon (-1.92 percent), and Kuwait (-2.35 percent).

The findings of such regional modeling and remote sensing studies are generally consistent with smaller-scale, country-level, and field-based studies. The analyses consistently find that the use of groundwater far exceeds recharge rates, resulting in a decline in water table levels across the MENA region. In fact, published studies for every country in the region highlight problems with overuse and overexploitation of groundwater resources.

Social and Physical Impacts of Groundwater Use and Overuse

Discussions of groundwater utilization typically focus on the negative implications of the overexploitation just highlighted. However, it is important to note that increases in groundwater use can have positive, sometimes transformative, impacts on poverty reduction and food security around the world.[15] Within the MENA region, Allan was perhaps the first to highlight the important role of groundwater use, in the second half of the twentieth century, in providing a consistent source of water for drinking and irrigation,[16] increasing rural family incomes, and allowing younger family members to gain technical skills that facilitate urbanization and socioeconomic transitions. As part of this transition, groundwater emerged as an important element of overall water use in the MENA region. In some countries with no permanent rivers—Saudi Arabia, the United Arab Emirates, Oman, Kuwait, Bahrain, and Qatar—groundwater accounts for almost 100 percent of water use. In many other regional countries, it accounts for more than half of all use.

Agriculture irrigated by groundwater supports rural livelihoods in many parts of the MENA region. For example, Kuper et al. estimate that 1.75 million hectares of farmland and more than 500,000 farm holdings are supported by groundwater in Morocco, Algeria, and Tunisia.[17] Nonetheless, as the region urbanizes, agriculture's share of total employment has steadily declined, and groundwater's direct role in livelihood security has arguably diminished. However, the link between groundwater and food security, as well as food price stability, intensified due to increases in groundwater use for agriculture. The growing use of groundwater for agriculture is not without logic. Political stability in the MENA region is sensitive to food price changes.[18] Governments are aware of their dependence on volatile international grain markets and potential market disruption from trade sanctions (e.g., the 1980 US grain embargo of the Soviet Union); sudden restrictions by exporting countries with concerns for their own domestic price stability;[19] or blockades of trade routes by third parties (e.g., the 2017 blockade of Qatar's land, air, and sea borders). With these dynamics at play, the development of an independent national or regional food market is a significant economic, political, and social asset. However, coupling such an asset with a limited and rapidly declining resource such as groundwater creates major risks and costs in both the short and long terms.

First, the use of scarce groundwater resources to support generally low-value agricultural production, often grains, comes at the opportunity cost of much higher value than urban uses. In extreme examples, both Saudi Arabia and Qatar used policies to encourage the use of groundwater for low-value agriculture, while simultaneously expanding high-cost, energy-intensive desalinization to meet urban needs. While both countries drastically scaled back these policies, Saudi Arabia, with virtually no renewable water resources, became the world's sixth largest wheat exporter in the 1990s.[20]

Second, and more importantly, groundwater use in much of the region is greater than natural recharge or is based on wholly nonrenewable fossil groundwater. In other words, current use rates simply cannot continue indefinitely, and the immediate contributions to livelihood and food security are coming at the cost of greater insecurity in the future. Furthermore, the timeline for collapse—when groundwater resources run dry—is unknown because aquifers continue to be tapped without firm data on the volume of water available each year, let alone in the future.

Third, when groundwater is overused in normal conditions, its potential to provide a buffer to water supply in times of drought or low surface water availability is greatly reduced. The impact of this reduction is amplified as it occurs exactly when food production is most at risk and when food security concerns are already greatest. Depleted groundwater reserves and the co-occurrence of domestic drought and high international food prices are factors that have been associated with the 2011 Arab uprisings and the breakdown of the state in Syria, and are currently of concern in Iran.

Finally, groundwater overdraft brings with it a host of other costs, including the energy needed to pump to deeper levels, social inequalities in access and tensions that may result as neighbors compete for this common-pool resource, damage to infrastructure as land subsides, and ecosystem damage as the natural interface between surface and groundwater systems is disconnected. Overdraft can also have long-term, potentially irreversible costs to environmental services including loss of porosity (reducing future storage potential) and land subsidence (e.g., in Iran).[21] In coastal areas, aquifer drawdown leads to saltwater intrusion, making the previously freshwater useless due to salinization. Coastal aquifers in North Africa, along the eastern

Mediterranean, and in the Persian Gulf are particularly prone to salinization (see Figure 1). The problem is exacerbated because these are the same regions of major population centers with high water demands not easily met by other sources. Saltwater intrusion has been identified as a significant issue in Morocco,[22] Oman,[23] and Syria,[24] for example.

Transboundary Aquifers

Aquifers as a potential transboundary water governance issue first received significant attention from the international community in the 1980s.[25] While recognition of the potential importance of transboundary aquifers has increased, these are meaningful only in rare cases when formal institutions are in place for their governance.[26] UN-ESCWA and Bundesanstalt für Geowissenschaften und Rohstoffe (BGR) were not able to identify one agreement on internationally shared aquifers in their detailed survey of twenty-two transboundary aquifers in West Asia.[27] Further, there was no recognition that many transboundary aquifers in the region are in fact shared by two or more states.

In the following section, we review knowledge and issues on transboundary aquifers in the MENA region. To do this, we consider two types of shared aquifers, those divided by an international boundary and those located within a single country but hydrologically connected to an internationally shared river.

Aquifers Divided by an International Boundary

The International Groundwater Resources Center (IGRAC) maintains the most comprehensive inventory of aquifers divided by international boundaries. To create its inventory, IGRAC overlays spatially explicit data from increasingly detailed geologic surveys and models with national political boundaries. In their most recent update in 2017, they identify 592 transboundary aquifers, including thirty-six in the MENA as shown in Figure 2. A separate, more detailed inventory of West Asia by UN-ESCWA and BGR identified additional transboundary aquifers in the region, primarily from further subdivisions of IGRAC work.[28] Differences in numbers based on level of detail simply highlight the complicated nature of groundwater hydrology, and that delineation, and likely management, of transboundary aquifers is more problematic than for transboundary surface waters.

It is clear from Figure 2 that transboundary aquifers form a significant share of the groundwater resources of every country in the region, with the possible exceptions of Turkey and Iran (though see below). Wada and Heinrich found that the MENA

Figure 5.2: Transboundary Aquifers in the MENA Region

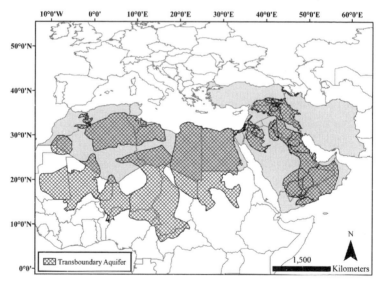

Source: Transboundary aquifers in the MENA region identified by the International Groundwater Resources Center, (IGRAC), UNESCO-IHP (UNESCO International Hydrological Programme). Originally published as "Transboundary Aquifers of the World [map]. Scale 1:50 000 000" in 2015, and revised in 2017.

region accounted for the vast majority of the most stressed trans-boundary aquifers in the world,[29] and particularly noted issues in the Paleogene and Cretaceous aquifers of Iraq, Jordan, Kuwait, Oman, Qatar, Saudi Arabia, Syria, the UAE, Yemen, and Bahrain, as well as the Mourzouk aquifer shared between Algeria, Libya, and Niger. Using information gathered from multiple sources, UN-ESCWA and BGR came to the general conclusion that transboundary aquifers in Western Asia (the MENA region, not including North Africa) were being rapidly depleted,[30] that the cross-border implications of high abstraction have been neglected, and that many aquifers will be exhausted before even being recognized as internationally shared resources.

Probably the most widely discussed of the problematic trans-boundary aquifers in the region are the Mountain Aquifer shared between the West Bank and Israel and the Coastal Aquifer under-lying Gaza and Israel's Mediterranean coast. As pointed out in Feitelson and Haddad,[31] negotiations between Israel and Palestine always include issues of their shared aquifer resources, but this aquifer also forms part of the larger transboundary water issues between Syria, Jordan, Israel, and Palestine over the Jordan River. Another relatively well-studied case is that of the Nubian Sandstone Aquifer, considered to be the world's largest fossil groundwater reserve, which is shared by Libya, Chad, Egypt, and Sudan.[32] Prior to Muammar Gaddafi's overthrow, overuse by Libya in particular of this and other shared aquifers was a source of tension in the region. Other examples include the Qa Disi aquifer, where overdraft by large commercial farms in Saudi Arabia have reportedly led to an increase in salinity with long-term negative consequences for both "upstream" Saudi Arabia and "downstream" Jordan,[33] and the Anti-Lebanon aquifer where it has been reported that overuse by Syria has caused gradual decreases in the discharge of freshwater springs serving as the main source of drinking water for Damascus.[34] UN-ESCWA and BGR provide additional case studies and examples.[35]

Sovereign Aquifers Associated with Transboundary Rivers

An aquifer located entirely within the sovereign territory of one state may also take on a transboundary nature if it is fed by or discharges into a transboundary river. As a case in point, the Nubian aquifer in Egypt, typically presented as a fossil aquifer, receives modern recharge from the Nile River, whose waters are supplied by rainfall from countries further upstream.[36] Conversely, groundwater use in Iran contributes to the desiccation of the Hamoun lakes,[37] on the border with Afghanistan, but also the Helmand River in Afghanistan.

The Tigris-Euphrates system provides another example and a case study of the potential international political dimensions. Both the Tigris and Euphrates begin in Turkey and flow downstream through Syria (the Euphrates) and Iraq (both) before joining together in southern Iraq. A number of rivers also flow into the system from Iran. All three riparian states depend heavily on the Tigris-Euphrates system for irrigation, and there has long been tension on how the water should be equally shared. Tensions increased as Turkey began unilateral implementation of its Greater Anatolia Project (GAP) in the 1990s, which involves the construction of more than twenty dams on the headwaters of both the Tigris and Euphrates Rivers and allows Turkey to increase substantially its water consumption.[38]

Most literature on the international politics of the Tigris-Euphrates focuses on the surface waters in the river itself. However, Voss et al. highlight how the availability of surface water is also connected to groundwater outcomes.[39] They found that, over the 2003–2009 period, groundwater use intensified and depletion accelerated in response to reduced surface water availability. In total, they estimated that approximately 20.5 km^3 of groundwater was "lost" from the region each year with a total loss of 91 km^3 over the study period. Of that loss, 40 percent was due to drying conditions during the drought, but 60 percent was due to increased abstraction, particularly in Syria, Iraq, and western Iran. Groundwater use in Turkey did not intensify as much because, as the upstream state and in the absence of water-sharing agreements, it could continue to rely on surface water access.

After Voss et al.'s study was published,[40] several other papers using longer timelines and new data followed. Joodaki combined GRACE and land-surface hydrologic models with newly available in-situ groundwater well data from western Iran to estimate groundwater change over a larger area.[41] That paper found that Iran lost ~25 Gt/year of water, whereas Iraq lost ~2Gt/year, and northern Saudi Arabia, southern Saudi Arabia, and eastern Turkey each lost ~5 Gt/year from 2003–2015. They separated groundwater loss due to a reduction in natural recharge versus a reduction due to increased human use, and estimated that more than half the loss in Iran was due to increased use. Chao also provided an update to the region and reconfirmed that groundwater abstraction was increased as a means of maintaining agricultural productivity during the drought.[42] The paper found that in total, ~115 Gt of groundwater was removed from the Tigris-Euphrates region from 2003 to 2015.

These studies highlight several issues related to the interrelationship between internationally shared surface waters and groundwater. First, transboundary groundwater issues involve more than simply aquifers bisected by international boundaries; the surface waters that provide recharge to the aquifers are also important. Second, as in transboundary surface waters, upstream states have a clear advantage in water access, particularly when principles for water sharing have not been agreed upon. Third, the studies show that access, or lack thereof, to shared surface/ groundwater systems may add a layer of tension to internal conflicts, as has been suggested in Syria.[43] Finally, the papers highlight the importance of scale in terms of international water conflict and cooperation. The impacts of the drought and subsequent groundwater depletion are notably local and subnational. Even if a formal transboundary agreement was in place for the Tigris-Euphrates Rivers, subnational, internal conflict may still be exacerbated by the interplay of local surface and groundwater scarcity, food security, and tension from emerging actors, such as Iraqi Kurdistan. Tensions driven by drought, water scarcity, and food security are largely the burden of rural, agricultural communities, and the impact of economic collapse at this scale can ripple out to disrupt national and regional stability.

To summarize, the impacts of drought and subsequent groundwater depletion occur on a scale at which transboundary agreements have little or no potency, but there remains a critical need for cooperation among stakeholders to deter conflict and to equitably manage the limited water resources that do exist, particularly as they support local and regional food markets.

Discussion and Conclusion

A major issue of groundwater in the MENA region—and across the globe—is that it is an invisible, hidden, common-pool resource that is difficult to manage or even understand.[44] While lack of knowledge and difficulty in accessing the available data pose significant obstacles to effective groundwater governance, recent advances in the use of satellite technologies, particularly as associated with the GRACE mission, are changing how groundwater data are collected and shared. Some of the first applications of these advances were in the MENA region, for example, Moore and Fisher's work in Yemen.[45]

Voss et al.'s work in the Tigris-Euphrates demonstrated that the same approaches could be used to overcome physical limitations in data availability and data sharing across international borders.[46] Their work sparked other studies in the same region that provide longer timelines with new data.[47] The impetus for the new data availability—particularly at the local-scale—was in part insights from the previous satellite work. A small explosion in studies coupling GRACE with other techniques to look at groundwater in the region is now underway, as examples since 2017 demonstrate.[48]

This outcome shows how technology can provide new data, bypass previous channels of data control, and bring forward additional data from other, more traditional sources. The experience also raises important questions: since it is border-blind, does the availability of remotely sensed regional data provide the leverage to improve monitoring of national groundwater resources? Can scientific data, especially remotely sensed data, provide a foundation for new cooperation in transboundary waters, including shared aquifers, particularly those where data is seen as a valuable political asset?

Of course, the availability of better groundwater data does not equate to the solution of groundwater problems, as the experiences of California, northwest India, and the North China Plain demonstrate. As Moore and Fisher summed up for Yemen, before the current crisis hit, "advances in remote sensing serve to illustrate that the technical capacity to detect changes in water resources far outstrips the institutional capacity to manage them."[49] There are in fact very few examples of successful, sustainable groundwater management anywhere in the world, including cases where data and information is reasonably strong. The few cited examples of "good" groundwater governance typically involve relatively small-scale use within already established communities and governance systems.[50] While this does not suggest that we should give up on improved management and governance for other cases, it does suggest that we should consider focusing efforts as much on reducing the social and political risks of poor groundwater management as managing the groundwater itself, particularly in the realm of interconnections between water and food security.

In the shorter term, the social and political risks in the MENA region are related primarily to the foregone value of groundwater as a buffer against drought.[51] When groundwater is managed sustainably, users turn to it when surface water supplies are limited. But when groundwater is depleted under normal conditions, it cannot be easily drawn on in times of drought. Compounding the issue, it is exactly in times of drought when domestic food supplies are likely to be under pressure and when food prices likely to rise. Further, the potential risks from groundwater overdraft on food supply and price stability during drought may not yet be fully realized, given that the nature and extent of the groundwater problem is relatively new, the pressure on groundwater is not yet fully recognized, and climatic conditions in the region may be changing. For example, Joodaki showed that in 2013 groundwater tables in western Iran had still not recovered from their pre-2007 drought levels despite a return of rains.[52] The primary reason was continued over abstraction. When the next drought hits, the option to use groundwater as a water supply buffer will be limited or insufficient.

In the drinking-water sector where control is typically with a single government entity, better management of groundwater to mitigate short-term risks such as drought is possible and promising. For example, both the UAE and Qatar are strategically implementing managed aquifer recharge as part of their overall water security strategies. For agricultural water use, options outside the groundwater sector may be more fruitful. For example, increased consideration of food stocks and stock release policies, implementation of external trade or financial agreements to ensure supplies and price stability at critical times, and a reexamination of domestic food policies could all contribute. For example, many countries in the region subsidize the provision of basic foodstuffs regardless of income level.[53] This approach mutes scarcity signals and exacerbates price risk in critical times, such as during drought. Reexamining the mechanisms used to ensure food security to the most vulnerable populations in both "normal" and drought periods will help mitigate the impacts of continued groundwater governance failure.

In the longer term, the primary risk of continued groundwater overdraft is the sourcing of future food supplies. Even with groundwater overdraft, food imports for most countries in the region are already high. Without tapping groundwater resources, dependence on food imports will only increase. As groundwater resources decline further, the trade-off between current groundwater use and future food security will emerge, and a policy for increased food imports will become a necessity. While the calculus for how to approach the import question will vary by state—and wealthier states will have a wider set of options—all states in this water-scarce region must carefully examine the interrelationships between water, food, and energy, and how, within that nexus, they can best use their scarce and diminishing water resources. Part of this examination involves the recognition that food self-sufficiency and food security are not synonyms. Producing low-value, low-water productivity grains for domestic consumption rather than higher-value, higher-water productivity fruits and vegetables to generate export revenues, does not necessarily make a state more food or water secure in the long term. However, moving away from food-grain self-sufficiency strategies also means exposure to increased risks from international market disruption.[54] National-level strategies for mitigating short-term risks of groundwater overuse apply here as well, but there is also a role for the international community to ensure orderly grain trade and, in particular, to oppose the use of food trade as a political weapon.

Finally, the ubiquitous presence of transboundary aquifers in the MENA region would seem to make groundwater governance and management even more complex and more contentious. However, we know that internationally shared surface waters have at least as much potential to promote cooperation between states as they do to serve as the impetus for conflict.[55] But we also know that to move from potential conflict to cooperation requires a recognition and physical understanding of the shared resources as well as institutional mechanisms to serve either as forums for discussion or to establish use rules. General principles for these institutions have been difficult for the international community to establish for surface waters, and they will be even more problematic for shared groundwater. Movement has instead come from states sharing individual basins; many have come together to establish hundreds of treaties to manage specific conditions.[56] For groundwater, these efforts lag not only in the MENA region, but also around the globe. While the challenges are great, there are broad efforts toward understanding the region's internationally shared groundwater resources and promoting discussion around them;[57] opportunities to learn from oil and gas sectors;[58] and aquifer-level work on how cooperation can be achieved, all of which provide a way forward.[59]

6

COMMUNITY-BASED WATER PRACTICES
IN YEMEN

Helen Lackner

Yemen's water shortage is extreme and, despite the current war, still attracting attention.[1] This chapter examines the transformations in customary water management approaches in recent decades in the context of state water management strategies since the establishment of the Republic of Yemen in 1990. It concentrates on the impact of these changes on the population with respect to the sustainability of this very scarce resource and its ability to respond to basic needs. Given that 90 percent of Yemen's water is used in agriculture, this sector will get most attention, though the mechanisms for provision of both rural and urban domestic water will also be given considerable attention.

The mismanagement of Yemen's water resources has been a major underlying contributing factor to the social tensions that exploded first in the uprisings of 2011 and later the descent into civil war since 2015. Alongside other neoliberal interventions, water management policies were major elements in the emergence of acute social differentiation between a microscopic group of beneficiaries who enriched themselves massively at the expense of the vast majority of Yemenis. This has happened thanks to the synergy of political decisions supporting the powerful, combined with modern water extraction technologies. While policymakers, analysts, and citizens still frequently call for the revival of traditional water management mechanisms, these are no longer applicable in their original form due to the technological changes of the past half-century. Therefore, any revitalization of these practices must include significant adjustments, even fundamental transformation in view of the combination of socioeconomic polarization with technological innovations.

In the post-war Yemen that will eventually emerge, addressing the people's basic needs for water will be essential if most of the country's population is to remain in situ. An understanding of the complex details of Yemen's water situation is essential to identifying and promoting viable solutions to this problem both for Yemenis and for their neighbors who will otherwise be faced with the prospect of mass emigration from a desertified country.

Background

Some basic facts need to remain at the forefront of readers' minds when thinking about the problem: first, about 70 percent of Yemen's population lives in rural areas and more than 55 percent of them depend on agriculturally related activities for their survival, hence water is essential not only for domestic use but also for their economic life. Second, although the war has probably caused a small reduction in pumping due to fuel shortages,[2] Yemen is currently using about 3.4 billion m³ of water annually;

one-third of which is from nonrenewable fossil aquifers and most of the rest is from shallow aquifers, as there are no permanent river flows.[3] Third, the availability of water in Yemen, at $85m^3$ per capita per annum, is significantly below the $1,000m^3$ considered essential for reasonable living conditions by the World Health Organisation (WHO). Fourth, only about 8 percent of water is used for domestic consumption and 2 percent for industry, a situation that provides the basis for a solution to basic survival: a small transfer of water out of agriculture and into domestic use would have a major impact on the ability of Yemenis to continue living in their homeland.

While the overall situation is dire, there are significant differences within the country depending on both geological and climatic factors: the areas with the greatest scarcity of groundwater are those with the highest population density, namely the western highlands. The political and social implications of this situation have not been addressed adequately in either analysis or planning. The country has no nationally managed interconnected domestic water supply infrastructure, neither urban nor rural. As pointed out by Christopher Ward, Yemen's geography, and the conditions of its water basins, make it a "naturally decentralized country" whose "topography has broken the country up into thousands of little valleys and isolated settlements,"[4] which would make a single system both extremely costly and technically inappropriate. This also has major political and social implications.

One feature of the grave water situation that Yemen faces is climate change. Although it will not be discussed further here, its implications and consequences need to be kept in mind when discussing the water situation. Climate change in Yemen is primarily manifested through the water crisis: worsening irregularity of rain episodes and of the timing and duration of rainy seasons prevents people from planning their agricultural cycle for rain-fed agriculture. More violent downpours reduce infiltration, and thus the replenishment of the water table, as well as destroying agricultural and other infrastructure, from *wadi* banks to terraces, creating a snowball effect that accelerates deterioration.[5] "Exceptional" storms took place in 2015 and 2018; each year had two consecutive events within days. More frequent droughts and floods reduce the resilience of the population, particularly the poor, who do not have the financial or material resources to prepare for such future disasters in agricultural production, thus worsening poverty. Finally, rising sea levels are likely to both increase salinity of coastal plains water tables as well as render many coastal cities, towns, and villages uninhabitable.

Have State Policies Really Integrated Customary Water Management Principles?

Even today, officially, water management is based on a number of principles of *'urf*, or "customary" law, which are community-based and in conformity with Islamic rules and law. There is no inherent clash between *'urf* and Islamic rules with respect to water management in Yemen. The country's geography does not facilitate centralized management—and therefore management of water sources—and the extraction mechanisms have remained localized, numerous, and varied. The management mechanisms have been neatly summarized by Ward:[6]

– Water is *mubah*, the property of no one—but the *usufruct* can be appropriated by those who develop it;
– Upstream riparians have priority: *al 'ala fa al 'ala*;
– Water may not be alienated from the land;
– Wells must be spaced a certain distance apart, outside a "protection zone" or *harim*;
– No one can deny a person drinking water—"Right of Thirst."

These principles were relatively easy to implement when water extraction mechanisms were small in scale, using technology with limited capacity—shallow wells and human- or animal-drawn power—as their impacts were extremely localized within a sub-basin. The introduction of increasingly powerful technology over the past half a century has meant that extraction anywhere impacts on much larger areas, up to large-scale basin levels. This means that water use in one location can affect very different remote and unrelated, possibly even hostile, communities. Alongside these technological changes, the rapidly growing urban populations have created new problems due to the need for rural-urban transfers of water.

Since the country's unification in 1990,[7] state strategies have been neoliberal; initially, they were characterized by laissez-faire, allowing increasing overexploitation of the resource by the more powerful landowners. A water law was passed in 2002 after many years of debate and struggle between the different ministries and institutions concerned.[8] The fact that its bylaws were only issued in 2011 demonstrates both successful resistance from powerful water users and the low priority given to the issue by the regime. These bylaws focus primarily on the distribution of responsibilities between the various macro-institutions. Both the law and bylaws recognize customary rules and therefore they fail to address the fundamental problems arising from the new social, political, economic, and technological environment.

The numerous institutions involved with water add opportunities for inter-institutional rivalries and problems: the National Water Resources Authority (NWRA), the Ministry of Agriculture and Irrigation (MAI), the General Authority of Rural Water Supply Projects (GARWSP), and the National Water and Sanitation Authority (NWSA), which deals with urban matters. A further four ministries have a say: the Ministry of Planning and International Cooperation (MOPIC), the Ministry of Finance, the Ministry of Local Government, and the Ministry of the Interior. The water law's bylaws give NWRA the responsibility for dealing with conflicts despite the fact that it is an organization staffed primarily by engineers; it should transfer unresolved issues to the Ministry of the Interior, i.e., the police. While a good understanding of engineering and hydrology issues is essential to solve water-related conflicts, other skills are equally important, namely deep knowledge of local history, legal precedents, and social, political, and economic relations.

The main strategy document is the National Water Sector Strategy and Investment Program (NWSSIP) 2005–2009, updated three years later. Although jointly issued by the Ministries of Water and the Environment (MWE) and Agriculture and Irrigation (MAI), it ignores the rivalry between the two institutions. NWSSIP was developed at the initiative, and largely under the influence, of the main international financiers of the sector: the World Bank, and the Dutch and German governments, which sponsored a series of meetings with national and international concerned officials. It summarizes water-sector management objectives as follows:

a) Meeting the basic domestic water needs;
b) Facilitating water use by higher return sectors of the economy (e.g., industry and tourism);
c) Maximizing income per cubic meter of water used in agriculture;
d) Protection of the environment and sustainability of the resource (protection against both pollution and depletion).[9]

'Urf management mechanisms are an integral part of the strategy. Although they have operated for many centuries and have been adapted to varying circumstances, the implications of the fundamental technological transformations of recent decades have not been addressed. Official discourse about water management in recent years has frequently promoted a return to customary procedures to solve conflicts over access and exploitation of water,

regardless of the fact that they are no longer fit for purpose. Participant observers like Ward have advocated a decentralized "community based" approach to addressing the problem.[10] In his book, Ward states that "the problem is a local problem and therefore it is local people who have the incentives to fix it. Local—and location-specific—solutions are needed... Stakeholders have to agree together on a framework of rules, regulation and incentives."[11] Similar views have been expressed by other external experts like Gerhard Lichtenthaeler and Chris Handley.[12]

The NWSSIP made this approach official and presented an idealized version of institutions from an undefined past, which may itself be an idealized version of earlier reality when it asserted:

> The state, however, cannot adopt (especially for groundwater extractions) a top-down command-and-control approach that would replace indigenous institutions and substitute a formal legal code for customary water laws. Historically, these institutions and norms have been proven effective in regulating water use and ensuring sustainability. A more pragmatic approach is for government institutions to forge a partnership with decentralized community-based organizations for co-management of water resources.[13]

This emphasis on local and community-based approaches was also reflected in the last prewar official statement on water policy. The 2011 Sana'a Declaration was adopted by the Saleh regime, most likely precisely because it did not challenge the inequitable distribution of the limited water resources or the ability of the most powerful to continue controlling and monopolizing much water for their own benefit. The declaration states among its four basic principles that "communities and local initiatives shall take on their responsibility for water resource management," and the first of its six proposed measures is: "water resources management must be based on democratic participation and commonly-agreed objectives as well as on partnership initiatives with the GOY [Government of Yemen] through a combination of bottom-up and top-down management approaches."[14] While well-meaning, this approach was unlikely to succeed as it assumes a willingness on the part of the powerful to give up their advantages in the interests of the community, a characteristic that has not been prominent in Yemeni (or indeed any other) society in the current era dominated by a worldwide philosophy of "winner takes all." Particularly in the face of intensifying competition over increasingly limited resources, leading to stress and worsening living conditions for the majority of people, altruism is currently not the prevailing social norm.

A detailed analysis of the impact of the implemented strategies on society was carried out in 2007. It focused on both sustainability and poverty reduction aspects, and concluded that:

> There is an anti-poor disparity between better off and poorer Yemenis in terms of both access to safe water and sanitation, and the price paid for it. The vulnerability of poorer people is greater, and the share of their income directed to getting adequate water higher. In agriculture, ownership of a water source is correlated with higher income, and development of groundwater resources in recent years has contributed to growing income disparities as the better off have been able to capture the lion's share of the resource. The health consequences for the Yemeni population are severe—for instance, mortality of children under the age of 5 years is twice that of other countries in the MENA region, and half of these deaths of children are due to diarrhea. The gender and educational enrollment impacts are also considerable, with women and girls spending large parts of each day fetching water.[15]

The same study acknowledged the failure of previously applied measures, despite the fact that some of its main authors had been actively involved in both their design and implementation. Although drafted very diplomatically, the message is clear: while the strategy had intended to achieve a significant reduction of the rate of groundwater overdraft, results will only be notable in the long term as "the pace of change at the local level is extremely slow" on the issue of reduced agricultural use, while maintaining rural incomes "getting more farm income per drop will require considerable effort beyond what is currently being done." With respect to the ability of increased diesel prices to "promote efficiency and intensification of water use ... rural people have reacted to the price rises by reducing water use,"[16] but domestic water prices have increased with "a negative impact on incomes and welfare, particularly for the poor." The report's conclusion about reforms impact in assisting the poor is that "so far the evidence points the other way (consolidation of existing wealth and income patterns, unequal access to rents and subsidies, and negative impacts on employment and incomes of the poor),"[17] a damning indictment of this attempt at combining neoliberalism with popular participatory approaches.

Rural Water

In view of the demographic and economic importance of rural areas, giving additional attention to this sector is imperative. There are many situations in which the same water source is used for both agricultural and domestic uses. The main sources[18] are the following:

– Direct rainfall used immediately on fields and filling water cisterns for domestic use (60 percent of Yemen's agricultural land is rain fed);
– Diverted rain water into channels for spate irrigation, including both traditional earth channels, which are rebuilt after each major flood, as well as the "improved" modern structures designed by irrigation projects and built of cement with gates and all the paraphernalia; most of these have been financed with support from the International Financial Institutions (IFIs);

- Shallow wells used for both agriculture and domestic purposes using "surface" aquifers;
- Springs used primarily for domestic use, but in some cases for agriculture; in the past, they were a main source of agricultural irrigation;
- In the past half century, a new form of irrigation has expanded exponentially: deep boreholes. They are used in rural areas primarily for agriculture but also for domestic use, while those drilled for urban supply (in Sana'a, Ta'iz, Aden, Mukalla, etc.) are usually excluded from use locally on site for both agriculture and domestic uses, creating significant social problems and conflicts.

Each of these systems has its distribution mechanism and ownership status, which create a wide range of opportunities for both conflict and cooperation. 'Urf rules have been subject to significant local variation, while retaining their fundamental principles: for example, the spacing between wells varies from one place to another, and the rules of priority access and usufruct also allow for a range of interpretations. However, technological modernization has fundamentally transformed the socioeconomic landscape as well as the relationships between water users: in many cases, water resources can no longer be managed at the level of a single small community—be it a tribe, a group of related tribes, or a mixed community of tribal and non-tribal people. With deep boreholes, actions in geographically distant sites directly impact people in other areas, in particular those living downstream, something that is not necessarily visible or easily perceived. While along a wadi bed, it is possible to see who is responsible for upstream extraction, in a large and wide basin, this is not the case.

Changes in recent decades have not led to the formal replacement of 'urf regulations; in practice, these rules have undergone significant adaptations that have actually transformed them from mechanisms increasing equity to mechanisms decreasing it. An additional very important factor affecting the application of the rules has been population increase, which has meant greater demand for water. In particular, the vastly expanding cities require significant transfers of water from rural to urban areas, a fundamental social, political, and economic change.

Water Management in Agricultural Development

Most agricultural investments have been primarily foreign financed, thus subject to the conditionalities and "suggestions" of the financiers.[19] The majority of projects have focused on irrigation and the promotion of export-oriented cash crops, primarily fruit (mangoes, bananas, strawberries) and vegetables. Though the latter were mostly for local consumption, all are very thirsty crops, demonstrating that these policies were determined without consideration of sustainable use of the country's very scarce water resources. Regardless of original intentions, the projects have, in most cases, favored the stronger political elements at the expense of smallholders and, thus, at the expense of equitable distribution. The main investor has been the World Bank often with co-financing from other multilaterals—e.g., the International Fund for Agricultural Development, the OPEC Fund for International Development, the Islamic Development Bank— who subscribe to the same principles and believe that World Bank design and approval guarantees "good" practice. Support for agriculture involved considerable infrastructure investments in spate irrigation, as well as, more recently, some support for the introduction of water-saving irrigation methods at the farm level and extremely limited support to rain-fed agriculture. These will be discussed in turn.

Spate Irrigation Improvements

In the middle reaches of Wadi Tuban in Lahej governorate, farmers interviewed between 1995 and 2005 increasingly complained of the lack of water from the major spate irrigation scheme that had been "modernized" and rehabilitated with external funding. Complaints clearly linked the problem with the establishment of new, privately owned, large farms upstream, after unification in 1990.[20] These were allocated first priority to receive water from the spates, thus depriving the midstream and downstream farmers of the water they would have received had these new farms not been established, following "upstream first" traditional prioritization. Downstream smallholders suffered additionally from the fact that their local wells produced very saline water as a result of coastal seawater intrusion, due to the increasing number of wells drilled both for agriculture and for supply to Aden.

The investments that have had the greatest impact both on the availability of water nationally and on the country's social structure have been focused on the development of "modern" cement infrastructures for spate irrigation.[21] These have been introduced or modernized through a series of projects on all the major wadi systems in the country: those reaching the Red Sea coast in the Tihama, implemented via the Tihama Development Authority (TDA) and financed by most of the major IFIs, and others along the west of the Arabian Sea coast, on wadis Tuban and Bana.

In the interior, projects were financed in Jawf and Mareb, the latter using water from the reconstructed Mareb dam. In the latter cases, resistance from strong local tribal communities prevented implementation, largely because the populations concerned realized that the new structures would transform the management mechanisms to the detriment of the majority of smallholders, and they had the political and military clout to enforce their views. Their successful resistance to the "foreign" projects also resulted in increased tension with government institutions, sometimes including minor armed confrontations.

The Tihama projects have been most recently discussed by Ward, who is sympathetic to the World Bank's objectives and modus operandi, and summarizes the situation as follows:

> The development of improved upstream diversion structures on spate schemes in a series of public projects from the 1950s up to the 1990s led to a *de facto* change in the spate water allocation rules. More land is now irrigated at the head of the schemes and less at the tail. The negative distributional effect of this is stronger because the head-enders (for example in Wadi Mawr and Wadi Rima) are generally better-off, larger landowners. A survey showed that more than 80% of farmers in Wadi Rima were at best no better off after the 'improvement' project. Instead, head-enders took all the baseflow, increased their cropping intensity, and grew higher value crops, including the water-intensive bananas, which require irrigation seven times a month.[22]

In the last decade, Bonzanigo and Borgia carried out a detailed study of projects in Wadi Siham;[23] their findings confirm the above statements, as well as observations and experience of this author throughout Yemen. They discuss these aspects from the Imamate period onwards,[24] and illustrate how such projects accelerated social differentiation by assisting the more powerful and weakening the smallholders whose access to irrigation water was severely restricted, or even completely terminated, as a result of the technical "improvements" brought about by the project. While the official customary methods of water management supposedly continued, the transfer of authority and power from the community-based water shaykhs and village *aqils* to officials and engineers from the TDA and new state-supported powerful individuals enabled the latter to divert water and technical support for their own benefit.[25] They also point out that, beyond political influence, "other factors, such as socio-economic changes, institutional reforms, the opening up of society, changes in the needs and priorities of local people, and impoverishment, have also determined changes in water control and access. Overall however, most conflicts and reactions that arose were dictated by a differentiated access to water."[26] Further, they examine in some detail the issue of upstream colonization of land by new, wealthy entrants into the agricultural sector, supported by the regime.

The projects' main management innovation was the introduction of Water Users' Associations (WUAs), a mechanism promoted worldwide by the major International Financial Institutions. In Yemen, these have been failures: as long as WUAs were financially supported, they were partially functional, but, even then, they contributed to the consolidation of power and control by the stronger social elements. But, based locally, they were unable—constitutionally or in practice—to address the issue of upstream diversion of water at the expense of downstream users. They were also in many cases subject to political pressures: they ceased to function as soon as financial and technical support ended, clearly demonstrating that they were not integrated into local institutional structures, and were not perceived by their members to fulfill any useful function. Even the Poverty and Social Impact Analysis (PSIA) recognized the largely anti-poor bias of operational WUAs: "experience with user associations has been that larger farmers and asset owners may either refuse to join, or may join and dominate: either case undermines the basic rule of a WUA which is equitable water management for mutual benefit."[27] Thus, it is clear that the associations failed to alleviate the social stresses resulting from the increasingly inequitable distribution of water.

While theoretically applying procedures operating for decades or even centuries, modern spate irrigation projects effectively transferred management and conflict-resolution power and authority to new state "bureaucracies," to authorities such as the TDA, NWRA, and others, as well as to powerful political/military figures.

In summary, projects in recent decades have transformed rural relations, bringing to the fore social tensions due to the worsening impoverishment of the majority, as:

– They consolidated the power and influence of larger landowners, either by ensuring that irrigation water reliably reached their lands, leaving smallholders' lands dry or with insufficient water, as was the case in wadis Siham, Zabid, and others in the Tihama. While in Tuban and Bana, additional factors resulted from the political changes due to the reprivatization of land after unification.

– The expansion of upstream spate-irrigated areas significantly reduced water flows downstream. Previously uncultivated land upstream was purchased by wealthier people, often powerful military individuals, while downstream landholders suffered as a result.

– Spate-irrigation systems reduce water availability downstream in the main escarpments, whether along the Red Sea coastal plain or on the western edge of the Arabian Sea, along wadis Tuban, Bana, and even Hassan. While people on the coastal plains were previously using mainly groundwater that flowed from the highlands during the rainy seasons, less of this is now reaching them. This has led to the emergence of a problem of intrusion of saline water from the seas, which obviously affects the quality and quantity of usable water in these populated areas, whether for agriculture or domestic consumption.

– The main innovation in water management, the WUAs, merely consolidated the tendencies of concentration of wealth and power. They failed to revitalize the management procedures in favor of the majority of smallholders and sharecroppers. In particular, they failed to introduce a democratic element to water management,[28] which might have led to more equitable distribution.

Tube Wells

State support for deep tube wells was primarily indirect, in the form of cheap credit from the Cooperative and Agriculture Credit Bank (CACB) for the purchase of equipment and subsidized diesel for their operation. Beneficiaries were landowners with the personal influence or wealth to access these loans. This century, foreign-financed agricultural development projects have also been initiated to reduce water use by promoting efficient on-farm irrigation technology. Tube wells extract water from deep aquifers, whether fossil or renewable, and are expensive to drill, equip with pumps, and operate. They are mostly located in the large plains, and the exploitation of their water affects the availability of water in the basins. With the rare exception of groups of smallholders with contiguous land plots agreeing to work together and jointly purchasing and operating them, they are primarily owned by wealthier owners of much larger holdings of more than 10 hectares.

Their operations have negative side effects resulting from the lowering of the water table. First, rapid extraction of water requires frequent deepening of wells, sometimes on an annual basis. This is both expensive initially and also incurs additional running costs for fuel and more expensive pumps that need to be renewed more frequently.[29] In addition to the fact that these requirements are only accessible to wealthy, large landholders, it also means that only the highest-value cash crops can economically be cultivated; in many cases, *qat* is grown rather than fruits and vegetables. In Amran, in the late 2000s, I was told that that the water table in some areas was dropping by over ten meters a year. In the Sana'a basin, which also supplies the city of Sana'a, the water table is estimated to have dropped at the rate of 6–8 m/year.

Second, the operation of deep wells has a direct and immediate impact on neighboring smallholders dependent on shallow wells and supplementary irrigation; as the water table drops, their wells dry up. Unable to cultivate, they have few options and often end up selling their land and becoming even more impoverished in a vicious cycle of poverty, leading to the sale of assets, which worsens poverty and results in the sale of more assets, etc. This is not the only problem: downstream springs and water tables also suffer, thus making life in some cases impossible in areas that have lost all of their water. Most importantly, in the long term, extraction of water beyond replenishment capacity threatens the very ability of an area to sustain life, let alone agriculture, and thus will result in significant population displacement—a process that has already started. Among others, beautiful villages and areas where I worked in al-Bayda governorate near Rada' in the early 1980s have now been abandoned,[30] as they have run out of water. Tube wells are the main water-use sector in which the larger and more powerful landowners have been least challenged. These are clear causes of social tensions and conflicts on different scales.

On-Farm Water Saving Irrigation Technologies

The introduction of improved on-farm irrigation technologies was promoted mainly for deep-well irrigated operations: from about the year 2000 onwards, support was targeted at holders of deep wells that were cultivating high-value crops. While the World Bank and others were busy putting pressure on the government and the regime to stop subsidies for fuel and basic commodities, their projects were providing subsidies effectively targeted to the rich rather than the poor. The prime example of this was the Ground and Soil Conservation Project (GSWP) that allocated $12 million for the "supply and installation of buried PVC pipes and overground galvanized iron (GI) pipes to improve water conveyance and distribution efficiency and reduce conveyance losses from existing tube wells and on existing farms. It would also provide localized on-farm irrigation systems (drip, bubbler, or sprinkler) for a part of the project area to further reduce on-farm losses."[31] While not explicitly targeted at the larger farmer, smallholders do not have tube wells. By comparison, another component of this project, for water harvesting and groundwater recharge focused on small-spate schemes, wadi bank protection, and terrace rehabilitation, etc., was only allocated $2.6 million.

Rain-fed Agriculture and Research

Until the 2000s, agricultural support completely ignored rain-fed crops, whether in research or projects. Since then, only one agricultural project with a component for rain-fed agriculture was implemented, the Rain-fed Agriculture and Livestock Project (RALP) that was jointly funded by the World Bank and the International Fund for Agricultural Development (IFAD). However, even this project had only a small component for the development of local landraces for rain-fed crops,[32] while the bulk of its investment went into "community development" activities. Although the latter include terrace rehabilitation, which contributes to water conservation and rain-fed agriculture, direct support to local landraces received only $3.4 million of the total $42.7 million.[33] This component involved collecting seeds of basic staple crops (sorghum, millet, wheat) throughout the country, but there was no research into high-value crops that might enable smallholders on rain-fed land to increase their incomes significantly or deal with issues of drought and short-ened rainy seasons, i.e., the consequences of climate change.

Domestic Rural Water Supply

The Reality on the Ground

There are thousands of examples of nonoperational domestic rural water projects that illustrate the social, political, and technical complexities of this synergy. A few of them follow: about ten years ago, in Hadda district in the eastern part of Dhamar gover-norate in the central highlands in a water-scarce plain area, three large villages were located within one kilometer of each other. GARWSP had provided a project to serve the villages, with a well located between them and a water tank and household-level dis-tribution system. The scheme cost about $500,000 to serve a population of more than 3,000 people. It functioned for about one day before people damaged the pump. GARWSP staff had either failed to understand the social relations among the groups and failed to check up, or, alternatively, had been successfully misled. The three villages had long-standing feuds between them, and were unwilling to cooperate or share the water.

In 1996, Ta'iz city water supply was so scarce that those in the urban network received water only once every forty days or so. In the complex and highly problematic efforts to find new sources in the neighboring rural areas, as part of a World Bank-financed project, "agreement" was reached for a village water-supply proj-ect in exchange for permission to drill wells to supply the city. Addressing only engineering aspects, suitable sites were identi-fied for the well, pump, storage tank, and conveyance mecha-nism. Of course, everyone agreed in advance to cooperate. However, once the structures were built, the owner of the land where the tank was situated insisted on his personal rights and access to all the water, as did the owner of the land where the well was located, while the conveyancing system and the targeted villages were left dry. This illustrates the risks inherent in a superficial and formal participatory approach that ignores the fundamental sociopolitical issues prevailing in any social group, small or large.

I found a contrasting case in Wadi Hadramaut in the late 1990s. Here, a water project was efficiently managed and shared in a village inhabited by *sada* (or Hashemites; descendants of the Prophet Muhammad)—who had recovered their high status and authority after unification—and low-status *fellaheen*—in Hadramaut, a low-status ascribed group of agriculturalists traditionally excluded from land ownership. Although they explicitly stated their hostility toward each other, they jointly operated a fully functioning water project, justifying this with the idea that everyone needs the water, so all had to agree on this.

Effective cooperation was the characteristic of another organization in Ta'iz governorate, which was by far the most effective community organization I ever saw in Yemen or elsewhere. It financed, built, and managed a complex set of institutions and provided water, electricity, medical services, and education to its community for decades, using primarily funds from its men working abroad and in cities in Yemen. With respect to water, the villages were situated on top of a mountain with no groundwater resources. In the 1970s, they purchased plots of land in the valley below and dug boreholes, equipping them with powerful pumps that brought the water up to their villages where standpipes were available to all—but only those households with installed sanitation systems were allowed to have house connections. Prices were affordable and covered operational and staff costs, and the poorest members received free water.

When I first visited in 1996, the community needed to replace its powerful pumps in the valley below, and funds from migrants' remittances had been severely curtailed by the crisis with Gulf states after the 1990 Kuwait problems, as many had returned and their financial situation had significantly deteriorated. As I was involved with the World Bank-funded Ta'iz project, and there was interest in supporting successful community-based activities, we suggested that the bank might help the community finance new pumps. We were surprised to meet with refusal on the grounds—and according to a World Bank staffer—that they were already well organized, so did not need any help. While the bank and other agencies were active in promoting this example as a success in its publications and meetings, this aspect was not included in the public relations documentation.[34]

As was demonstrated yet again in 2017, the absence of clean water and adequate sanitation is a major source of disease: the country suffered the world's worst cholera epidemic, with more than one million cases by the end of that year. With at least 70 percent of Yemen's population living in rural areas, rural domestic water supply and sanitation are problems for both the people and the state. As explained earlier, a national water network would not be appropriate in a country with Yemen's geological and topographical conditions. Some agricultural water sources—mostly pump-equipped wells—are also used for domestic supply, and this is where women and children are seen queuing for long periods under the sun, waiting for the pumps to be operated. Other smaller schemes, particularly springs with small outputs, are intended to be exclusively for domestic use. The main points to be remembered are: first, no effective national policies have been implemented to ensure equitable access to water for all; and, second, the wide range of sources and types of distribution systems all require specific approaches appropriate to their sociotechnical conditions. The following paragraphs illustrate some of the issues that need to be addressed.

Financing and Institutions

Given its close relationship to health, domestic water has received significant international investment. The main financier has been the government of the Netherlands, which has supported the General Authority for Rural Water Supply Projects in the decades before the war,[35] despite this institution's debatable reputation with respect to both efficiency and transparency. The Netherlands was thus perceived to be the main supporter of rural water projects as it provided imported pumps and engines, and was therefore considered responsible for project failures. Although GARWSP projects dominated the sector, there was a lack of popular confidence in its capacity. Other implementers of rural water schemes included local councils at governorate and district levels; the Social Fund for Development (SFD), itself the favorite institution of foreign financiers; UNICEF; the Public Works Project, like SFD, funded by numerous bilaterals and multilaterals, but primarily the World Bank; and even the World Bank directly, with the Rural Water Supply and Sanitation Project. While all of these nowadays claim to use beneficiary participatory approaches, none do so in a manner that would induce success, nor do they combine in-depth synergy between technical and social aspects.

The NWSSIP's stated objective for rural water supply was rapid expansion of services to reach more than five million people by 2015 in a sustainable manner.[36] As elsewhere, but more appropriately, NWSSIP promoted decentralization and "enhancement of beneficiary community role" as well as "adopting a demand responsive approach."[37] However, it acknowledged its failure in ensuring inclusion of compulsory sanitation components in rural water supply projects.

The Poverty and Social Impact Analysis (PSIA) analysis of rural water supply projects pointed out the following risks:

limited access by the poor due to their lack of political influence in the local council,[38] and the length and complexity of procedures involving at least three institutions. It mentions the extreme example of a project in the Tihama that was conceived in 1987, but was only completed in 2004.[39] However, having promoted the "demand driven approach" (DDA), the PSIA acknowledges that the problems of inequity, politically influenced decision-making, and risks in implementation are "implicit" to this approach.[40] Another widespread failure of the DDA has been its inability to increase the influence of women in decision-making, despite the fact that women are the main water collectors.

A major issue in domestic supplies is the choice of technology. To ensure sustainability of the resource, using technologies that extract more water than is replenished should be avoided. However, this is extremely unpopular for a number of reasons: first, communities consider that they are given "second best" if they are not offered the most modern and powerful technologies. Second, with the increase in population, demand almost always exceeds the sustainable use of any source. To address this situation, the SFD decided early this century to restrict its support to small-scale water-harvesting projects. While this decision may be wise for environmental protection, it is certainly not popular.

A census of rural domestic water-supply projects examined the status of 5,214 projects, including boreholes, shallow wells, springs, rainwater harvesting, and dams.[41] It found that 31 percent of both mechanized borehole and mechanized well projects were nonfunctional, and of all types of projects, those that had the highest ratio of functionality were those financed and implemented by the communities themselves (86 percent), while only 57 percent of projects implemented by GARWSP were operational. Problems with technology, specifically either with pumps or generators, were the major reasons given (41 percent of cases) for projects not operating,[42] followed by the source being dry (28 percent). The census estimated that only 33 percent of rural people have access to improved water, but less than 20 percent in five governorates. This survey did not address social or nonengineering problems, something which casts doubt on these findings, as social and political problems are known to be major reasons for failure of projects.

The discussion above shows that implementation strategies have given far too little attention to the important synergy between technical and social aspects, reflected in the fact that most rural people are still dependent on unreliable, unclean water, and lack sanitation facilities, exacerbating the health risks associated with water.

Urban Water

The media often reports that Sana'a is likely to be the first capital to run out of water, though the water crisis at the world level is now bringing other cities to the fore.[43] The urban water emergency had been a feature of daily life in Ta'iz for over two decades prior to the war.[44] As early as the mid-1990s, the 40 percent or so of households in Ta'iz connected to the network received water once every forty days, most of it from Hayma, a neighboring rural area. Deprived of water by tube wells supplying the city, agriculture dried up and the population was impoverished, as the limited "compensation" offered had been monopolized by a local leader. Attempts to drill in the neighboring district led to military conflict with the population, and produced far less water than required for Ta'iz, while causing considerable antagonism locally due to lack of support to the local communities who had neither water nor electricity, even though the electricity cables traveled across their land. By 2015, despite multiple projects, connected households received water every sixty days or so, despite the fact that Ta'iz is in the area of Yemen that receives the highest rainfall.

Interestingly, it is not only the poorer areas that lack connections to municipal water networks. In Sana'a, for example, a new residential area around Attan was officially allocated for housing. Although it was explicitly excluded from future connections to the Sana'a urban water and sanitation network, this has not prevented it from becoming a very upmarket area where many notables and other wealthy people have built large villas, even "palaces." In Aden, up to the 1980s, domestic water flowed directly into homes from the urban supply storage. Today, everyone, including those living in small apartments, has carefully locked and cared for domestic water tanks, as water distribution is erratic, to say the least. The vast majority of urban households purchase water by the tanker load, either for all or part of their use.

Some smaller towns have benefited from German-funded projects, which, to their credit, do focus on the need for sanitation alongside the supply of water, thus avoiding the major problem of disease-breeding stagnant water ponds. While sanitation structures are also being built in other towns and cities, they lag behind water supply.

Only towns and cities are covered by municipally managed integrated networks, using local water resources. By the early 2010s, these rarely supplied more than 50 percent of households, often far less. All have significant areas unconnected to networks, and those that are connected only receive supplies for limited periods, leading all households to install storage tanks of different capacities and keep water in containers within their flats and houses. Moreover, there is no systematic link between the provision of water and that of sanitation systems, leading to frequent seepages of sewerage water into the water table from which domestic water is extracted, and so there is significant pollution of the water coming from taps. This contributes to explaining the 2017 cholera epidemic. Drinking water needs to be purified everywhere in the country, and the inability of millions to afford to buy clean water has contributed to the spread of waterborne diseases. Neighborhoods on the network received water only once or twice a week prior to the war.

As urban populations grow, the need to bring water from neighboring rural areas will increase, and the problems witnessed by Ta'iz may well occur elsewhere. With the disappearance of water in the highlands, more people are likely to move to coastal areas. There, desalinated sea-water will have to become the main source of water in future decades. Thanks to improved technology, its cost should become more accessible even for municipalities with limited funds, though international investment funding will certainly be essential. However, the highland main towns and cities will need different strategies.

Conclusions: Postwar Priorities

Given the urgency and importance of the water crisis in Yemen, new approaches are essential. I do not believe that an exclusively "community-based" approach is either feasible or helpful. The problem must be addressed in different ways according to the nature and scope of the source to ensure the equitable distribution of water for basic needs. There is, however, no doubt that a significant shift in water use out of agriculture is essential to enable the fifty million or so Yemenis alive by the middle of this century to stay in the country. This also means that alternative, low-water-demanding economic activities must emerge, which requires a population with far higher levels of education and skills.

To enable Yemenis to continue living in the country, specific but different measures must be taken according to the particular conditions of each aquifer. This is not a case where a "one-size-fits-all" strategy can work. What is needed is an asset of complementary strategies, ranging from strong state intervention at the macro-level associated with more democratic participatory approaches at the micro-level. Overall, this will also require a significant reduction of water use for agriculture to prioritize water first for human drinking and other domestic needs, and then for livestock and possibly industry. Such a policy requires enforcement capacity of the state to prevent private interests from monopolizing water at the expense of the majority. Once this macro-level need has been addressed, local communities can decide on the next level of distribution for "their" water—though ensuring access to all, including the weak and marginalized, must remain a state-enforceable priority. Water can, and indeed should, be managed as democratically as possible, allowing all "stakeholders"—in this case, everyone, including women—to have a say in the distribution of the resource between human drinking and domestic, livestock, agriculture, and industrial uses. Put simply, at the macro-level, the state needs to be in charge, while at the micro-level, users should be given responsibility in a democratic manner, on the principle of "one person, one voice," ensuring equity.

Customary water management procedures in the country remained suitable and appropriate for many centuries. The fundamental technological changes of recent decades have transformed the terms of the discourse. Only small communities using a single source where people are in regular contact with each other and have long-established relations—whether of cooperation or hostility—can manage their water at the micro-level. At the macro-level of multi-water basins and large, deep aquifers, management must be determined and enforced at the state level. The same goes for basin-level management, which might involve one or more governorates, or possibly regions in a future federal Yemen. Small- and medium-scale rural domestic water schemes must be managed according to the most appropriate system; for example, as in the case of a village with a single cistern or a committee for schemes supplying a number of communities. Basically, the underlying principles must include flexibility and the implementation of the most appropriate mechanism at each level, as well as a deep synergy between technological and sociopolitical approaches.

In the past, agricultural development policies have been biased in favor of the neoliberal development agenda, and provided immediate benefits to the few at the expense of long-term sustainability for the majority, by giving priority to thirsty, high-value, export crops. Although the IFIs and bilateral funders have played their role in this scenario, they were in full concordance with the priorities of the Yemeni regime, seeking lasting support from powerful landowners who benefited from these policies; equity was not an objective or strategy of the Saleh regime.

Domestic rural water supply is the most urgent aspect of water management for the survival of the rural population; finding effective mechanisms to provide people with the water and sanitation they need for healthy lifestyles is essential. The approaches used in the past have failed for a number of reasons. First, they failed to develop mechanisms suited to the specific technical circumstances of the water source. A successful management mechanism for an open cistern replenished by rain-water and supplying a single village of densely built highland houses must clearly be different from that for a large project using a pump and borehole supplying a number of villages distant from each other on a plain. Each needs an approach that responds to the social and political dynamics of the concerned beneficiary community. Participatory community approaches are clearly suitable in the case of the first, whereas in that of the second, the power relationships and ownership issues of the land where the well, storage tank, and the pipes are located have implications for management that most likely require the involvement of the state as a third party.

Second, decision-making has been dominated by engineers and hydrologists, with an exclusively technical vision. Evidence has demonstrated that successful management of rural domestic water requires the combined skills of technologists and social scientists. While both the state and funding agencies have adopted "participatory" and "demand-driven" approaches, these have strengthened the powerful at the expense of the poor and at the expense of social equity. Unless the social and power relations of concerned individuals and groups are clearly understood, there is potential for conflicts and waste of invested funds on failed schemes. In recent decades, "beneficiary participation" and the involvement of social development specialists have been limited to ensuring that beneficiaries contribute payments and comply with decisions made elsewhere. People hired in these positions have almost always been junior in their own hierarchies, including many women, which further reduces their level of authority within the community and within their institutions.

The issue of rural-to-urban water transfers also needs to be addressed equitably: urban areas must be provided with the water needed for domestic needs. In the highlands, this will have to come from local sources at the expense of agriculture. Rural communities losing their water must be compensated adequately through investments in economic sectors, allowing their people to earn a reasonable income in activities that require no or little water; whether this is called compensation or something else is the least of the problems.

Writing at a time when there is no immediate prospect of peace in Yemen, nor any clarity of the type of regime likely to emerge from the war, it is difficult to assess the likelihood of these essential approaches being implemented by future Yemeni state entities. However, unless new sustainable water management is implemented at the country level, Yemen's neighbors are likely to experience a significant influx of "climate/water" refugees across their borders within a generation or less.

7

WEAPONIZING WATER IN THE MIDDLE EAST

"LESSONS LEARNED" FROM IS

Tobias von Lossow

The Weaponization of Water in Syria and Iraq

In recent Middle Eastern conflicts, the weaponization of water has gained new momentum.[1] In Syria and Iraq, for instance, with few exceptions, of all the warring parties have been using water as a weapon—in various ways, for multiple reasons, and with different impact in scale and scope. Driven by political motives and military considerations, this practice has resulted in severe humanitarian, environmental, and economic consequences. The use of water as a weapon diminishes water availability and access (attacks on wells, networks, pumping stations, etc.), hampers food production (particularly irrigated agriculture), and threatens energy production (i.e., hydroelectricity).

In Syria and Iraq, the so-called Islamic State (IS) became a kind of frontrunner of frequently and systematically weaponizing water in order to achieve its political and military goals.[2] After the defeat of the militia as a territorial force in Iraq and its massive military push-back in Syria, this contribution seeks to more broadly contextualize the weaponization of water by IS, reviewing it as a closed case study. Providing detailed assessment of this case against historical and regional records contributes to a better understanding of the phenomenon of weaponizing water during contemporary armed conflict. From the analysis, broader implications can be derived for current and future conflicts in the Middle East with regard to the role of water resources and water infrastructures in warfare contexts. A better understanding of the risks, threats, and mechanisms of the weaponization of water may potentially allow the prevention of such acts in future.

This contribution draws on works about the weaponization of water in Syria and Iraq, paying special attention to the role of IS.[3] In order to provide comprehensive analysis, it also refers to water and security research that focuses on supplies in urban areas, sheds light on water infrastructures, reflects historical cases, and uncovers regional political and security dynamics.[4] Finally, country specific articles, reports, and other contributions feed into the analysis, particularly sources that document what has been happening on the ground in the armed conflicts of Syria and Iraq.

To clarify differences between various terms, approaches, and concepts of utilizing water in fragile or violent contexts, the following definition is used: "water as a weapon," or the "weaponization of water," is defined as direct (ab)use of water resources as an instrument of war during armed conflict and as a tool to achieve strategic political and/or tactical military goals.[5] The manipulation of water flows, reserves, and supplies, for instance, is a strategic act of warfare that serves a certain purpose. In most cases, this requires control of the water resources in the first place, and often involves water infrastructures to execute.

The weaponization of water differs from intentionally or unintentionally targeting, damaging, or destroying—by an airstrike, for example—water infrastructures such as treatment plants, pumping stations, or dams. In the case of such a deliberate attack, the demolition of installations is a one-off matter; it is means and ends at the same time. As the weaponization of water is usually applied in contexts of violence or armed conflict, it differs also from what can be subsumed under the "instrumentalization of water." In this case, rather, political long-term strategies deprive certain regions or parts of the population by preventing them from water access. At the national level, it often occurs under autocratic regimes and in fragile contexts as well as in times of stability.

Nonetheless, the various terms, related approaches, and concepts of (ab)using water to deliberately cause harm are not clear-cut. Blurring lines between the actual practices, differences in various regional contexts and overlap in means, impact, and consequences make it sometimes difficult to precisely name these kinds of phenomena as they might look similar in intention and outcome.[6]

Regional Waters under IS Control

During its rise and expansion as a territorial force in Syria and later Iraq, IS had gained control over important water resources, and had been repeatedly using water as a weapon to further its strategic political as well as tactical military aims.[7] It began in 2012, when militant groups that joined or merged into IS at a later stage weaponized water sporadically and limited to certain areas. These groups seized important water infrastructures and all major dams along the Euphrates in Syria in 2013.[8] The capture of large dams on the Euphrates and Tigris—the region's most important water resources—turned out to be a central pillar of IS's expansionist strategy. This became particularly obvious when the militia rapidly overran Iraq in 2014.[9] Within a few months, and with the only exception being Haditha dam, IS quickly and easily gained control over all the large Iraqi dams on the Euphrates and Tigris upstream of Baghdad—at least for a certain period of time (see Table 1).

Table 7.1: Major Dams under IS control

Dam	Under IS Control
Syria	
Tishrin Dam	11/2012–12/2015
Euphrates Dam/Tabqa Dam	02/2013–05/2017
Baath Dam	02/2013–06/2017
Iraq	
Mosul Dam	August 7–18, 2014
Haditha Dam	–
Samarra Dam	04/2014– 10/2015
Ramadi Dam	05/2015– 01/2016
Fallujah Dam/Nuaimiya Dam	02/2014– 06/2016

Source: The table is based on information in Tobias von Lossow, "The Rebirth of Water as a Weapon: IS in Syria and Iraq," *The International Spectator* 51, no. 3 (2016): 82–29.

In August 2014, the prominent capture of Mosul dam marked a turning point also for external actors outside the region. The largest dam in the Middle East, generating the biggest share of Iraq's hydro-electricity, was and still is in bad physical shape, requiring daily reparation measures. The United States (US) decided to intervene militarily and thereby de facto expanded its—originally humanitarian—mandate to support Kurdish forces in protecting the Yezidi population in the Sinjar Mountains. The US henceforth provided massive close air support to Iraqi security forces and Kurdish Peshmerga units to retake Mosul dam after ten days.[10] Moreover, the US launched massive airstrikes to prevent Haditha dam from being captured by IS, which made huge efforts to capture Iraq's second largest dam. Later on, in 2016 and 2017, when intensified efforts and large campaigns of the anti-IS coalitions in Syria and Iraq finally succeeded in fighting back the terrorist group, dam after dam had to be retaken. With the recapture of Tabqa dam (Euphrates dam) and Baath dam upstream of Raqqa during the Raqqa campaign, the last major dams under IS control were "liberated" in May and June 2017.[11]

Analysis of IS' weaponization of water has found that the militia repeatedly applied water as a weapon in a targeted, systematic, consistent, and, at the same time, flexible manner.[12] IS used water as a weapon in various forms in order to further its political aims by targeting civilian populations and thus putting the Syrian and the Iraqi governments under pressure. These acts were meant to break resistance, demonstrate power, and exert de facto control over certain territories.[13] IS also benefitted from the psychological effect of the water weapon, which manifests itself in the mere fact of control over water resources: the potential use of the destructive force of water already has an impact, regardless of whether water is actually weaponized or not.[14] The fact that IS controlled several important water resources and water infrastructures that could potentially have been used as weapons was threatening and reinforced their political and military aims and ambitions. The weaponization of water also served IS' tactical military purposes; for instance, when flooding was applied either offensively to drown opponents' positions, or defensively to turn areas impassable and thus halt hostile combatants from approaching further into IS-controlled territories.

Differentiating the immediate impact, IS weaponized water in three ways.[15] The militia either made sure that there was *too little water* available in the targeted areas by retaining water at dams, diverting it, or cutting supplies for communities. Alternatively, IS arranged for *too much water* when flooding certain territories by releasing large amounts of water at once, or by blocking the water flow at barrages thus drowning the riverbanks behind the dam. Furthermore, water has been rendered unusable for drinking and agricultural purposes by *contaminating resources*—with oil, for instance.[16] During the period of its territorial expansion until autumn 2015 and the establishment of its so-called caliphate, IS mostly deployed the water weapon by manipulating quantities in the form of too little or too much water—using large dams to increase the impact of either strategy.[17] This practice shifted when the militia was pushed back and lost its strongholds as well as most of the territorial heartlands in 2016 and 2017. At this point, water quality and the contamination of water resources became more relevant and frequently applied as part of IS' scorched earth tactics. In this context, and beyond the weaponization of water, the militia also looted, intentionally damaged, and destroyed water infrastructures in Iraq.[18]

The example of Fallujah dam illustrates in a nutshell the broad spectrum, variety, multiplicity, simultaneity, and gravity of how IS weaponized water. Even if this example was quite exceptional by IS standards, it gives an idea and overview of the logics and mechanisms of the water weapon. In April 2014, IS closed the gates at Fallujah dam in order to withhold water, threatening and deliberately depriving the largely Shi'a population at the lower reaches of the river basin, thus affecting one of the most important agricultural centers of the country. By retaining water, IS simultaneously submerged Iraqi government and military facilities at the banks, increasing the reservoir's water table behind the barrage.[19] Two days later, the militia diverted these retained waters over an irrigation channel into a side valley and flooded land up to 100 kilometers away. The city of Abu Ghraib was up to four meters under water, 10,000 houses and 200 square kilometers of fertile farmland were destroyed, the harvest for 2014 was lost, the livestock killed, and about 60,000 people forced to flee.[20] By flooding these large territories, IS also prevented the rapid advance of follow-on units of the Iraqi army from approaching IS positions near Fallujah. In addition, this move also hampered the parliamentary elections held on April 30, 2014; as a consequence of the flooding, only a third of the polling stations in Anbar province—the largest by area—were able to open on election day.[21]

The Bigger Picture: Revisiting IS and the Weaponization of Water

The weaponization of water by IS in Syria and Iraq received intense political and media attention. It raised broader awareness for this phenomenon and brought it prominently back on the agenda of water and security discourses. IS applied this practice in an unprecedented way in many regards; it weaponized water to a new level in the way that it integrated water with all its facets into the portfolio of its day-to-day warfare operations.[22]

Then again, the act of weaponizing water is by no means a new phenomenon. Additionally, in the recent conflicts in Syria and Iraq, IS has not been alone in using water as a weapon; this tactic has been used by most warring parties. Particularly in Syria, for example, water has been weaponized more often by government forces or other actors backing the regime. Revisiting the case of IS in a larger context gives a more distinct picture of the unique ways in which the militia actually used water as a weapon and what role this practice played in regional conflict dynamics.

International Attention, Media Presence, and Propaganda

A specific feature of the IS case was the high level of political attention and global media coverage it attracted. IS was among the first actors in the conflicts to openly and proudly admit weaponizing water, and exploited this practice for its broader propaganda purposes. IS presented the water weapon to its fellow fighters and followers as a demonstration of power and used it as a means of attracting potential recruits from all over the world. The militia's information channels—the news agency Amaq, the propaganda magazine *Dabiq*, and its social media presence on Twitter and Facebook—played an important role here by commanding the world's attention.[23]

IS's historically rather unique openness about weaponizing water matched the world's perception of the group as an unprecedentedly brutal, extraordinarily reckless, and highly aggressive actor. The self-marketing of the militia aimed continuously at promoting and upholding an image of being the most powerful and dangerous force among all the warring factions in Syria and Iraq. The increasing number of terrorist attacks in Europe and elsewhere in the world reaffirmed this perception. As concerns in political circles rose worldwide, IS quickly became the central enemy in the conflicts—and the only one that the international community could relatively easily agree on, given the highly complex and complicated setting, particularly in Syria.

In addition, IS's exceptional self-marketing and its pathological desire for attention and recognition made it relatively easy to verify its acts of weaponizing water. While first hints often came from the population on the ground through social media channels, IS shortly after publicly claimed responsibility through its news channels and propaganda organs. Regularly, Russian, US, or other international sources confirmed instances of water weaponization by referring to or publishing satellite footage.[24] Such multifold, unitarian, and non-contested confirmation of the use of water as a weapon is unique in recent history. When warring parties have been accused of intentionally damaging water facilities or weaponizing water during armed conflict over the past decades, they have usually either denied such an accusation, or framed it as collateral damage. This has been the case, for example, with aerial bombing campaigns perpetrated by Israel and NATO.[25]

Historic Regional Context: Hydrology and Politics

The effectiveness and impact of weaponizing water depends on the climatic and hydrological parameters as well as the political setting and capacities to manage water supplies, access, and the various users' needs. The more harmful the potential impact of the water weapon in a specific environment, the more effective, powerful, and attractive it is to have it ready for deployment.[26] The water weapon is particularly effective in water-scarce environments such as the arid and semi-arid lands of the Middle East. The notorious water crisis in the region had, and has, multiple implications for the security situation and for stability in the region.[27]

Both Syria and Iraq are exposed to little and irregular rainfall, recurring droughts, and unevenly distributed water resources within the countries. Both countries highly depend on very few water resources, particularly on the Euphrates and Tigris, which originate outside these countries.[28] Moreover, the high dependence on large, mostly irrigated, agriculture, outdated and centralized water infrastructures, and policies failing to adequately address these challenges have made the societies of Iraq and Syria even more vulnerable—and the water weapon even more effective.

In this region, the (ab)use of water as such is nothing new. Even if IS enhanced the use of water in various ways, it followed a continuum—a certain "traditional" pattern of considering and using water more strategically in politics, conflict, and warfare. The Middle East gives examples of various types of politicizing, instrumentalizing, weaponizing, and targeting water, applied along lines of center-periphery, geography, tribes, ethnicity, or socioeconomic cleavages. The political instrumentalization of water supplies, access to resources, and subsidies favoring certain parts of the population over others have been commonplace in the Middle East over the past decades.[29]

In Syria, for instance, the regime's investments in the water sector focused mainly on cities and urban centers, while the rural population and remote areas of the country remained rather neglected. During the heavy drought between 2006 and 2010, and compounded by the global economic crisis, the subsidies on diesel had to be cancelled in 2008. This withdrew one of Syrian farmers' key assets: they relied on diesel motor pumps to extract groundwater for irrigation,[30] crucial equipment that was even more necessary during the drought.

In Iraq, water has even been used as a means of punishing certain populations. In the 1990s, Saddam Hussein had the marshes in the south drained to take revenge on the local, mostly Shi'a population for rising up against his regime.[31] It resulted in a humanitarian, socioeconomic, and environmental disaster, requiring tremendous efforts to restore about 50 percent of this unique ecosystem about a decade later. The marshes were targeted once more when IS withheld Euphrates water in Syria and at the Iraqi upper branches of the Euphrates and Tigris in order to hit the Shi'a population as well as one of the country's agricultural centers.[32] Over the last few decades, large parts of the population have been forced to abandon the marshes since environmental degradation, decreasing water inflow, and increasing salination of water and soil have made it one of the most vulnerable areas in the country today.

In the region and throughout history, water and water infrastructure have time and again been targeted, damaged, destroyed, or used as a weapon to gain military advantages on the battlefield. Cyrus the Great is said to have diverted the water of the

Euphrates in order to invade Babylon in 539 BC. After the water level dropped, his forces crossed the dried-out riverbed, then entered and took over the city in the early morning hours, overpowering the highly protected city, which was unprepared for such an attack.[33]

The "Dual-Use" Character of Water

The control over water resources and infrastructures is a precondition for the weaponization of water. At the same time, it comes with necessities, obligations, and responsibilities with regard to water access, supply services, and maintenance. Dealing with these issues in a sustainable way is of fundamental importance for warring factions that hold territories and control over a population. Particularly in arid or semi-arid regions, and specifically during armed conflict, the provision and management of basic supplies can itself become desirable in order to reach mid-term and long-term goals. This sets clear limits for deploying the water weapon.

Although regularly using water as a weapon, IS faced just such—in this case, practical and ideological—constraints and competing goals in Syria and Iraq.[34] Its military expansion and control over seized territories required basic supplies. On the one hand, the militia simply needed water and hydroelectricity from local sources for its military operations. On the other hand, IS was providing supplies for the population living in the conquered territories, which helped to neutralize potential opposition or even gain support, particularly in areas that had been neglected before the arrival of the group. In a few cases, IS even increased hydroelectricity production or improved water supplies.[35]

Water was key for IS to gain legitimacy in the conquered territories and to consolidate the proclaimed caliphate. The provision of water and electricity—usually state-run services—in a winning-hearts-and-minds attitude increased the militia's credibility amongst its ranks. Fellow fighters, new recruits, and supporters from all over the world wanted to see the caliphate project realized in the IS-controlled territories.[36] Even if the militia did not really invest in supply systems, it promoted the provision of such services and increased its popularity and the legitimacy of its rule with such state-building measures. Since the caliphate was an important foundation of the IS ideology, the provision of water and electricity served as an important showcase for their ability to establish a state-like entity and demonstrated the will and capacity to actually run it.

Besides providing water in IS-controlled areas affected by drought and suffering from insufficient water access, the resource also played a role in the militia's recruitment efforts in the region, particularly in Iraq. IS offered support to the population in 2011–2012 during the drought, spread rumors, and provided alternative income opportunities when water shortages made agricultural activities nearly impossible. The group managed to easily recruit desperate farmers who could hardly envision alternatives to joining the militia.[37]

Given the multiple benefits of water, IS frequently and flexibly used water as a weapon, but restricted this to a limited period of time or to certain areas. A closer look shows that the militia did this mostly cautiously, not causing irreparable, long-standing, large-scale damage in the territories captured or in those it planned to seize in the near future. In many cases, IS simply cut off water supplies after it had conquered cities or communities and resumed supplies a few days later having blackmailed support from, or at least the neutrality of, the population.[38] Only on very few occasions, as in the previously mentioned example at Fallujah dam, did the militia cause large-scale damage through flooding or retaining water.

Since water was so vital for IS and was weaponized rather rationally, the often-cited and feared worst-case scenario of a dramatic and apocalyptic blowing-up of a major dam did not materialize. This was highly unlikely to happen at the time when the militia was controlling larger territories and implementing the caliphate project.[39] Instead, the risk of larger damage resulting from weaponizing water, and also from targeting infrastructures, increased when the anti-IS coalitions in Syria and Iraq stepped up their efforts and started broader offensives in 2016. Damaging and looting water installations became more prevalent when the militia had to retreat under military pressure.[40]

The dual-use characteristics of water have implications: since weaponizing water requires its control in the first place, this means in turn that every actor controlling water resources, installations, and infrastructures is technically in a position to potentially use water as a weapon. The weaponization of water is not so much about state or non-state actors, as the IS case indicates.[41] It is rather about any kind of actor that is both capable and ready to use water as a weapon in order to achieve political or military goals at a certain point in time. In the case of Syria, available figures illustrate how all actors—state actors, non-state actors, and hybrids alike—have frequently used water as a weapon. Incidents for which government forces and actors fighting for the regime have presumably been responsible by far outnumber incidents for which IS had been responsible.

Against this background, it is debatable if, or for how long, the so-called "liberation" of dams and water infrastructures in Syria prevented these installations from being used to weaponize water. After IS had been forced to hand over water installations, it was mostly Syrian government forces or the Free Syrian Army (FSA) that took over—both actors that frequently weaponized water—continuing up to the time of writing.

Reaction and Prevention: Protection of Critical Infrastructures

The case of IS in Syria and Iraq shows that measures to prevent an actor from weaponizing water are rather limited. After the group seized and controlled various dams and installations, it was relatively easy for them to weaponize water. Interventions at diplomatic and political levels hardly had any impact. Since the militia's intervention in the Syrian and Iraqi water supplies explicitly intended to violate international norms, laws of war, international humanitarian law, and human rights law, an international plea and condemnation, for instance by the UN, did not have any effect.[42]

Technical and hydrological interventions in the Euphrates and Tigris river system have worked on a handful of occasions, but are extremely risky with effects that are hard to calculate. In one instance, the Iraqi government, controlling the mouth of Lake Habbaniya, successfully increased the water released into the Euphrates at the lower end of the lake. For a few days, it was possible to outbalance the river flow, which had decreased by 50 percent after IS had diverted Euphrates water into the same lake further upstream.[43] In another example, such an intervention had dramatic unintended consequences: when IS withheld water at Fallujah dam in April 2014, the Iraqi government increased the amount of water released further upstream at Haditha dam in order to put IS under pressure.[44] The group's positions, indeed, were threatened, but the militia released the water into a side valley, as outlined earlier. Through this countermove, also involving weaponizing water, the Iraqi government de facto intensified the IS-triggered flood, which became the worst in the area since the 1950s.[45]

It was primarily military intervention that proved to be effective and had a decisive impact. The airstrikes of the anti-IS coalition made a difference, but also required enormous military efforts on the ground by Kurdish units, the FSA, and the Iraqi army. Retaking—or in case of Haditha dam, holding—key dams and important water installations came at high costs, because IS also heavily invested militarily with manpower and material in capturing, holding, and defending these sites. Haditha dam had been put under siege by IS for about two years, which it repeatedly attacked in several offensives and a series of suicide attacks.[46] The dam could only be held due to US close air support. In most cases, the water infrastructures had finally been liberated as part of the larger anti-IS campaigns—as, for instance, for the cities of Ramadi, Fallujah, and Raqqa. Particularly, the recapture of Tabqa dam illustrated how difficult, risky, and dangerous such battles over dams are. After taking Tabqa airport, the US-backed anti-IS forces approached Tabqa dam in March 2017, just before moving on to Raqqa. A few days of heavy fighting led to a fire in one of the control rooms, for which both parties blamed each other. While the anti-IS forces, mainly FSA fighters, seized the southern control tower at the dam, IS was able to hold the northern tower on the other side. During inspections and maintenance works initially agreed on by both sides, two engineers were killed at the dam. The situation remained tense but stable for about six weeks, with both sides facing each other—the frontline literally crossing the dam crest.[47] In this situation, it was not possible to further engage militarily without putting the dam at risk. The final, relatively smooth capture of the northern tower indicated that an IS withdrawal with safe conduct had been negotiated.[48]

Since all of the outlined, rather reactive, measures to prevent water from being weaponized have only limited impact and carry high risks and costs, they are mostly a means of last resort. A far more effective way is the protection of water infrastructures in times of peace, in potential pre-conflict settings, or at the beginning of armed conflict. Dams, pumping stations, treatment plants, and other water infrastructure, including hydroelectric power plants, usually fall under the heading of critical infrastructure that, theoretically, should be protected against attacks or during civil strife or armed conflict. In practice, however, such water infrastructure is a comparatively soft target; the sites are physically vulnerable given their sheer size and visibility, they are relatively easily accessible, and the hired staff is often just superficially vetted beforehand. IS took control of the Iraqi dams in quick and easy surprise coups, often more or less overrunning these installations, illustrating their vulnerability and the need to better protect these military targets.

The protection of water infrastructures is a crucial element that needs to be better addressed in the (post-) conflict settings in Iraq and Syria. This should be better reflected in the countries' security and defense strategies and concepts.[49] Beyond the physical vulnerability of water infrastructure, installations are also threatened by chemical and cyber attacks. Attempts to poison water resources, or to hack the control systems and modules of reservoirs, networks, distribution systems, and dams are regularly observed around the globe.

Rule Rather than Exception: Violation of Norms and Law

Over the past few decades, the weaponization of water has increasingly lost prominence as a means of warfare, even if it has continued to play a role in some conflicts—during the wars in the former Yugoslavia, for instance. Generally, states are increasingly hesitant to deploy the water weapon, and tend—at least officially—to not enact it, especially since practices of weaponizing water had been addressed more explicitly in international humanitarian law and banned by the 1977 Protocols Additional to the Geneva Conventions of 1949 (Protocol I & Protocol II).[50]

In most past cases, the weaponization of water was portrayed as a one-off matter—as an exceptional act to achieve a military breakthrough, enacted as a game changer or as means of last resort.[51] States targeting water infrastructure or weaponizing water in recent decades have referred to collateral damage as unintended. When the damage caused is not extraordinarily high, it has also been argued that the concept of proportionality, which makes water installations a legitimate military target, in case they are used militarily by opponents.

The armed conflicts in Syria and Iraq clearly broke with this behavioral attitude and marked a shift to this practice becoming more common and frequently used. The conflicts in Libya and Yemen also saw, and continue to see, water being weaponized, and infrastructures targeted, damaged, and destroyed.[52] IS was one of the first warring parties to weaponize water on a day-to-day basis and demonstrated an explicit noncompliance with, and violation of, international norms, humanitarian law, and laws of war. Weaponizing water provoked an outrageous outcry and was portrayed as a perverted warfare tactic by IS, neglecting the fact that nearly all parties in Syria and Iraq have been using water as a weapon—state actors and non-state actors, state-financed hybrids, and external actors alike. Aleppo, for instance, has been hit several times by the water weapon, deployed by different actors attempting to overtake the city.[53]

Over the course of the conflict in Syria, the Syrian Army and other forces loyal to the regime, supported by international actors like Russia, as well as the FSA and various other rebel groups, all turned out to be even more rigorous in weaponizing water than IS. Particularly from 2016 onwards, the other conflict parties have increasingly been weaponizing water in a targeted way, as systematically, consistently, and flexibly as IS did in the first place. The figures illustrate that incidents committed by actors other than IS by far outnumber those cases in which IS was responsible. Driven by a spiral of increasing brutalization in a climate of constantly increasing levels of violent disinhibition deliberately targeting civilians, the weaponization of water became more and more common—the rule rather than the exception.

This shift is also the result of broader trends and developments in the warfare context of Syria and Iraq. Over time, the weaponization of water became less exceptional and less scandalous and, at a certain point, turned into a subordinate element in the larger warfare strategy of siege and scarcity of water, food, electricity, medical services, and shelter. It explicitly targeted, and still targets, civilians and became commonly and frequently applied.[54] In this climate of committing a series of war crimes and crimes against humanity, the weaponization of water is just one facet. Against the background of what happened in Aleppo, Eastern Ghouta, and Afrin—to mention a few prominent cases—the weaponization of water by IS in 2014 and 2015 gave just an inkling of what would subsequently unfold in Syria from 2015 onwards.

Conclusion

Belligerent parties have always weaponized water in one way or another throughout history; the weaponization of water is not a new phenomenon. Particularly in the water-scarce Middle East, water plays a specific strategic role that makes it attractive for warring parties to apply as a weapon in armed conflicts. Still, to a certain extent, IS can be seen as a frontrunner in using water as a weapon, since the militia applied it systematically and frequently. In addition, IS exploited and promoted these acts for its propaganda, to further its image as a powerful and reckless actor, and to gain international attention. But the IS ambition to establish a state-like entity also set limits and vividly illustrated the dual-use characteristics of water and water infrastructures in armed conflicts. The militia found itself in a dilemma of either committing war crimes by weaponizing water or investing in its state-building efforts by providing basic water and electricity supplies as means of gaining support from the population. Both these highly rational approaches used by IS to achieve its political and military aims had to be balanced during its territorial expansion.

Over the course of the conflicts, the weaponization of water made another swift turn: when IS was militarily pushed back, the group increasingly contaminated water resources and damaged water infrastructure. Even more problematic was the fact that, in Syria, the weaponization of water has become part of a broader strategy of scarcity in the context of siege warfare—a military approach that explicitly targets the civil population and constantly undermines minimal humanitarian standards, violating international law. Increasing the population's suffering became a goal in and of itself, parties to the conflict intentionally targeted schools, hospitals, and residential areas—with the weaponization of water as a subordinate element. While IS was among the first actors to weaponize water in Syria and Iraq, it turned out that nearly all of the conflict parties in the region adopted this practice over the course of the conflict, some of whose actions even exceeded IS practices in scale and scope.

The distinction between state and non-state actors is not useful since the Syrian Army and pro-government forces with support of international actors like Russia have been using water as a weapon to the same extent as the various opposing groups, including IS. Despite the extreme attention that IS gained, and which it was actively seeking, it would be rather misleading to link the weaponization of water too much with non-state actors. Over the course of the conflict, a rising number of actors increasingly neglected international law, standards, and norms. A similar development can be observed in Yemen, where government forces as well as airstrikes by Saudi Arabia have been repeatedly attacking water installations. Even if systematic data and research is lacking in some cases, such as Yemen, various incidents suggest that the use of water as a weapon, as observed in Syria and Iraq, is becoming a "trend" shaping present and future warfare and war-making in the Middle East.

8

IN PURSUIT OF SECURITY AND INFLUENCE

THE UAE AND THE RED SEA

Nael Shama and *Islam Hassan*

Control of the sea by maritime commerce and naval supremacy, means predominant influence in the world; because, however great the wealth product of the land, nothing facilitates the necessary exchanges as does the sea.[1]

Introduction

For over a decade, there has been a significant change in the evolving foreign policy of the United Arab Emirates (UAE), which has become more assertive and active than ever before. The interplay of changes in the domestic and international environments; the 2004 change in the Emirati political leadership; and the 2011 Arab uprisings have triggered this development, which includes not only a change in foreign policy goals, but also in foreign policy means. One central tool used to achieve the new foreign policy goals has been a dominant presence in and around the Red Sea. The UAE has been heavily engaged in establishing military bases and acquiring operational and management rights over ports and economic zones in the region. This foray into the Red Sea, one of the most important global shipping lanes, has been coupled with a significant naval military presence in the Gulf of Aden and the Bab al-Mandab Strait as well as the presence of private Emirati security companies in the region to conduct anti-piracy operations and provide protection for UAE ships.

This study adds to the burgeoning literature on the international relations of the Persian Gulf in two distinct ways. First, it addresses the understudied topic of foreign policy change in small states. Second, by exploring the nature and motivations of Emirati activism in the Red Sea, the chapter addresses the unexplored trend of the securitization of water-space and shipping lanes in the Middle East.

The UAE's "gun and purse" diplomacy in the Red Sea region is advanced by supplying economic aid, building ports, providing maritime services, and establishing military and naval bases in various spots in and around the region. In order to understand this peculiar policy, this chapter explores several factors that have led to the overall changes in the country's foreign policy: the coming to power of a new leadership in 2004, the massive economic wealth the country has generated over the past decade or so, the faltering of traditional regional pillars of influence, the ensuing vacuum in the regional order, the intense rivalry with Qatar, and the rise of Islamist militant groups in the Middle East and North and East Africa. All these factors have contributed to the vast transformation in the UAE's foreign policy, which not only includes a change in the identification of pressing problems, but also in the means used to achieve foreign policy goals.

This study argues that following the ascendance of President Sheikh Khalifa bin Zayed Al-Nahyan and the Crown Prince of Abu Dhabi Sheikh Mohamed bin Zayed Al-Nahyan (MBZ) to power, in order for the UAE to maintain domestic stability in a volatile region, secure its trade, and expand its regional influence, it has adopted a more active and assertive foreign policy. A significant tool of such foreign policy is maintaining a strong economic and military presence on the sea-lanes of the Red Sea and the Gulf of Aden.[2] The study begins with a theoretical framework that discusses the notion of foreign policy change. It then examines two domestic variables—the change in leadership, and the increase in the country's economic and military capabilities—that have contributed to the transformation of the UAE's foreign policy. The study then investigates the effect of regional dynamics—particularly the 2011 Arab uprisings and regional relationships with the United States (US)—on the reformulation of Emirati foreign policy. It concludes with an investigation of the various Emirati activities in the Red Sea and East Africa in recent years, explaining why these areas have attracted the attention of the UAE's leadership in their pursuit of security and influence.

Foreign Policy Change

Change is a fundamental aspect of foreign policy that has received scant scholarly attention. While Holsti attributed this negligence to the concentration of researchers on the apparent stability of the Cold War structure, Gilpin explained that it is due to scholars' belief that static theory is more important and easier to prove than dynamic analysis—their normative bias in favor of stability, and their conviction of the futility of studying change.[3] Writing about the massive changes that engulfed the world as the Cold War era was coming to an end, Hoffmann observed that "there are periods of history when profound changes occur all of a sudden, and the acceleration of events is such that much of what experts write is obsolete before it gets into print. We are now in one of these periods."[4] The same words could, no doubt, be said of the current dramatic changes that have taken place in the Middle East since the 2011 Arab uprisings. Studying the nature, sources, and consequences of such change is imperative.

The current literature on foreign policy change includes several models, but few can be applied to the foreign policy of the UAE. Some models are disposed towards inertia, focusing more on factors that hinder change than those that facilitate it. Goldmann, for example, deals with "stabilizers" in the decision-making process that act as barriers to change.[5] Other models deal with the environment, international or domestic, focusing exclusively on factors such as the impact of shifts in the balance of power or changes in the political system on foreign policy change, while disregarding the leaders who make that change. For example, Skidmore concentrates entirely on structural reasons, and pays no attention to the foreign policy decision-making process.[6] Other models focus on specific issues like the relationship between structure and agency (Carlsnaes), or the cyclical aspect of change, championing the argument that periods of stability are followed by periods of transition over the long term (Holsti).[7]

The theoretical framework used in this chapter is premised on the belief that, in foreign policy analysis, different levels of inquiry should be considered simultaneously, including regional and systemic effects, domestic influences, and the role of leadership. It therefore takes into account systemic factors, domestic developments, and the dynamics of the decision-making process. Inspired by the outstanding works of Gustavsson and Hermann, it assumes that foreign policy change comes about as a result of the convergence of three sources of change: changes in the domestic and international environments; a change in the political leadership that runs foreign affairs; and an element of external crisis that stimulates and/or accelerates change.[8] Other sources of change, such as bureaucratic politics and advocacy groups, are excluded because the foreign policy decision-making process in the UAE is highly centralized. Since its establishment more than four decades ago, the UAE and its foreign policy have been run by the man at the helm of the state, with the help of, at most, a few close confidants.

We therefore argue that sources of foreign policy change include the following: a substantial change in the economic and political capabilities of the state; appearance of crises in the regional and international environment; and a change in the leadership of the state.[9] These changes on the domestic, regional, and international levels are subsequently digested and interpreted through the convictions, idiosyncrasies, and worldviews of the principal foreign policy decision-maker. If (s)he believes that these changes create a new situation, posing as either a threat or an opportunity or both, then foreign policy change is to be expected. This is because developments on these three levels can lead to the birth of new paradigms of thinking, including the reconceptualization of new threats, the shuffling of foreign policy objectives, and the inception of new foreign policy strategies and plans of action. Figure 1 illustrates the components and dynamics of the model.

In this study, measuring the level of foreign policy change follows the typology developed by Hermann, which differentiates between four degrees of change: adjustment changes where minor changes result from a change in the level of efforts thrust into a policy; program changes in which foreign policy goals remain unchanged, but changes occur in the means or methods used to address a problem; problem or goal changes where a change occurs in the identification of problems and goals, which

Figure 8.1: Dynamics of Foreign Policy Change

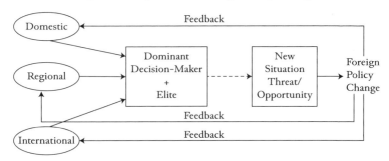

often unleashes a change in the foreign policy means used to achieve the new goals; and change in international orientation, where there is an entire restructuring in the state's orientation towards world politics.[10] We demonstrate that the change in the UAE's foreign policy, as evidenced by its increased intervention in the Red Sea and East Africa, corresponds to the third level of change, entailing not only a change in the identification of problems and goals, but also in means and methods.

The UAE after Zayed: Diplomacy of the Gun and the Purse

Despite developing a large and well-trained foreign affairs bureaucracy over the years, foreign policy making in the UAE is still run in the same fashion as it has been since the federation's genesis. Running of foreign affairs lies in the hand of the ruler, the president of the federation, who is committed to achieving consensus among the seven emirates on the general direction of foreign affairs. The main responsibility of the bureaucracy in this "prince state" is to execute policies already designed by the ruler rather than to propose policies or make new initiatives. As Kamrava explains, individuals at the helm in this type of state "have not just replaced institutions. They have become institutions."[11] This *modus vivendi*, not unusual in Arab states, means that major shifts in foreign policy usually follow a change in top leadership.

A major shift in the foreign policy of the UAE took place in 2004 after the death of Sheikh Zayed Al Nahyan, the country's founding father. During the long years of Sheikh Zayed's rule, 1971–2004, the UAE's foreign policy was more idealistic than realistic, more reactive than proactive. It toed the line of the Gulf Cooperation Council (GCC) and Arab countries, developed amicable relations with most world nations, avoided entanglement in the quarrels and rivalries of other states, focused on diplomacy and mediation to solve regional disputes, and gave top priority to the Palestinian question.

Obviously, during the early, precarious years of the federation, Zayed had to contend with the basic challenges of state formation. He realized that in order for the federation to survive, let alone flourish, he had to direct his efforts and resources towards two main goals: maintaining the unity of the UAE, and seeking regional and international recognition of the nascent union. After being elected as President of the Federation in 1971, Sheikh Zayed's main focus was to ensure the sustainability of the union. Further, Iran's forceful establishment of authority over the strategically located Abu Musa, Lesser Tunb, and Greater Tunb islands two days before the proclamation of the UAE meant that the newly established federation "was put on test from the first day of its formation."[12]

To obtain regional and international recognition, Zayed avoided confrontations with neighboring states. In a statement summarizing his foreign policy views, Sheikh Zayed said:

> We, in the Gulf, build our foreign policy in two parallel lines. Our relation with Arab and Islamic countries is a brotherly relationship within the Islamic context, and we deal with these countries in the way as brothers deal with each other. Our second line deals with non-Islamic countries on purely humane criteria. We treat them as

humans, respect them as humans, as much as they have friendship and kindness for us.[13]

In addition, Zayed followed the political trends in the Arab and Muslim worlds. Generally speaking, the foreign policy of the UAE was pan-Arabist at the zenith of pan-Arabism in the 1970s; turned slightly pan-Islamist in the heyday of pan-Islamism in the 1980s; and then became increasingly pragmatic in the decades that saw the decline of socialist, communist, Nasserist, Ba'thist, and Islamist ideologies, in the 1990s and thereafter.

This quiet, and quintessentially reactionary, foreign policy was gradually discarded after the rise of Sheikh Khalifa bin Zayed to power in 2004, together with his younger brother, MBZ, the Crown Prince of Abu Dhabi.[14] By the time this new generation came to power, the UAE was no longer the small, vulnerable union it was in 1971. By the early 2000s, the UAE had become a consolidated federation, its economy a regional powerhouse, and its socioeconomic outlook inspired other countries in the region and beyond.[15] The challenges of state-building were substantially overcome and replaced by ambitions for establishing a modern, secular state geared towards economic liberalization at home and expanded influence in the region.

Because of the frail health of Khalifa, MBZ had become the de facto ruler by 2014. On a personal level, the overly ambitious MBZ has a regional and international outlook that is conspicuously different from his reserved father. MBZ has tended to be more pragmatic, realistic, and confrontational in dealing with regional challenges. Under his leadership, the UAE followed an independent, confident, and initiative-based foreign policy that— unlike other small states that only guard their home turf—goes beyond the country's natural strategic realm and seeks a foothold in faraway regions. So, rather than merely focusing on diplomacy, mediation, dialogue, and foreign aid, which Sheikh Zayed used as a tool to win regional and international recognition, the new leadership has sought influence through military engagement, massive foreign direct investments (FDI) internationally, and military and naval presence beyond the country's vicinity, particularly in the Red Sea, East Africa, Yemen, and Libya.

No less significantly, since 2004, the UAE's economy has become much more robust, thanks to a massive influx of petrodollars following the upsurge of oil prices from US$22 per barrel in 2002 to US$147 in 2008.[16] The country's GDP has more than doubled since the new leadership came to power: it amounted to US$150 billion in 2004, then increased by around 271 percent to US$407 billion in 2017, and is estimated to further increase by around 119 percent to reach US$485 billion by 2020.[17] Such significant economic growth has prompted the UAE's pursuit of foreign direct investment in promising markets.

Foreign Direct Investment (FDI) outflow has increased dramatically since the new leadership came to power in 2004. While FDI levels decreased between 2008 and 2011 because of the global financial crisis, Emirati FDI increased significantly once again after the 2011 Arab uprisings. The seven Red Sea basin countries received more than 14 percent of the UAE's total FDI

Figure 8.2: UAE's Foreign Direct Investments 2000–2016

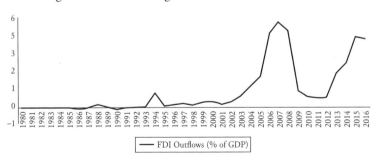

Source: "United Arab Emirates—Foreign Direct Investment," IndexMundi, www.indexmundi.com/facts/united-arab-emirates/foreign-direct-investment.

outflow, reflecting the importance of the seven countries as promising markets, and areas of strategic interests for the UAE. As illustrated later in this article, investments in ports made up a significant portion of UAE's outward FDI to the Red Sea basin countries.

Table 8.1: UAE's Foreign Direct Investments in Red Sea Basin Countries 2003–2015

Hosting Countries	Companies	Projects	Jobs Created	Cost (Million $US)
Djibouti	4	4	2,545	1,695
Egypt	64	99	44,827	32,378
Eritrea	N/A	N/A	N/A	N/A
Saudi Arabia	135	201	32,140	13,489
Somalia	1	1	18	11
Sudan	12	17	2,673	706
Yemen	6	7	2,425	596
Total	–	**329**	**84,628**	**48,875**
Total UAE Global outward FDI	–	**2,456**	**572,296**	**297,365**

Source: *The United Arab Emirates: Inward and Outward FDI*, report, The Arab Investment & Export Credit Guarantee Corporation (Dhaman), 2, http://dhaman.net/wp-content/uploads/2016/02/UAE.pdf; *Somalia: Inward and Outward FDI*, report, The Arab Investment & Export Credit Guarantee Corporation (Dhaman), 2, http://dhaman.net/wp-content/uploads/2016/02/Somalia.pdf; *Sudan: Inward and Outward FDI*, report, The Arab Investment & Export Credit Guarantee Corporation (Dhaman), 2, http://dhaman.net/wp-content/uploads/2016/02/Sudan.pdf; and *Yemen: Inward and Outward FDI*, report, The Arab Investment & Export Credit Guarantee Corporation (Dhaman), 2, http://dhaman.net/wp-content/uploads/2016/02/Yemen.pdf.

Flush with cash and high on ambition and bravado, the UAE has also sought to become a major regional military power. Over the decade that followed the death of Sheikh Zayed, the UAE's military expenditures increased by about 234 percent, compared to an increase of 204.5 percent and 207.5 percent in the military expenditures of Saudi Arabia and Egypt, respectively.[18] Today, the UAE is frequently described as "Little Sparta," for its small-sized yet efficient and well-equipped military force.[19] The Emirati army is made up of roughly 65,400 active troops, but its recent fighting experience in Yemen and Libya has made it a somewhat battle-hardened army.[20] In 2014, the UAE also imposed compulsory military conscription on all Emirati men aged between eighteen and thirty.[21] The Emirati army still, however, relies heavily on the services of mercenaries, which have helped the Emirati leadership mitigate the challenge of having limited human resources at home, insofar as the army is concerned, and allowed the country to avoid possible domestic opposition to its military operations by conscripted Emiratis.[22]

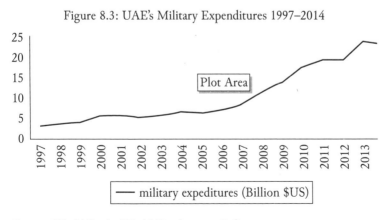

Figure 8.3: UAE's Military Expenditures 1997–2014

Source: World Bank, *World Development Indicators*.

The country's military acquisition budget doubled between 2009 and 2015,[23] and the new leadership has made sure to endow its army with state-of-the-art weaponry and training.[24] In 2016, Emirati military expenditures were estimated at around US$21.8 billion, with the Air Force receiving the lion's share, making it the second most advanced in the Middle East.[25] Particularly after 2016, the UAE has been investing heavily in its naval forces too. The Emirati naval forces now operate corvettes, submersibles, coastal defense craft, mine warfare craft, amphibious vehicles, offshore patrol vessels, and rolling airframe missiles.[26] At the time of writing, the UAE's navy is ranked fourth in the Middle East, third in the Persian Gulf region (after Iran and Qatar respectively), and thirty-third globally. In addition, according to the Stockholm International Peace Research Institute, 19 percent of all major arms purchases in the Middle East between 2008 and 2012 were made by the UAE.[27] The US Department of Commerce expects that the UAE's defense budget will continue to increase in the coming years, reaching US$41 billion by 2025. As a result, the UAE has been listed in the world's top fourteen defense spenders over the past three years.[28]

Not only has the UAE spent massively on modern weapons systems, it has also aspired to become a major arms producer in the region. Insofar as the Emirati naval forces are concerned, MBZ took part in establishing Abu Dhabi Ship Building (ADSB), a company that "specializes in the construction, repair and refit of naval, military and commercial vessels."[29] Today, the UAE manufactures armored vehicles, drones, arms and ammunitions, and patrol vessels; and also repairs, overhauls, and upgrades military aircraft and warships domestically.[30] All these diplomatic and military efforts have been accelerated by two pivotal developments: the crisis moment of the 2011 Arab uprisings and the rising frictions in the UAE-US relations.

IN PURSUIT OF SECURITY AND INFLUENCE

The Shock of the 2011 Arab Uprisings

A pan-Arab awakening that crossed borders with ease, and unleashed deep forces of change, the 2011 Arab uprisings sent shockwaves throughout the ruling establishments of the Arab monarchies of the Persian Gulf, representing a typical example of what Hermann dubbed an "external shock."[31] Fear of potential spillover effects rose meteorically when, following the downfall of Ben Ali and Mubarak, local Islamists "started to become more politically active."[32] In a hitherto unthinkable move, in March 2011, more than 100 activists submitted a petition to the UAE government demanding an elected parliament with legislative powers. They called for the reform of the Federal National Council, which, as one signatory told the *Wall Street Journal*, should be given "more authority," including "legislative powers as well as powers of accountability."[33] Using language that is unusual in the politics of the UAE, she added that "elections should be a right of every citizen."[34]

In the context of the vocal calls for reform and equality during the Arab uprisings, the UAE's potential Achilles heel was the relatively less developed and less affluent northern Emirates, such as Ajman, Sharjah, and Ras Al-Khaimah. The grievances produced by the socioeconomic disparities between Abu Dhabi and Dubai—which account for around 90 percent of the UAE's GDP—on one hand, and these emirates, on the other, carried the potential of turning into the kind of wide-ranging popular resentment that ignited the 2011 Arab uprisings in other states across the region. The income gap between both groups of emirates has been growing at alarming rates. In 2007, for instance, the per capita income of Abu Dhabi was six times that of the emirate of Ajman, whilst, in 2000, it was only five-and-a-half times as much.[35] In 2011, the GDP per capita of Abu Dhabi and Dubai were estimated at around US$110,000 and

US$41,670, respectively, while it was only US$22,100 in Sharjah and US$21,897 in Ras Al-Khaimah.[36] Further, the rate of unemployment reached 20 percent in the northern emirates, whereas the states' overall average was around 14 percent.[37] Particularly worrying to the Emirati leadership was the fact that it was in these states that the local Al-Islah Islamist movement, historically an offshoot of Egypt's Muslim Brotherhood (MB) group, was most active and influential. In the UAE's corridors of power, concerns that the MB would "export the revolution" to the emirates using its alleged ties to Al-Islah were very high, especially after the former's successes in Egypt's parliamentary and presidential elections in 2011 and 2012, respectively. In 2014, the UAE designated the MB a terrorist organization.

The UAE leaders have developed a great dread towards the MB, and Islamist groups at large, considering them to be a real threat to their country's national security. The UAE's Foreign Minister, Abdullah Bin Zayed, denounced the MB as "an organization which encroaches upon the sovereignty and integrity of nations."[38] Indeed, Islamists have not only been perceived as a threat, one of many, but rather as an existential threat. The UAE's ambassador to the US, Youssef Al-Otaiba, said it plainly: "We see extremism as an existential threat."[39] Undoubtedly, the 2011 petition, and the youth-led activism that accompanied it, touched a raw nerve among the UAE's perturbed ruling elite. Real or imagined, the UAE leadership sensed that it was facing a "ticking time bomb,"[40] a real threat, both at home and abroad.

To contain this threat, the UAE leadership devised a two-pronged policy: unchecked repression at home and combatting Islamists abroad,[41] including in faraway regions, such as the Levant, the Mediterranean, the Red Sea, and East Africa. In the meantime, the Arab landscape has changed dramatically since 2011. Some regimes were struck down, and others have been engulfed by bloody civil wars. The Arab-Israeli conflict ceased to be the driving conflict of regional dynamics, giving way to other intense conflicts, such as the Saudi-Iranian rivalry, and the huge, often violent, polarization between Islamist and non-Islamist forces. The reshaping of the region triggered a redefinition of states' foreign policy roles and rules of engagement.[42] Taking part in a collective security approach that relies on traditional Arab powerhouses was no longer possible. A weakened and inward-looking Egypt, a war-torn Syria, and a divided Iraq created a conspicuous vacuum in the region. Further, cracks in the unity of the GCC, caused by the divergent threat perceptions of its member states, undermined the council's ability to devise a joint institutionalized security strategy or to act as a united bloc vis-à-vis regional threats.[43] The UAE leadership thus attempted to stem the regional disorder, step into the vacuum, and control the nature and pace of regional change, either in cooperation with close allies—as in the 2017 blockade of Qatar and the war in Yemen—or, if necessary, using a go-it-alone approach.

Not only did the UAE leadership feel vulnerable to the domestic ramifications of the 2011 Arab uprisings, it also became anxious about a cascade of alarming regional developments, including the rising influence of Iran and the ensuing Sunni-Shiite rivalry; the birth and expansion of the so-called Islamic State in Syria and Iraq (ISIS); the eruption of bloody civil wars in Syria, Iraq, Libya, and Yemen; and the potential influx of refugees from these countries to the Arab states of the Persian Gulf. Expressing his concerns about the multiple security threats facing his country, the UAE's Minister of State for Foreign Affairs Anwar Gargash said: "We can't be a stable house if there is a brush fire around us,"[44] adding that:

> There is a very rapidly changing status quo in the region character-ized by political instability and violent extremism, and we have seen it since the Arab Spring started in 2011. *This added more risks in an already risky environment* ... There are many regional challenges ...

As [much as] the UAE and other countries need regional allies, we
have to start with our own self-power and potential.[45]

The new regional setting was ripe with both new threats and
fresh opportunities. On a quest for enhanced security and more
influence, the UAE abandoned its foreign policy traditions and
embarked on a substantial shift in the way it runs its foreign
affairs. The style of the UAE's policy changed from neutrality to
intervention, from lethargy to activism, from compromise to
intransigence, and from the use of aid and quiet diplomacy to a
distinctively hawkish approach that asserts its presence in
regional affairs using military means. The UAE's armed forces
intervened in Bahrain and Libya in 2011, fought ISIS in Syria
and Iraq in 2014, and have been partaking in the Saudi-led war
on Yemen since 2015. The UAE's foreign policy change involved
not only a change in goals (seeking security by combatting
Islamists and pursuing increased regional influence), but also a
change in means (from soft to hard power).

These two objectives—security and influence—have been the
driving motivations behind the UAE's intervention in the Red
Sea and East Africa. The UAE leaders, particularly MBZ, view
this region both as a source of threat to regional stability—in
light of the rising influence of militant Islamist groups, especially
the al-Qaʻida-linked al-Shabab group—and as an arena to project
Emirati hard power capabilities to gain more leverage vis-à-vis
other regional powers.

Tension with the Obama Administration

Cracks in the longstanding relationship with the US during the
second term of the Obama administration also fostered change
in the foreign policy of the UAE. As a small state with limited
demographic and military capabilities during the crucial decades
of state-building and state-consolidation, the UAE relied almost

exclusively on security arrangements with Western states, particularly the US, for its survival and security. A bilateral UAE-US defense pact signed in 1994 allowed US troops to be stationed in Al-Dhafra base in Abu Dhabi, and for US warships to visit and utilize the large Jebel Ali port.[46] The US presence in Al-Dhafra increased dramatically over the years: from around 800 troops in 2003, to 1,800 in the mid-2000s, to about 3,500 in 2014.[47] Moreover, the UAE soon became "the foremost US military partner in the Arab world."[48] With the exception of the US-led invasion of Iraq in 2003, it was the only Arab state to participate in all other US-led military coalitions over the past three decades; namely, in Kuwait, Somalia, Kosovo, Afghanistan, Libya, and the war against ISIS.

Three nearly simultaneous developments, however, poisoned the strategic UAE-US alliance. First, the gradual US shift from the Gulf region to the Asia-Pacific region, in what is usually termed the "pivot to Asia," and Washington's unmistakable efforts to lessen its dependence on energy supplies from the Arab states of the Persian Gulf, made UAE leaders ponder whether the Gulf states were still considered to be a priority in Washington's strategic calculations. Then came the US administration's tacit embrace of the 2011 Arab uprisings, and the powerful winds of change it unleashed. For the Gulf states, the fall of Mubarak "was a wake-up call...that traditional Western support could no longer be taken for granted and that more efforts would have to be invested in...taking care of their own security."[49] Third, the 2015 landmark nuclear deal with Iran, a traditional source of threat for the GCC, reinforced these concerns to a great extent.[50]

These three developments cast doubt on the US commitment to maintaining its long-standing security umbrella over the Arab states of the Persian Gulf. In an interview with *The Atlantic*, President Obama's reference to "free riders" who "aggravate" him further angered Gulf leaders, who thought the statement was aimed at them.[51] As early as 2013, the head of a UAE-based research center, Abdulaziz Sager, observed that: "it is not clear whether the GCC states can continue to rely on US policy...the prevailing mood appears to be that the terms are beginning to change to such a degree that the GCC states have no choice but to act on their own *and without consideration of US interests and concerns.*"[52]

In short, the fallout with Washington contributed to the UAE's strategic reformulation of its foreign policy, the contours of which began to emerge more clearly after 2011, including a disposition towards using military means, the orientation towards other regions, the pursuit of new security partners, and, if necessary, the employment of a go-it-alone security approach. The UAE's foray into the Red Sea and East Africa is a direct manifestation of this new foreign policy. With Donald Trump's election as president, UAE-US relations have significantly improved. At the time of writing, three years into his presidency (2020), Trump seemed to be adopting a Nixonian Doctrine in his Middle East policy by minimizing US commitments and relying on the UAE and Saudi Arabia to police their own region.

It could be argued that the UAE's control of sea-lanes and ports in and around the Red Sea was pursued to bolster the country's regional standing to an extent that would make it indispensable to US interests, and, accordingly, help the UAE recover its strategic alliance with Washington, but on different terms and with new roles assigned to Abu Dhabi. The US's significant military installations and substantial aid programs in the Red Sea region—such as Camp Lemonnier in Djibouti, the US-Somali-Kenyan base near Bar-Sanguuni in southern Somalia, and the United States Agency for International Development's (USAID) Famine, War, and Drought (FWD) campaign in East Africa— require "bases, overflight rights and port-of-call privileges abroad."[53] Hence, the UAE's control of ports and sea-lanes in the Red Sea makes the US dependent, to a certain extent, on its alliance with the UAE to continue its various operations in the region. It also gives the UAE a bargaining chip in its negotiations with the US since the US Navy, and hence the US Defense Department, would have a favorable stance towards the UAE.[54] Moreover, the UAE's control of sea-lanes and ports in the region contributes to stronger ties between the UAE and US businesses that operate in the Red Sea. This solicits support for the UAE by various business and interest groups in the US that can influence US government policies. Finally, strategically located naval bases put the UAE on equal footing with its regional archenemy, Qatar, which has used its Al-Udaid airbase to consolidate its ties with the US Air Force, in particular, and the US Department of Defense, in general. The UAE's stronger relations with the Trump administration, and its capitalization on its naval capabilities in the Red Sea to forge stronger ties with the economic and military orders in the US, have once again made the UAE an important, strategic ally to the US in the region.[55]

The aforementioned changes in the goals of the Emirati foreign policy meant that new spheres of influence were needed, and new foreign policy tools required. The Red Sea, with its vibrant sea-lanes, looked like an attractive opportunity.

Why the Red Sea?

A magnet that attracts power, the Red Sea has historically been an arena of competition among international forces because it provides a strategic link between Europe, Africa, and Asia. First the Egyptians, Greeks, Persians, Arabs, Romans, then in the nineteenth and early twentieth centuries, the British, French, Russians, and Germans, and later in the Cold War era the Americans and Soviets, all vied for the dominance of the Red

Sea, its littoral and entrances.[56] In the current scheme of things, it is the US and China and, interestingly, a number of regional powers, such as Turkey, Israel, Saudi Arabia, Qatar, and the UAE, that are scrambling for influence in the region.

In order to understand the UAE's quest for influence in the Red Sea and East Africa regions, one has to consider the position of Abu Dhabi and Dubai in the UAE's federation and their respective interests. The UAE is made up of seven Emirates of which Abu Dhabi and Dubai stand out as the key determinants of the country's political and economic policies. For the past decade, Abu Dhabi has been more concerned with regional politics, while Dubai has been directing its resources towards economic development. The UAE's strong presence in the Red Sea serves both Abu Dhabi's political regional interests and Dubai's economic and trade interests. The UAE has taken a special interest in the Red Sea region for two main reasons: to gain economic and geopolitical influence.

First, the Red Sea is a global sea-lane through which huge US and European hydrocarbon imports are transported, and through which traded goods between Europe and the thriving Asian market are shipped.[57] It is estimated that over 10 percent of the world's trade and over 30 percent of the world's container volume passes through the Red Sea,[58] which has two narrow chokepoints: the Suez Canal in the north and the Bab al-Mandab strait in the south through which 3.9 and 4.8 million oil barrels, respectively, flowed every day in 2017.[59] This makes the Red Sea a significant sea-lane for shipping oil, the lifeline of the UAE's economy.

Furthermore, the importance of the economies of the Red Sea countries has been rising in recent years and is expected to rise further in the future. It is estimated that between 2015 and 2050 the population of the countries that have a coastline on the Red Sea will increase from around 306.5 million to 551.7 million; the

GDP of their economies to triple from US$1.8 trillion to US$6.1 trillion; and their international trade to increase from US$881 billion to US$4.7 trillion.[60] Such enormous growth makes the Red Sea region an attractive market for the UAE, which owns a logistics industry worth US$27 billion, and which continually searches for increased political influence and foreign investment opportunities.[61]

The Red Sea, moreover, is currently one of the main trade routes for around 35 percent of the UAE's exports and 52 percent of its imports.[62] So, in addition to benefiting from the operation of ports and the provision of maritime services along the route, the UAE tries to maintain a significant military and naval presence in the region to thwart any attempt by rivals to take trade away from its strategic Jebel Ali port in Dubai, the ninth busiest seaport in the world.[63] The Emirati military and naval presence in the Red Sea is also aimed at securing the flow of Emirati imports and exports that have recently been at risk due to instability in Red Sea basin countries and Emirati military activities in the region, evidenced by the Houthis' targeting of an Emirati high-speed logistics vessel by the coast of Yemen in October 2016. Following this attack, the UAE has engaged in massive naval procurements to upgrade its naval capabilities and protect its trade and logistics activities in the Red Sea and Gulf of Aden.[64] Meanwhile, the UAE's economic aid to East African countries increased twentyfold between 2011 and 2013.[65]

Second, the overarching concern about the rise of Islamism and political Islam in the region has been another motive. One significant attribute of the UAE's current foreign policy is its ardent fight against Islamist and political-Islamic ideologies, and its promotion of politically secular and economically liberal policies.[66] In recent years, a number of militant Islamist groups have appeared in several East African countries, especially Somalia, Sudan, Eritrea, and Tanzania, causing tremendous instability in both East and North Africa.

Table 8.2: Militant Islamist Groups in East Africa

Militant Islamist Group	Location
Itihad al-Islami	Bosaso, Somalia
The Eritrean Islamic Jihad Movement	Eritrea
Justice and Equality Movement	Sudan
Al-Takfir wal-Hijra	Sudan
Jama'at Ansar al-Sunnah al-Muhammadiyah	Sudan
Al-Shabab	Somalia
The Islamic Courts Union	Somalia
Al-Qaeda in Sudan and Africa	Operates across Africa
Wilayat Sinai	Sinai, Egypt

Source: Angel Rabasa, *Radical Islam in East Africa* (California: Rand Corporation, 2009).

The rise of Islamists in East Africa, and their reported ties to ISIS,[67] has motivated the UAE to build stronger ties with local governments, support indigenous rival militant groups, and station active military forces in the region. All this amounts to an "added layer of protection" from the threat of militant Islamists, especially in light of a recent increase in terrorist threats against the UAE.[68] The UAE's foreign minister, Abdullah bin Zayed, put it bluntly: "As groups like Daesh [ISIS] develop ties to criminal networks and arms networks like al-Shabab, it is essential that we prevent them from expanding their operations into the sea and threaten vital channels such as the Strait of Hormuz, the Red Sea, Bab al Mandab and the Gulf of Aden."[69] Likewise, explaining the rationale behind his country's intervention in Yemen, the UAE's minister of state for foreign affairs, Anwar Gargash, said: "Our goal is to succeed in returning security to Yemen and to protect the security of the Gulf through Yemen."[70]

Third, besides the revenues the government-owned DP World and P&O Ports generate from managing ports across the globe, these two companies have contributed to the UAE's nexus with global markets. The two companies' managed ports have become major stops for ships and vessels across the globe, whatever their routes and destinations. This has not only contributed to the UAE's power in reshaping global navigation, but has also helped in branding the state as ships and vessels stop at a *Dubai*-managed port.

In sum, a number of incentives and threats have directed the UAE's purse and gun towards East Africa. To be sure, the waters of the Red Sea and the Gulf of Aden are vital for the foreign policy of the UAE because of the economic potential they promise and the security risks they carry. The instability in Yemen and East Africa has posed a threat to trade vessels navigating in the Red Sea and the Gulf of Aden, and so control of ports on these vital sea-lanes is crucial for providing security for trade. For the UAE, an active presence in the Red Sea and the Gulf of Aden's waterways and ports helps in limiting threats from Somali pirates and weakening the link between al-Shabab and al-Qa'ida in Yemen, whose arms purchases are often shipped by sea and transferred through ports.[71] Moreover, geopolitical expansion through economic investments and hard power projection in the Red Sea offer new promising business opportunities: it bestows bargaining power on the UAE leadership that can be used in future negotiations and conflict settlements, and it aids the branding efforts of the UAE, a small state that is frantically pursuing an influential role in the international system.[72]

The UAE in the Red Sea and East Africa

The UAE's efforts in the Red Sea have included establishing military bases, constructing and running ports, and providing maritime services. The UAE currently operates seaports in five of the seven main countries on the Red Sea (Egypt, Djibouti,[73] Somalia, Yemen, and Saudi Arabia), and runs military bases in at least three states (Yemen, Eritrea, and the self-declared state of Somaliland). The UAE naval and military presence in the region includes plans to set up a base for military training on the Yemeni island of Socotra; a naval presence on two islands in Bab al-Mandab; a military training center in Mogadishu; and two military bases in Berbera, the largest port in Somaliland as well as in Eritrea's Assab.[74]

Economically, the focus of the UAE has been on investment opportunities, new markets, logistics, and ports. As the chair-

Figure 8.4: The UAE in the Red Sea

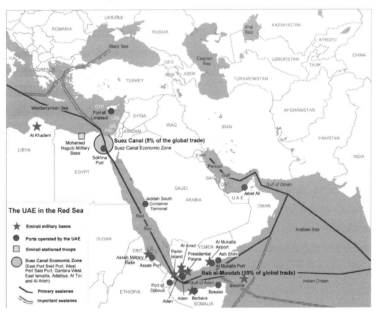

Source: Map designed by Mike Izady from information gathered by authors.

man and CEO of DP World Group, Sultan Ahmed Bin Sulayem, pointed out, trade and logistics infrastructure "are key pillars in diversifying economies supported by technology and automation."[75] The UAE began its efforts in 2008 by investing in the Ain Sokhna Port in Egypt, crucial for being the closest port to the Egyptian capital, Cairo.[76] Over the following years, Dubai Ports World (DPW), a company that operates maritime services and marine terminals predominantly owned and run by the UAE government,[77] developed the port's first basin, and built a second basin to double the capacity of the port, reaching up to 1.1 million twenty-foot equivalent units per year.[78] In November 2017, DPW expanded its operations in Ain Sokhna further by signing a partnership agreement with Egypt's Suez Canal Economic Zone (SCZone) "to develop an integrated industrial and residential zone at Sokhna."[79] This agreement came after DP World and SCZone established a joint development company in August 2017 that would carry on development plans for Ain Sokhna Port, East Port Said Port, as well as the regions of Qantara West, East Ismailia, West Port Said, Adabiya, Al Tor, and Al Arish.[80] Although SCZone owns the majority of shares in this company (51 percent), DPW has managing rights over the zone. In other words, DPW will be managing the strategic Suez Canal Zone from Port Said up north to Ain Sokhna in the south.

In 2000, DPW won a twenty-year concession from the Djibouti government to operate the Port of Djibouti.[81] This led to the establishment of a joint venture in 2006 with the Djibouti government to invest in the Doraleh Container Terminal, and a planned free zone in the area.[82] DPW also won concessions to operate two ports in the Gulf of Aden: Berbera Port and Bosaso Port. The former was a concession to manage and develop a port project in Berbera for thirty years with an automatic ten-year extension plan.[83] The joint venture DPW set up with the government of Somaliland gives it a 65 percent stake in the company in return for the hefty US$442 million investment from the Emirati company and the provision of US$5 million and 10 percent of the port's revenue to the Somaliland authorities each year.[84] In Bosaso, the Dubai-owned P&O Ports company signed a thirty-year contract with the authorities of Puntland—a region in northeastern Somalia that self-declared as an autonomous state in 1998—to operate the port,[85] an agreement that will translate into the investment of US$336 million.[86]

In Yemen, DPW signed a contract in 2008 to operate the port of Aden, but the company suspended its operations in 2012 after Yemen's anticorruption commission accused DPW of failure to fulfill its contractual investment obligations.[87] However, in 2015, the Saudi-led military coalition, to which the UAE armed forces have contributed, seized the port of Aden from the Houthi rebels and took control over the inflow of goods and aid.[88] Also in Yemen, Emirati forces captured the ports of Mukalla and Shihr in April 2016, and, a few months earlier, occupied two strategically located islands in the Bab al-Mandab strait, through which around four million barrels of oil pass every day.[89] In early 2017, Emirati troops seized the port of Mokha, and are now setting their sights on the port of Hodeidah, the largest Yemeni port, and the country's only major port the UAE has not yet controlled.[90] The significance of the Hodeidah port is derived from the fact that it is the entry point for around 70 to 80 percent of food imports currently coming into Yemen. This explains why the Saudi-led coalition and its local Yemeni allies launched a push toward Hodeidah in 2017 to capture it from Houthi forces.[91] The UAE has also seized Socotra Island, located in the Arabian Sea south of the Yemeni mainland, and has put forth plans to use the island as a base for military training.[92]

Furthermore, DPW won concessions from the Saudi government to operate the South Container Terminal at the Jeddah Islamic Port. In addition to the port's strategic location on the

Red Sea trade routes, it handles around 59 percent of Saudi Arabia's sea imports, thus serving the country's main commercial hubs.[93] Moreover, in 2017, DPW won a contract to develop the Jeddah Islamic Port as part of the NEOM mega project.[94] In the Mediterranean, the UAE has managed to win concessions to operate and provide marine services at Limassol port in Cyprus, one of the busiest ports in the Mediterranean, and, with Egypt's approval, has expanded its military presence in the Mohamed Naguib base, located west of Alexandria.[95]

Conclusion

The regional competition over the Red Sea, and its islands, ports, and straits, has intensified in recent years among Egypt, Turkey, Saudi Arabia, the UAE, and Qatar, and is likely to continue in the foreseeable future. The extensive economic and political endeavors of the UAE in the Red Sea and East Africa cannot be understood without examining the overall changes that the foreign policy of the UAE has undergone since 2004, particularly after the events of 2011. The accumulation of vast economic wealth, the fragmentation of Arab politics, the emergence of a vacuum in the regional order, the open confrontation with Qatar, the tacit competition with other claimants to influence in the Arab world, and the rise of Islamist militant groups have all created a novel situation that has been seen by the UAE's new de facto leader, Mohamed bin Zayed, both as a threat and an opportunity.

To safeguard its stability and security at home, thwart the threat of the burgeoning den of militant Islamists in Somalia, Yemen, and other East African states, secure its trade relations and oil transportation routes, and extend its regional influence, the UAE has decided to retain a strong foothold in East Africa. The control of ports and islands, and the establishment and administration of military bases, training centers, and economic zones in the Red Sea, the Arabian Sea, the Gulf of Aden, and the Mandeb Strait have offered the UAE a chance to achieve these objectives.

As illustrated by this study, the transformation that has taken place in the foreign policy of the UAE over the past few years has been dramatic. It has not only involved a change in the identification of new foreign policy problems and goals, but also a change in foreign policy means. Whether the UAE can sustain such a distant foothold in the Red Sea and East Africa given intense competition with regional and international powers, and whether it can maintain its close alliance with Saudi Arabia and Egypt, allowing it to be active in areas long considered to constitute the strategic depth of the two regional powerhouses, is left for time to tell.

9

CONCLUSION

CHANGING REGIONAL OUTLOOK
AND PATHWAYS TO PEACE

Marcus DuBois King

The scope of this volume is ambitious: a full exploration of the dynamics of the multitude of water conflicts and disputes in the Middle East in one edited volume. However, the diverse countries examined in the preceding chapters reflect a broad and purposeful design. Our goal was to inform better understanding of the range of how these countries are positioned in water conflicts, and thus to inform the reader about recent developments. We also encourage a reassessment of theoretical assumptions about power dynamics and the political geography in the field of water and conflict. The first three chapters explored the theoretical dimensions and conditions that contribute to hydro-hegemony, while other chapters presented additional contextual examples of contemporary conflict.

The volume's first case studies supported the proposition that increased water stress and competition over scarce water resources in the region may precipitate conflict in fragile states and societies. Chapter two on scarcity-induced conflicts elucidated a dynamic asserting that water competition has become more intense due largely to a significant increase in demand from burgeoning populations. This research challenged the prevailing empirical literature building on the historical record that tells us that cooperation around shared water resources dominates conflict and the proposition that this will continue in a linear progression on a national and international scale.

Second, chapter three on Turkish hydro-hegemony in the Euphrates and Tigris basin expanded on existing assumptions in the water and conflict literature. Prevailing negative assessments of the water hegemons were challenged by the case of Turkey. On the contrary, this chapter argued that, under certain circumstances, net positive outcomes are possible for riparian states in the face of actions by the dominant state.

The case studies in this volume have taken newly significant hydrologic assets and patterns of resource distribution into account. Chapter five on groundwater supply, use, and security implications brought a better understanding of potential conflict triggers based on the latest scientific assessment of aquifers. This work highlights a pathway for future research into how over withdrawal of groundwater will factor into the future hydropolitics of the Middle East, a discipline that has been historically dominated by analysis of surface water basins.

The volume described new and significant geopolitical conditions in the ever-changing Middle East. Chapter four assessed the implications of an emergent proto-state in Iraqi Kurdistan with abundant water resources. This entity has challenged the regional water and security architecture as well as that inside Iraq. Understanding this dynamic could be important in the reasonably likely event that additional regions and sub-regions gain resource autonomy in the coming decades. Additionally, chapter six maintained the geographical focus on community-level water governance in Yemen in the face of a weak centralized authority that will continue during the foreseeable future. This level of analysis has reinforced the conclusions of H.M. Ravnborg,[1] Peter Gleick, and others that have found water conflict is more common on an intrastate and local level.[2]

Likewise, chapter seven took into account how autonomous actors, including rebels such as the Free Syrian Army and extremists such as IS, took advantage of the conditions of the internal civil wars in Iraq and Syria. The case studies have shown that the chaos created by war also accelerates water scarcity in fragile states. Water scarcity has been a critical enabler for those seeking to weaponize water. Finally, the authors have expanded the notional extent of geopolitically contested water-space in the Middle East. The Red Sea is an area with critical maritime chokepoints where scholars have yet to critically examine hydropolitics in detail.

Time to improve many of the conditions causing water stress in the Middle East is short and the region has indeed reached a "watershed moment," as described herein. In sum, the authors all agree on one thing: the urgent need to address the water problems identified by these case studies. Doing so could mitigate the chances of water-based conflict in those Middle Eastern countries, which for the large part are already destabilized by non-water related factors. Lessons drawn from these case studies are also relevant to other regions of the world with similar socio-political and hydrological conditions. We hope that the insights in this volume will inform the work of scholars, practitioners, and others interested in conflict, water, and natural resource management alike as they seek to understand shifting power dynamics of hydropolitics and their importance in achieving a durable peace in the region.

NOTES

1. INTRODUCTION: NEW POWER DYNAMICS AND HYDROPOLITICS IN THE MIDDLE EAST

1. Peter H. Gleick, "Water, War & Peace in the Middle East," *Environment* 36, no. 3 (1994): 7–8.
2. Terje Tvedt. *The River Nile in the Age of the British: Political Ecology and the Quest for Economic Power* (London: I.B. Tauris & Co Ltd, 2004), 326.
3. Andrew Maddox, Robert Samuel Young, and Paul Reig, "Ranking the World's Most Water-Stressed Countries in 2040," *World Resources Institute*, August 26, 2015, www.wri.org/blog/2015/08/ranking-world-s-most-water-stressed-countries-2040.
4. "Syrian Civil War: the Role of Climate Change | ECC Factbook," *ECC Library*, January 16, 2018, http://library.ecc-platform.org/conflicts/syrian-civil-war-role-climate-change.
5. Aaron T. Wolf, Lynette Silvia, and Jennifer Veilleux C., "Transboundary Freshwater Dispute Database," Program in Water Conflict Management and Transformation, http://www.transboundarywaters.orst.edu/database/.
6. Ravnborg, H. M.; Bustamante, R.; Cissé, A.; Cold-Ravnkilde, S.M.; Cossio, V.; Djiré, M.; Funder, M.; Gómez, L.I.; Paz, T.; Le, P.; Mweemba, C.; Nyambe, I.; Huong, P.; Rivas, R.; Yen, N.T.B.; Skielboe, T. (2012). "The challenges of local water governance: The extent, nature and intensity of local water-related conflict and cooperation". Water

Policy (2011) 14 (2): 336–357. 1 April 2012. https://doi.org/10.2166/wp. 2011.097, and PBL (2018): *Linking water security threats to conflict*, The Hague, August 2018, http://www.pbl.nl/sites/default/files/cms/publicaties/3039%20Linking%20water%20security%20threats%20to%20conflict_DEF.pdf

7. Naho Mirumachi. "Study of Conflict and Cooperation in International Transboundary River Basins: The TWINS Framework." (2010). Department of Geography, King's College, London.

8. Peter H. Gleick, "Water, Drought, Climate Change, and Conflict in Syria". *Weather, Climate, and Society* 6 no. 3 (2014): 331–340. Francesco Femia, Troy Sternberg, and Caitlin E. Werrell, "Climate Hazards & Security in Syria & Egypt". *Journal of Diplomacy and International Relations* 16, no. 1 (2014).

09. Jan Shelby; Omar S. Dahi; Christiane Frohlich; and Mike Hulme, "Climate change and the Syrian civil war revisited". *Political Geography* 60 (2017): 232–244.

10. Zeitoun, M. & Warner, J. "Hydro-hegemony: a framework for analysis of transboundary water conflicts". *Water Policy*, 8 (2006).: 435–460. https://doi.org/10.1007/s10784–008–9083–5

11. Wolf, A.T., Yoffe, S.B., and Giordano, M. "International waters: identifying basins at risk". *Water Policy* (2003) 5(1): 29–60.

12. Femia, Sternberg, and Werrell, "Climate Hazards & Security in Syria & Egypt".

13. Water, Peace and Security Partnership. https://www.un-ihe.org/water-peace-and-security-partnership.

14. Susanne Schmeir et al, "Are water and conflict linked and what actually links them?". *Water, Peace and Security Partnership* (2018). https://flows.hypotheses.org/1801

15. Marien González-Hidalgo and Christos Zografos, "Emotions, power, and environmental conflict: Expanding the 'emotional turn' in political ecology". *Progress in Human Geography* (2019): https://doi.org/10.1177/0309132518824644

16. Khaled AbuZeid, "Green Water and Effective Legislation for Transboundary Water Management". *Euro-Mediterranean Space.* (2007) ... http://web.cedare.org/wp-content/uploads/2005/05/Green-Water-

and-Effective-Legislation-for-Transboundary-Water-Management-Khaled-Abu-Zeid-V3.pdf

17. Wolf, Yoffe, and Giordano, "International waters: identifying basins at risk".

18. Helle Munk Ravenborg et al. "The challenges of local water governance: The extent, nature and intensity of local water-related conflict and cooperation". *Water Policy* 14:2 (2012): 336–357. https://doi. org/10.2166/wp. 2011.097

19. Omar Naje, "Yemen's Capital 'will Run out of Water by 2025'," SciDev. Net, October 22, 2010, www.scidev.net/global/policy/news/yemen-s-capital-will-run-out-of-water-by-2025-.html.

20. Tobias von Lossow, "The Rebirth of Water as a Weapon: IS in Syria and Iraq," *The International Spectator* 51:3 (2016): 82–99.

21. Water, Peace and Security Partnership. https://www.un-ihe.org/water-peace-and-security-partnership

22. Susanne Schmeir, et al. (2018). "Are water and conflict linked and what actually links them?" *Water, Peace and Security Partnership.* https:// flows.hypotheses.org/1801

23. Femia, Sternberg, and Werrell, "Climate Hazards and Security." Peter H. Gleick. "Water, Drought, Climate Change, and Conflict in Syria". *Weather, Climate, and Society* 6: 3, (2014): 331–340.

2. MALTHUS IN THE MIDDLE EAST: SCARCITY-INDUCED WATER CONFLICTS

1. Peter H. Gleick, "Water, War & Peace in the Middle East," *Environment* 36, no. 3 (1994): 7–8.

2. Yacob Arsano, "Ethiopia and the Nile: Dilemmas of National and Regional Hydropolitics" (PhD diss., University of Zurich Center for Security Studies, Swiss Federal Institute of Technology, Zurich, Switzerland, 2007); Hussein Amery and Aaron T. Wolf, eds., *Water in the Middle East: A Geography of Peace* (Austin: University of Texas Press, 2000); Ashok Swain, *Understanding Emerging Security Challenges: Threats and Opportunities* (Routledge, 2013).

3. Peter H. Gleick, "Water, Drought, Climate Change, and Conflict in

Syria," *Weather, Climate and Society* 6, no. 3 (2014): 331–40; Swain, *Understanding Emerging Security Challenges.*

4. Francesca de Châtel, "The Role of Drought and Climate Change in the Syrian Uprising: Untangling the Triggers of the Revolution," *Middle Eastern Studies* 50, no. 4 (2014): 521–35.

5. Thomas Bernauer, Tobias Bohmelt, and Vally Koubi, "Environmental Changes and Violent Conflict," *Environmental Research Letters* 7, no. 1 (2012): 015601; Alex de Sherbinin et al., "Population and Environment," *Annual Review of Environment and Resources* 32 (2007): 345–73.

6. Bernauer, Bohmelt, and Koubi, "Environmental Changes," 015601; de Sherbinin, "Population and Environment," 345–73.

7. Food is also used to prop up and revive a political system that is battered by political or economic difficulties. Less than a year into the civil war in Syria, the *New York Times* reported that Russia's "steady supply of weapons, food, medical supplies and other aid" save the Assad regime from a certain defeat (David M. Herszenhorn, "For Syria, Reliant on Russia for Weapons and Food, Old Bonds Run Deep," *The New York Times*, February 18, 2012, www.nytimes.com/2012/02/19/world/middleeast/for-russia-and-syria-bonds-are-old-and-deep.html).

8. Hussein Amery, *Water Security in the Arab World: Threats and Opportunities in the Gulf States* (Cambridge, UK: Cambridge University Press, 2015); Emma Rothschild, "Food Politics," *Foreign Affairs* 54, no. 2 (January 1976): 285–307; J. R. Tarrant, "Food as a Weapon? The Embargo on Grain Trade between USA and USSR," *Applied Geography* 1, no. 4 (1981): 273–86; John Shaw, *World Food Security: A History Since 1945* (New York: Palgrave Macmillan, 2007).

9. Emily Thornberry, "Saudi Bombs are Decimating Yemen. Yet May's Glad-Handing Goes On," *The Guardian*, April 5, 2017, www.the-guardian.com/commentisfree/2017/apr/05/saudi-arabia-bombs-yemen-theresa-may-trade.

10. Kristin Romey, "'Engineering Marvel' of Queen of Sheba's City Damaged in Airstrike. The Ancient Great Dam of Marib is One of Several Cultural Casualties of Yemen," *National Geographic*, June 3, 2015, https://news.nationalgeographic.com/2015/06/150603-Yemen-ancient-Sheba-dam-heritage-destruction-Middle-East-archaeology.

11. Mohammed Ghobari, "Yemen's War-Damaged Hodeidah Port Struggles to Bring in Vital Supplies," *Reuters*, November 24, 2016, www.reuters.com/article/us-yemen-security-port-idUSKBN13J1OJ.

12. Areeb Ullah, "Syrian Air Force 'Purposely' Targeted Water Supplies in Wadi Barada: UN," *Middle East Eye*, March 14, 2017, www.middleeasteye.net/news/syrian-air-force-purposely-targeted-water-supplies-wadi-barada-un-854561645.

13. Kassem Eid, "I Survived a Sarin Gas Attack," *The New York Times*, April 7, 2017, www.nytimes.com/2017/04/07/opinion/what-its-like-to-survive-a-sarin-gas-attack.html.

14. Hussein Amery, "Islamic Water Management," *Water International* 26, no. 4 (2001): 1–9; Salma Taman, "The Concept of Corporate Social Responsibility in Islamic Law," *Indiana International & Comparative Law Review* 21, no. 3 (2011): 481–508.

15. Mustafa Saadoun, "Tribal Disputes Flare in Southern Iraq over Water Scarcity," *Al-Monitor*, February 15, 2018, www.al-monitor.com/pulse/originals/2018/02/water-security-iraq-tribal-conflicts.html.

16. Julia Harte, "New Dam in Turkey Threatens to Flood Ancient City and Archaeological Sites," *National Geographic*, February 21, 2014, https://news.nationalgeographic.com/news/2014/02/140221-tigris-river-dam-hasankeyf-turkey-iraq-water.

17. "Cost of Non-Cooperation on Water: Crisis of Survival in the Middle East," *Strategic Foresight Group*, India (2016).

18. UNEP, "How Dangerously Dirty Water is Threatening One of the World's Ancient Religions," United Nations Environment Programme, February 23, 2018, www.unenvironment.org/news-and-stories/story/how-dangerously-dirty-water-threatening-one-worlds-ancient-religions.

19. Tamer El-Ghobashy and Joby Warrick, "Islamic State Leaves a Toxic Farewell of Environmental Sabotage, Chronic Disease," *The Washington Post*, February 4, 2018, www.washingtonpost.com/world/the-islamic-states-toxic-farewell-environmental-sabotage-and-chronic-disease/2018/02/04/927ff2b6-05c8-11e8-ae28-e370b74ea9a7_story.html?utm_term=.005dfc7d928f.

20. "Turkey Denies Adverse Impact of Damming," *Financial Tribune* (Iran),

July 6, 2017, https://financialtribune.com/articles/environment/67739/turkey-denies-adverse-impact-of-damming.

21. El-Fadel et al., "The Euphrates-Tigris Basin: A Case Study in Surface Water Conflict Resolution," *Journal of Natural Resources Life Science Education* 31 (2002): 99–110.

22. International Crisis Group, "Turkey and the Middle East: Ambitions and Constraints," *Crisis Group Europe Report* no. 203 (April 7, 2010): 10, https://d2071andvip0wj.cloudfront.net/203-turkey-and-the-middle-east-ambitions-and-constraints.pdf.

23. Ibid, 13.

24. Stephen C. McCaffrey, *The Law of International Watercourses, Non-Navigational Uses* (Oxford: Oxford University Press, 2001).

25. Marwa Daoudy, "Asymmetric Power: Negotiating Water in the Euphrates and Tigris," *International Negotiation* 14, no. 2 (2009): 361–91.

26. Marwa Daoudy, "Hydro-Hegemony and International Water Law: Laying Claims to Water Rights," *Water Policy* 10, S2 (2008): 89–102.

27. Ibid.

28. James Cooksey, "Conflicts over Water as a Resource," Defense Technical Information Center, Naval War College, Newport, R.I., April 23, 2008, https://apps.dtic.mil/dtic/tr/fulltext/u2/a484294.pdf.

29. Ibid., 10.

30. Ghada Ahmed, "Syria Wheat Value Chain and Food Security," *Duke MINERVA*, Policy Brief no. 8 (March 2016).

31. de Châtel, "The Role of Drought," 521–35.

32. Robert F. Worth, "Earth is Parched Where Syrian Farms Thrived," *The New York Times*, October 13, 2010, www.nytimes.com/2010/10/14/world/middleeast/14syria.html.

33. Ibid.

34. Ibid.

35. Robert F. Worth, "Earth is Parched Where Syrian Farms Thrived," *The New York Times*, October 13, 2010, www.nytimes.com/2010/10/14/world/middleeast/14syria.html.

36. Colin P. Kelley et al., "Climate Change in the Fertile Crescent and Implications of the Recent Syrian Drought," *Proceedings of the National Academy of Sciences* 112, no. 11 (2015): 3241.

37. Ibid.

38. Ibid., 3243.

39. Jessica Barnes, "Managing the Waters of Ba'th Country: The Politics of Water Scarcity in Syria," *Geopolitics* 14 (2009): 510–30.

40. de Châtel, "The Role of Drought," 521–35; Ahmed, "Syria Wheat Value Chain and Food Security."

41. de Châtel, "The Role of Drought," 522.

42. Kelley et al., "Climate Change in the Fertile Crescent," 3242.

43. Ibid.

44. Hammoudeh Sabbagh and M. Ismael, "President Al-Assad Lays Foundation Stone for Tigris River Water Drawing Project," Syrian Arab News Agency (SANA), March 7, 2011.

45. Arsano, "Ethiopia and the Nile," 69; see also Swain, *Understanding Emerging Security Challenges*.

46. Mwangi Kimenyi and John Mukum Mbaku, "The Limits of the New 'Nile Agreement,'" Brookings, April 28, 2015, www.brookings.edu/blog/africa-in-focus/2015/04/28/the-limits-of-the-new-nile-agreement.

47. "One River One People One Vision," Nile Basin Initiative, 2016, www.nilebasin.org.

48. Dereje Mekonnen, "The Nile Basin Cooperative Framework Agreement Negotiations and the Adoption of a 'Water Security' Paradigm: Flight into Obscurity or a Logical Cul-de-sac?" *European Journal of International Law* 21, no. 2 (May 2010): 421–40; Salman M. A. Salman, "The Nile Basin Cooperative Framework Agreement: The Impasse is Breakable!" International Water Law Project, 2017, www.internationalwaterlaw.org/blog/2017/06/19/the-nile-basin-cooperative-framework-agreement-the-impasse-is-breakable.

49. Daniel Abebe, "Egypt, Ethiopia, and the Nile: The Economics of International Water Law," University of Chicago *Public Law & Legal Theory Working Paper* no. 484 (2014); Swain, *Understanding Emerging Security Challenges*.

50. Rising quality of life manifests itself in different ways including a shift in people's dietary preferences in favor of higher consumption of proteins. Beef is extremely water intensive.

51. This is almost three times more than the power produced by the Hoover Dam in Arizona; Abebe, "Egypt, Ethiopia, and the Nile"; Jean-Daniel Stanley and Pablo L. Clemente, "Increased Land Subsidence and Sea-Level Rise are Submerging Egypt's Nile Delta Coastal Margin," *GSA Today* 27, no. 5 (2017): 4–11.

52. Richard Conniff, "The Vanishing Nile: A Great River Faces a Multitude of Threats," *Yale Environment 360*, April 6, 2017, https://e360.yale. edu/features/vanishing-nile-a-great-river-faces-a-multitude-of-threats-egypt-dam; Stanley and Clemente, "Increased Land Subsidence," 4–11.

53. Ibid.

54. Aaron Maasho, "Paying for Giant Nile Dam Itself, Ethiopia Thwarts Egypt but Takes Risks," *Reuters*, April, 23 2014, www.reuters.com/article/us-ethiopia-energy-insight/paying-for-giant-nile-dam-itself-ethiopia-thwarts-egypt-but-takes-risks-idUSBREA3M0BG20140423.

55. Arsano, "Ethiopia and the Nile," 222.

56. "Toshka Project—Mubarak Pumping Station," *Water Technology*, www.water-technology.net/projects/mubarak; Patrick Werr, "Egypt's Land Reclamation Plan Should Heed History Lesson," *The National*, October 14, 2015, www.thenational.ae/business/egypt-s-land-reclamation-plan-should-heed-history-lesson-1.90770?videoId=5719243807001.

57. Jared Malsin, "Egypt's President Sisi Touts Megaprojects Ahead of March Vote," *The Wall Street Journal*, February 12, 2018, www.wsj. com/articles/egypts-president-sisi-touts-megaprojects-ahead-of-march-vote-1518431400.

58. Steve Solomon, *Water: The Epic Struggle for Wealth, Power and Civilization* (New York: Harper Collins, 2011).

59. Malsin, "Egypt's President Sisi Touts Megaprojects."

60. Werr, "Egypt's Land Reclamation Plan."

61. Ibid.

62. Bradley Hope, "Egypt's New Nile Valley: Grand Plan Gone Bad," *The National*, April 22, 2012, www.thenational.ae/world/mena/egypt-s-new-nile-valley-grand-plan-gone-bad-1.402214.

63. Bart Hilhorst, "Water Management in the Nile Basin: A Fragmented but Effective Cooperative Regime," *CIRS Occasional Paper* no. 17

(Doha: Center for International and Regional Studies, Georgetown University in Qatar, 2016).

64. Campbell MacDiarmid, "Egypt to 'Escalate' Ethiopian Dam Dispute," *Al Jazeera*, April 21, 2014, www.aljazeera.com/news/middleeast/2014/04/egypt-escalate-ethiopian-dam-dispute-201448135352769150.html.

65. Mu Xuequan, "Ethiopia's Grand Renaissance Dam 62 pct Complete," *Xinhua News*, October 21, 2017, www.xinhuanet.com/english/2017–10/21/c_136694651.htm.

66. "The Grand Ethiopian Renaissance Dam Fact Sheet," International Rivers, January 24, 2014, www.internationalrivers.org/resources/the-grand-ethiopian-renaissance-dam-fact-sheet-8213.

67. Abdi Latif Dahir, "A Major Geopolitical Crisis is Set to Erupt over Who Controls the World's Longest River," *Quartz Africa*, January 16, 2018, https://qz.com/africa/1181318/ethiopia-egypt-sudan-and-eritrea-tensions-over-grand-ethiopian-renaissance-dam-on-nile-river.

68. "Egyptian Warning over Ethiopia Nile Dam," *BBC*, June 10, 2013, www.bbc.com/news/world-africa-22850124.

69. MacDiarmid, "Egypt to 'Escalate' Ethiopian Dam Dispute."

70. Michael B. Kelley and Robert Johnson, "Stratfor: Egypt is Prepared to Bomb all of Ethiopia's Nile Dams," *Business Insi*der, October 13, 2012, www.businessinsider.com/hacked-stratfor-emails-egypt-could-take-military-action-to-protect-its-stake-in-the-nile-2012–10.

71. Heba Saleh, "Egyptian Farmers Hit as Nile Delta Comes under Threat," *The Financial Times*, September 3, 2018, www.ft.com/content/b43bfd4a-a54c-11e8–8ecf-a7ae1beff35b.

72. Ibid.

73. Kelley and Johnson, "Stratfor: Egypt."

74. Ibid.

75. Ibid.

76. MacDiarmid, "Egypt to 'Escalate' Ethiopian Dam Dispute."

77. Milena Veselinovic, "Ethiopia's $5bn Project that Could Turn it into Africa's Water Powerhouse," *CNN*, October 20, 2015, www.cnn.com/2015/03/06/africa/grand-reneissance-dam-ethiopia/index.html.

78. Dahir, "A Major Geopolitical Crisis."

79. Mohamed Mahmoud, "Egyptian Farmers Fear Drought, and Dam: 'Without the Nile There is no Life,'" *Middle East Eye*, January 13, 2017, www.middleeasteye.net/in-depth/features/egyptian-farmers-without-nile-there-no-life-egypt-765842704.

80. Amir Dakkak, "Egypt's Water Crisis—A Recipe for Disaster," *EcoMENA*, July 22, 2017, www.ecomena.org/egypt-water.

81. Ibid.

82. Fred Pearce, "Win-Win Deal Helps Avoid War over Ethiopia's $5 Billion Nile Dam," *New Scientist*, May 27, 2015, www.newscientist.com/article/mg22630235-700-win-win-deal-helps-avoid-war-over-ethiopias-5-billion-nile-dam.

83. MacDiarmid, "Egypt to 'Escalate' Ethiopian Dam Dispute."

84. Oli Brown and Michael Keating, "Addressing Natural Resource Conflicts: Working Towards More Effective Resolution of National and Sub-National Resource Disputes," Chatham House, the Royal Institute of International Affairs, London, 2015.

85. Ashok Swain, "Ethiopia, the Sudan, and Egypt: The Nile River Dispute," *The Journal of Modern African Studies* 35, no. 4 (1997): 675–94; John Waterbury, *Hydropolitics of the Nile Valley* (Syracuse, NY: Syracuse University Press, 1979).

86. Mark Zeitoun et al., "Transboundary Water Justice: A Combined Reading of Literature on Critical Transboundary Water Interaction and 'Justice,' For Analysis and Diplomacy," *Water Policy* 16, no. S2 (2014): 174–93.

87. Ana Elisa Cascão, "Changing Power Relations in the Nile River Basin: Unilateralism vs. Cooperation?" *Water Alternatives* 2, no. 2 (2009): 245–68.

88. Daniel Nisman, "China's African Water Scramble," *Huffington Post*, December 7, 2012, www.huffingtonpost.com/daniel-nisman/chinas-african-water-scra_b_2248874.html.

89. Noha Samir Donia, "Development of El-Salam Canal Automation System," *Journal of Water Resource and Protection* 4, no. 8 (2012): 597–604; "As-Salam Canal," Egypt State Information Service (ESIS), November 19, 2000, www.us.sis.gov.eg/Story/26487?lang=en-us.

90. Ingjerd Haddeland et al., "Global Water Resources Affected by Human

Interventions and Climate Change," *Proceedings of the National Academy of Sciences* 111, no. 9 (2014): 3251–6.

91. Saleh, "Egyptian Farmers Hit as Nile Delta Comes under Threat."

92. Khalid Al Ansary, "Iraq Wheat Farmers May Slash Plantings as Turks Fill New Dam," June 25, 2018, *Bloomberg News*, www.bloomberg.com/news/articles/2018–06–25/iraq-wheat-farmers-may-slash-plantings-as-turkey-fills-new-dam.

93. "Cost of Non-Cooperation on Water: Crisis of Survival in the Middle East."

94. "Counting the Cost: Agriculture in Syria after Six Years of Crisis," Food and Agriculture Organization of the United Nations (FAO), April 2017, 1, www.fao.org/3/b-i7081e.pdf.

3. TURKISH HYDRO-HEGEMONY: THE IMPACT OF DAMS

1. Mark Zeitoun and Jeroen Warner, "Hydro-Hegemony—A Framework for Analysis of Transboundary Water Conflicts," *Water Policy* 8, no. 5 (2006): 451.

2. Gary Winslett, "Substitutability, Securitization, and Hydro-Hegemony: Ontological and Strategic Sequencing in Shared River Basins," *Conflict, Security & Development* 15, no. 3 (2015): 287.

3. Peter H. Gleick, "Water and Conflict: Fresh Water Resources and International Security," *International Security* 18, no. 1 (1993): 89.

4. Paul A. Williams, "Turkey's Water Diplomacy: A Theoretical Discussion," in *Turkey's Water Policy: National Framework and International Cooperation*, eds. Aysegul Kibaroglu, Waltina Scheumann, and Annika Kramer (Berlin: Springer-Verlag, 2011), 201.

5. Republic of Turkey, Prime Ministry, State Planning Organization [hereafter, SPO], GAP: The Southeastern Anatolia Project Master Plan Study: Final Master Plan Report, Vol. 2 (Tokyo, Japan and Ankara, Turkey: Nippon Koei Co. Ltd. and Yüksel Proje A.Ş., April 1989), Tables 5.3 and 5.4, http://yayin.gap.gov.tr/guneydogu-anadolu-projesi-master-plan-calismasi-master-plan-nihai-raporu-cilt-2-yayin-87aa7418bd.html.

6. "Turkey's Baghdad Ambassador Reassures Iraqis over Ilisu Dam, Says

will Continue to Share Water," *Daily Sabah*, June 5, 2018, www.dai-lysabah.com/diplomacy/2018/06/05/turkeys-baghdad-ambassador-reassures-iraqis-over-ilisu-dam-says-will-continue-to-share-water.

7. Natasha Beschorner, "Water and Instability in the Middle East" Adelphi *Paper Series* 273 (London: Brassey's for International Institute for Strategic Studies, 1992/1993), 42.

8. Jeroen Warner, "Contested Hydrohegemony: Hydraulic Control and Security in Turkey," *Water Alternatives* 1, no. 2 (2008): 284.

9. Özden Zeynep Oktav, "Turkey's Water Policy in the Euphrates-Tigris Basin," in *Environmental Change and Human Security in Africa and the Middle East*, eds. Mohamed Behnassi and Katriona McGlade (Berlin: Springer-Verlag, 2017), 245.

10. Arda Bilgen, "A Project of Destruction, Peace, or Techno-Science? Untangling the Relationship between the Southeastern Anatolia Project (GAP) and the Kurdish Question in Turkey," *Middle Eastern Studies* 54, no. 1 (2017): 94–113.

11. Erhan Akça, Ryo Fujikura, and Ciğdem Sabbağ, "Ataturk Dam Resettlement Process: Increased Disparity Resulting from Insufficient Financial Compensation," *International Journal of Water Resources Development* 29, no. 1 (2013): 102.

12. Paul Williams, "Euphrates and Tigris Waters—Turkish-Syrian and Iraqi Relations," in *Water Resource Conflicts and International Security: A Global Perspective*, ed. Dhirendra K. Vajpeyi (Lanham, MD: Lexington, 2012), 44.

13. Aysegul Kibaroglu and Waltina Scheumann, "Euphrates-Tigris Rivers System: Political Rapprochement and Transboundary Water Cooperation," in Kibaroglu, Scheumann, and Kramer, *Turkey's Water Policy*, 277–8.

14. Kibaroglu and Scheumann, "Euphrates-Tigris Rivers," 277–8.

15. T.C. Orman ve Su Işleri Bakanliği Devlet Su Işleri Genel Müdürlüğü [hereafter, DSI, which stands for Devlet Su Isleri or "State Water Works"], *2006 Yili Faaliyet Raporu* (Ankara: DSI, 2006), 150, 378; and idem, *2016 Yili Faaliyet Raporu* (Ankara: DSI, 2016), 39–40, www.dsi.gov.tr/stratejik-planlama/faaliyet-raporlari.

16. DSI, "Turkey Water Report 2009," (Ankara: DSI, 2009), 16, www2.dsi.gov.tr/english/pdf_files/TurkeyWaterReport.pdf.

17. "GAP Regional Development Administration [hereafter, GAPRDA]," South-Eastern Anatolia Project Action Plan (2014–2018), 3, www.gap.gov.tr/en/action-plan-page-5.html.

18. 1.64 million hectares appears in the 1989 GAP Master Plan, with the higher total of 1.8 million hectares reflecting inclusion of "ungrouped" projects, with those finished by 1989 essentially "grandfathered" into GAP. SPO, GAP: Final Master Plan Report, Executive Summary, 2, and DSI, *2008 Yili Faaliyet Raporu* (Ankara: DSI, 2008), 86–8, www.dsi.gov.tr/stratejik-planlama/faaliyet-raporlari.

19. SPO, *Final Master Plan Report*, vol. 2, Table 5.1.

20. SPO, *Final Master Plan Report*, vol. 2, Table 5.8; and DSI, *2017 Yili Faaliyet Raporu* (Ankara: DSI, 2017), 70, www.dsi.gov.tr/stratejik-planlama/faaliyet-raporlari.

21. DSI is "State Water Works," an agency now under the auspices of Turkey's Ministry of Forestry and Water Affairs; GAPRDA, *Guneydogu Anadolu Projesi (GAP) 1992 Durum Raporu* (Ankara: GAPRDA, 1993), 9, http://yayin.gap.gov.tr/1992-gap-son-durum-yayin-91764d9b91.html.

22. Sources of data for author's estimates include: DSI, *2017 Faaliyet Raporu*, 44–50; idem, 8th (Erzurum), 9th (Elazig), 10th (Diyarbakir), 15th (Şanliurfa), 16th (Mardin—Ilisu Dam), 17th (Van), 19th (Sivas), and 20th (Kahramanmaraş) Regional Directorate menus; Enerji Atlasi, Hidroelektrik Santralleri, www.enerjiatlasi.com/hidroelektrik; Google Earth; and International Commission on Large Dams (ICOLD) Turkish National Committee, *Dams of Turkey* (Ankara, Turkey: DSI Foundation, 2014), 470–519 and 554–84.

23. Asaf Savaş Akat, "The Political Economy of Turkish Inflation," *Journal of International Affairs* 54, no. 1 (2000): 267.

24. SPO, *Final Master Plan Report*, vol. 1, 9.

25. Jeroen Warner, "The Struggle over Turkey's Ilisu Dam: Domestic and International Security Linkages," *International Environmental Agreements* 12 (2012): 240.

26. SPO, *Final Master Plan Report*, vol. 2, Table 5.9.

27. SPO, *Final Master Plan Report*, vol. 2, Table 5.8.

28. GAPRDA, *Güneydoğu Anadolu Projesi Son Durum 2018*, 36, http://

yayin.gap.gov.tr/2017-gap-son-durum-yayin-13a66a26b5.html, for GAP output; and Turkish Statistical Institute, "Electricity Generation and Shares by Energy Resources," www.turkstat.gov.tr/PreIstatistik Tablo.do?istab_id=1578.

29. GAPRDA, *Güneydoğu Anadolu Projesi (GAP) 1993 Durum Raporu* (Ankara: GAPRDA, 1994), 36, http://yayin.gap.gov.tr/1993-gap-son-durum-yayin-3374e25355.html; and idem, *Son Durum 2018*, 35.

30. Akat, "Turkish Inflation," 267–9.

31. Waltina Scheumann et al., "Sustainable Dam Development in Turkey: Between Europeanization and Authoritarian Governance," in *Evolution of Dam Policies: Evidence from the Big Hydropower States*, eds. Waltina Scheumann and Oliver Hensengerth (Berlin: Springer-Verlag, 2014), 153.

32. Scheumann et al., "Sustainable Dam Development," 155.

33. Mehmet Masum Suer, "Trilyonlar Guneydoğu'ya," *Milliyet*, April 3, 1992, 12.

34. Taha Akyol, "Süriye ve Terör," *Milliyet*, October 30, 1993, 18.

35. Winslett, "Substitutability, Securitisation and Hydro-Hegemony," 294, 297.

36. GAPRDA, *1993 Durum Raporu*, 39.

37. DSI, *2006 Faaliyet Raporu*, 176–7.

38. GAPRDA, *1993 Durum Raporu*, 73.

39. SPO, *Final Master Plan Report*, vol. 2, 3.5.

40. SPO, *Final Master Plan Report*, vol. 2, 6.10–6.11.

41. SPO, *Final Master Plan Report*, vol. 2, 6.3, 6.11.

42. GAPRDA, *Güneydoğu Anadolu Projesi'nde Son Durum (Eylül 1996)*, 4, http://yayin.gap.gov.tr/1996-gap-son-durum-yayin-ba81a7544e.html; and idem, *Güneydoğu Anadolu Projesi'nde (GAP) Son Durum (Kasim 2007)* (GAPRDA: Ankara, 2007), 27, 29, 40, http://yayin.gap.gov.tr/2007-gap-son-durum-yayin-6bfce04ec6.html.

43. Aysegul Kibaroglu and Waltina Scheumann, "Evolution of Transboundary Politics in the Euphrates-Tigris River System: New Perspectives and Political Challenges," *Global Governance* 19, no. 2 (2003): 298; and Leila M. Harris, "Contested Sustainabilities: Assessing Narratives of Environmental Change in Southeastern Turkey," *Local Environment* 14, no. 8 (2009): 705.

44. GAPRDA, 1992 Durum Raporu, 74; and DSI, *2007 Yili Faaliyet Raporu* (Ankara: DSI, 2007), 96, www.dsi.gov.tr/stratejik-planlama/faaliyet-raporlari.

45. Author's calculations based on DSI, *2007 Faaliyet Raporu*, 98–9.

46. "Turkey: First and Second Reviews under the Stand-By Arrangement, and Request for Waiver of Nonobservance of Performance Criteria and Rephasing of Purchases," International Monetary Fund *Country Report No. 06/268*, July 2006, 28, www.imf.org/en/Publications/CR/Issues/2016/12/31/Turkey-First-and-Second-Reviews-Under-the-Stand-By-Arrangement-and-Request-for-Waiver-of-19469.

47. GAPRDA, *Son Durum 2018*, 18; and World Bank, "GDP (Constant 2010 US$)," http://api.worldbank.org/v2/en/indicator/NY.GDP.MKTP.KD?downloadformat=excel.

48. GAPRDA, Action Plan (2008–2012), 5, 58.

49. Ibid., 56–58.

50. GAPRDA, *Güneydoğu Anadolu Projesi Son Durum Raporu 2013* (Şanliurfa: GAPRDA, 2013), 44, http://yayin.gap.gov.tr/2013-gap-son-durum-yayin-4e49d53fdf.html; and idem, *Son Durum 2018*, 29.

51. GAPRDA, *Son Durum 2018*, 32.

52. Author calculations based on DSI, *2008 Faaliyet Raporu*, 86–8; and idem, *2017 Faaliyet Raporu*, 96.

53. DSI reports have put this project's completed hectares at 57,253 ha and first year of operation as 2014, while GAPRDA reports have cited 61,883 ha (including a DSI supplement of 4,630 ha) and the year 2011.

54. Tarim Işletmeleri Genel Müdürlüğü (TIGEM), Ceylanpinar Tarim Işletmeleri Müdürlüğü, www.tigem.gov.tr/Sayfalar/Detay/b664d80a-00ca-46a5-9768-e4f47496d958.

55. Williams, "Euphrates and Tigris Waters," 42.

56. Ibid.

57. Kibaroglu and Scheumann, "Euphrates-Tigris Rivers," 263.

58. Ibid., 287.

59. Williams, "Turkey's Water Diplomacy," 204.

60. Leila M. Harris and Samer Alatout, "Negotiating Hydro-Scales, Forging States: Comparison of the Upper Tigris/Euphrates and Jordan River Basins," *Political Geography* 29, no. 3 (2010): 150–1.

61. Kibaroglu and Scheumann, "Euphrates-Tigris Rivers," 283–5.

62. Bilgen, "A Project of Destruction, Peace, or Techno-Science?" 96; and Henri J. Barkey and Graham E. Fuller, *Turkey's Kurdish Question* (Lanham, MD: Rowman & Littlefield, 1998), 31–2.

63. Ihsan Dortkardeş et. al., "Başarili operasyon," *Milliyet*, March 3, 1987, 8; and "Eşkiya 3 eri öldürdü," *Milliyet*, June 5, 1987, 13.

64. Syrian Arab Republic and Turkey, Protocol on matters pertaining to economic cooperation, signed at Damascus on 17 July 1987, *Treaty Series: Treaties and International Agreements Registered or Filed and Recorded with the Secretariat of the United Nations*, vol. 1724 (1993), 4–8, https://treaties.un.org/doc/Publication/UNTS/Volume%201724/v1724.pdf.

65. "Hazro'ya PKK baskini," *Milliyet*, August 28, 1987, 9.

66. Paul Williams, "Turkey's H$_2$O Diplomacy in the Middle East," *Security Dialogue* 32, no. 1 (2001): 30.

67. Ibid.

68. Ibid., 33.

69. Ibid., 30.

70. "Midyat'ta 6 sehit," *Milliyet*, November 13, 1992, 1; and GAPRDA, *1993 Durum Raporu*, 39.

71. Syrian Arab Republic and Turkey, Joint Communiqué on Cooperation, signed at Damascus on 20 January 1993, in United Nations, *Treaty Series*, 16–7.

72. "PKK baraja saldirdi: 8 er şehit," *Milliyet*, 2 October 1994, 23.

73. Williams, "Turkey's H$_2$O Diplomacy," 30–1.

74. "Öğretmen katliami," *Milliyet*, October 2, 1996, 14.

75. "Şam, Birecik'i uçuracak!,"*Milliyet*, April 14, 1998, 11; and "Özlüce Baraji'na PKK saldirisi," *Milliyet*, June 18, 1998, 30.

76. Warner, "Turkey's Ilisu Dam," 239–43.

77. Kibaroglu and Scheumann, "Euphrates-Tigris Rivers," 287.

78. Williams, "Euphrates and Tigris Waters," 43.

79. Andreas Atzl, "Transnational NGO Networks Campaign against the Ilisu Dam, Turkey," in *Evolution of Dam Policies: Evidence from the Big Hydropower States*, eds. Waltina Scheumann and Oliver Hensengerth (Berlin: Springer-Verlag, 2013), 205–6.

80. Warner, "Turkey's Ilisu Dam," 243.
81. Atzl, "Transnational NGO Networks," 206–7.
82. Warner, "Turkey's Ilisu Dam," 239, 244.
83. Atzl, "Transnational NGO Networks," 209.
84. Scheumann et al., "Sustainable Dam Development," 165.
85. Ibid., 154, 167.
86. Waltina Scheumann et al., "Environmental Impact Assessment in Turkish Dam Planning," in *Turkey's Water Policy: National Framework and International Cooperation*, eds. Aysegul Kibaroglu, Waltina Scheumann, and Annika Kramer (Berlin: Springer-Verlag, 2011), 143.
87. Waltina Scheumann et al., "Turkish Dam Planning," 145–6.
88. Scheumann et al., "Sustainable Dam Development," 143.
89. Williams, "Euphrates and Tigris Waters," 44.
90. Warner, "Turkey's Ilisu Dam," 238–39; and "Ilisu Baraji'nin gövde dolgusu bitti! PKK'yi bogacak proje," *Güneş*, July 30, 2017, www.gunes.com/ekonomi/ilisu-baraji-nin-govde-dolgusu-bitti-pkkyi-bogacak-proje-807639.
91. In lists of expropriated land, DSI has appended parenthetical labels "(GAP)" to Şirnak's Uludere-Balli, Kavşaktepe, and Musatepe-Çetintepe projects and "(DAP)" to Hakkari's Aslandağ-Beyyurdu. See DSI, *2014 Yili Faaliyet Raporu* (Ankara: DSI, 2014), 294–95, www.dsi.gov.tr/stratejik-planlama/faaliyet-raporlari.
92. Visual representations and informational snapshots of the Ortasu cascade can be found from the dashboards of the DSI's 10th district HQ in Diyarbakir, and its 17th district HQ in Van.
93. "DSI Genel Müdürlüğü Teröre Inat Calişmaya Devam Ediyor," *DSI Haberler*, May 8, 2017, www.dsi.gov.tr/haberler/2017/05/08.
94. Scheumann et al. "Sustainable Dam Development," 137.
95. Author's calculations based on DSI activity reports of 2013–2017.
96. "Ilisu Baraji ve HES Altinda Kalacak 4 Ildeki 990 Parsel Için Acele Kamulaştirma Karari," *Hürriyet*, October 14, 2016, www.hurriyet.com.tr/ilisu-baraji-altinda-kalacak-dort-ildeki-990-pa-40248495.
97. Scheumann et al. "Sustainable Dam Development," 137.
98. Kibaroglu and Scheumann, "Euphrates-Tigris Rivers," 294–5.
99. Joost Jongerden, "Dams and Politics in Turkey: Utilizing Water, Developing Conflict," *Middle East Politics* 17, no. 1 (2010): 138.

100. Oktav, "Turkey's Water Policy," 245.

101. Jongerden, "Dams and Politics," 140.

102. Kibaroglu and Scheumann, "Euphrates-Tigris Rivers," 295.

103. Marwa Daoudy, "Asymmetric Power: Negotiating Water in the Euphrates and Tigris," *International Negotiation* 14, no. 2 (2009): 383.

104. Aysegul Kibaroglu, "An Analysis of Turkey's Water Diplomacy and its Evolving Position vis-à-vis International Water Law," *Water International* 40, no. 1 (2015): 164.

105. Author's own counts based on Google search results include mainly incidents that sources have explicitly identified as occurring in relationship or close proximity to named installations.

106. "KCK ateşkesin bittiğini açıkladı: Bundan sonra tüm barajlar gerillanın hedefinde olacaktır," *T24*, July 11, 2015, http://t24.com.tr/haber/kck-ateskesin-bittigini-aicikladi-bundan-sonra-tum-barajlar-gerillanin-hedefinde-olacaktir,302608.

107. Leila M. Harris, "Water and Conflict Geographies of the Southeastern Anatolia Project," *Society & Natural Resources* 15, no. 8 (2002): 755.

108. This corroborates an overall figure for 2015 quoted by DSI's 10th Regional Directorate head, as cited in "Atatürk Barajı'ndan sonra en büyük sulama barajı: Silvan Barajı," *CNNTurk.com*, March 28, 2017, www.cnnturk.com/ataturk-barajindan-sonra-en-buyuk-sulama-baraji-silvan-baraji.

109. "PKK'nın saldırıları Silvan Barajı'nı durdurdu," *Yeni Akit*, August 9, 2015, www.yeniakit.com.tr/haber/pkknin-saldirilari-silvan-barajini-durdurdu-86003.html.

110. See "Atatürk Barajı'ndan sonra en büyük sulama barajı"; and "DSI Genel Müdürlüğü Teröre İnat Calışmaya Devam Ediyor."

111. "Thirst Wars: Turkey Applies Political Pressure by Cutting Off Water to Syria," *Sputnik International*, March 8, 2017, https://sputniknews.com/middleeast/201703081051370769-turkey-syria-water-euphrates; and Zaid Sabah, "Iraq, ISIS Angered as Turkey Hoards Euphrates Water," *Lebanon Daily Star*, July 6, 2015, www.dailystar.com.lb/News/Middle-East/2015/Jul-06/305304-iraq-isis-angered-as-turkey-hoards-euphrates-waters.ashx.

112. Metin Gurcan, "Turkey Takes on Kurds in Evolving Qandil Operation,"

Al-Monitor, June 15, 2018, www.al-monitor.com/pulse/originals/2018/06/turkey-iraqi-kurdistan-sustain-qandil-operation.html.

113. "Bakan Eroğlu TGRT Haber'de açıkladı: Bütün araç gereçlerimiz Hatay sınırına sevk edildi," *TGRT Haber*, January 25, 2018, www.tgrthaber.com.tr/politika/bakan-eroglu-tgrt-haberde-acikladi-butun-arac-gereclerimiz-hatay-sinirina-sevk-edildi-222907.

114. Harris, "Water and Conflict," 747.

115. Bilgen, "A project of Destruction, Peace, or Techno-Science?" 104.

4. A WATERSHED MOMENT: ASSESSING THE HYDROPOLITICS OF IRAQI KURDISTAN

1. Arun P. Elhance, *Hydropolitics in the Third World: Conflict and Cooperation in International River Basins* (Washington, D.C: United States Institute of Peace Press, 1999), 3.

2. Ofra Bengio, *Kurdish Awakening: Nation Building in a Fragmented Homeland* (Austin: University of Texas Press, 2015).

3. Kenneth Katzman, "The Kurds in Post-Saddam Iraq," Congressional Research Service, October 1, 2010, https://fas.org/sgp/crs/mideast/RS22079.pdf; "Kurdistan Map," The Kurdish Project, https://thekurdishproject.org/kurdistan-map.

4. Mehrdad R. Izady, *The Kurds: A Concise Handbook* (Washington: Crane Russak, 1992).

5. Raymond H. Anderson, "Limited Local Autonomy Granted to Kurds in Iraq," *The New York Times*, March 12, 1974, sec. Archives, www.nytimes.com/1974/03/12/archives/limited-local-autonomy-granted-to-kurds-in-iraq.html.

6. George Black, *Genocide in Iraq: The Anfal Campaign against the Kurds*, Middle East Watch Report (New York: Human Rights Watch, 1993).

7. Michael M. Gunter, *The A to Z of the Kurds* (Lanham: Scarecrow Press, 2009), 116.

8. Christopher M. Blanchard, "Kurds in Iraq Propose Controversial Referendum on Independence," Congressional Research Service, September 21, 2017, https://fas.org/sgp/crs/mideast/IN10758.pdf; Martin Chulov, "More than 92% of Voters in Iraqi Kurdistan Back

Independence," *The Guardian*, September 27, 2017, www.theguardian.com/world/2017/sep/27/over-92-of-iraqs-kurds-vote-for-independence.

9. "Kurdish VP Accuses Certain PUK Leaders of Fall of Kirkuk, Calls Them 'Apostates,'" *Rudaw*, October 18, 2017, www.rudaw.net/english/kurdistan/181020171.

10. "Masoud Barzani to Step down as KRG President," *Al Jazeera*, October 30, 2017, www.aljazeera.com/news/2017/10/masoud-barzani-step-krg-president-171029161347180.html.

11. "The Map of Estimated Population of Kurdistan Region 2017," Kurdistan Region Statistics Office, 2017, www.krso.net/Default.aspx?page=article&id=1680&l=1.

12. "Text of the Draft Iraqi Constitution," *The New York Times*, August 24, 2005, www.nytimes.com/2005/08/24/international/middleeast/text-of-the-draft-iraqi-constitution.html.

13. Ibid.

14. Michael Georgy, "Defiant Kurds Shrug off Risk of Trade War after Independence Vote," *Reuters*, October 18, 2017, www.reuters.com/article/us-mideast-crisis-iraq-kurds-economy/defiant-kurds-shrug-off-risk-of-trade-war-after-independence-vote-idUSKBN1CN0QS.

15. Frederick Lorenz and Edward J. Erickson, *Strategic Water: Iraq and Security Planning in The Euphrates-Tigris Basin* (Quantico, Virginia: Marine Corps University Press, 2013).

16. "Drought: Impact Assessment, Recovery and Mitigation Framework and Regional Project Design in Kurdistan Region (KR)," United Nations Development Programme, Iraq, January 2011.

17. Lorenz and Erickson, *Strategic Water*, 144.

18. Zoran Stevanovic and Miroslav Markovic, *Hydrogeology of Northern Iraq, Climate Hydrology, Geomorphology and Geology*, vol. 1 (Rome: Food and Agriculture Organization, UN, 2004).

19. Hannah Lynch, "When It Comes to Kurdistan's Water, Problems Flow but Not Solutions," *Rudaw*, July 26, 2017, www.rudaw.net/english/kurdistan/250720175.

20. Ibid.

21. Alessandro Tinti, "Water Resources Management in the Kurdistan

Region of Iraq," Institute of Regional and International Studies *Policy Report*, 2017, http://auis.edu.krd/iris/sites/default/files/Water%20Policy%20Report%20IRIS_FINAL%20ES.pdf.

22. Betsy Otto, "Aqueduct Water Risk Atlas," World Resources Institute, October 2013, www.wri.org/resources/maps/aqueduct-water-risk-atlas.

23. Ibid.

24. Lorenz and Erickson, "Strategic Water," 146.

25. "Baghdad Sends Salaries to Kurdistan's Dam Employees, also Medical Supplies," *Rudaw*, December 27, 2017, www.rudaw.net/english/kurdistan/27122017.

26. Lynch, "When It Comes to Kurdistan's Water."

27. Robert O. Keohane and David G. Victor, "The Regime Complex for Climate Change," *Perspectives on Politics* 9, no. 1 (March 2011): 7.

28. Mark Zeitoun and Jeroen Warner, "Hydro-Hegemony—a Framework for Analysis of Trans-Boundary Water Conflicts," *Water Policy* 8, no. 5 (September 2006): 443.

29. Aaron T. Wolf, Shira B. Yoffe, and Mark Giordano, "International Waters: Identifying Basins at Risk," *Water Policy* 5, no. 1 (2003): 29–60.

30. "Transboundary Freshwater Dispute Database (TFDD)," Oregon State University, https://transboundarywaters.science.oregonstate.edu/content/transboundary-freshwater-dispute-database

31. Zeitoun and Warner, "Hydro-Hegemony," 446.

32. Marcus D. King and Julia Burnell, "The Weaponization of Water in a Changing Climate," in *Epicenters of Climate and Security: The New Geostrategic Landscape of the Anthropocene*, eds. Caitlin E. Werrell and Francesco Femia (The Center for Climate and Security: 2017), 67–73.

33. Zeitoun and Warner, "Hydro-Hegemony," 443.

34. Ibid.

35. Kerim Yildiz, *The Future of Kurdistan: The Iraqi Dilemma* (London: Pluto Press, 2012).

36. "Baghdad Sends Salaries to Kurdistan's Dam Employees, also Medical Supplies," *Rudaw*, December 27, 2017, www.rudaw.net/english/kurdistan/27122017

37. King, "The Weaponization of Water in Iraq and Syria," 156.

38. Abdul Rahman, "A Case for an Independent Kurdistan" (The George Washington University, October 10, 2017).

39. "Convention on the Law of the Non-Navigational Uses of International Watercourses" (United Nations, May 21, 1997), http://legal.un.org/ilc/texts/instruments/english/conventions/8_3_1997.pdf.

40. David P. Forsythe, "Water and Politics in the Tigris-Euphrates Basin: Hope for Negative Learning?," in *Water Security in the Middle East: Essays in Scientific and Social Cooperation*, ed. Jean Cahan (Anthem Press, 2017), 173, www.cambridge.org/core/books/water-security-in-the-middle-east/water-and-politics-in-the-tigriseuphrates-basin-hope-for-negative-learning/731D00E86F1F57877A6D71E9C25E15FF.

41. Zanko Ahmad, "Water, a New Battleground between Kurds and Arabs in Iraq," March 30, 2011, http://ekurd.net/mismas/articles/misc2011/3/state4921.htm.

42. "Water, a New Battleground between Kurds and Arabs in Iraq."

43. "Water, a New Battleground between Kurds and Arabs in Iraq"

44. "Twenty New Dams to Offset Shortage of Water in Kurdistan, Minister Says," *Rudaw*, March 19, 2017, www.rudaw.net/english/business/19032017.

45. "Baghdad Sends Salaries to Kurdistan's Dam Employees," *Rudaw*.

46. "AQUASTAT Website," *Food and Agriculture Organization of the United Nations (FAO)*, 2016, www.fao.org/nr/water/aquastat/main/index.stm.

47. "The Kurdistan Region of Iraq: Assessing the Economic and Social Impact of the Syrian Conflict and ISIS," The World Bank, 2015, http://documents.worldbank.org/curated/en/579451468305943474/pdf/958080PUB0Apri0PUBLIC09781464805486.pdf.

48. "The People of the Kurdistan Region," Kurdistan Regional Government, www.gov.krd/p/p.aspx?l=12&p=214.

49. "Kurds & the Refugee Crisis," *The Kurdish Project*, https://thekurdishproject.org/infographics/kurds-and-the-refugee-crisis.

50. "The Kurdistan Region of Iraq," The World Bank.

51. Peter Schwartzstein, interview, November 24, 2017

52. Tinti, "Water Resources Management in the Kurdistan Region of Iraq," 4.

53. "Multi-Sector Needs Assessment of Syrian Refugees in Camps: Kurdistan Region of Iraq," *Assessment Report*, UNHCR, REACH Initiative, September 2014, https://reliefweb.int/sites/reliefweb.int/files/resources/Multi-SectorNeedsAssessement%28MSNA%29ofSyrianRefugeesinCampsSeptember2014KurdistanRegionIraq.pdf.

54. "Saving Water in the Refugee Camps of Iraqi Kurdistan," *ACTED*, October 11, 2016, www.acted.org/en/saving-water-refugee-camps-iraqi-kurdistan.

55. "Iraq Displacement Profile" Reliefweb, July 4, 2014, https://reliefweb.int/sites/reliefweb.int/files/resources/iraq_displacement_profile_4_july_2014.pdf.

56. Haifa Zangana, "Refugees in Their Own Country: Iraq's Ticking Time Bomb," *The New Arab*, March 26, 2015, www.alaraby.co.uk/english/comment/53ac546c-886e-432b-a05f-f600e4c2db0e.

57. Diary Muhamad, "Updates from the Waterkeeper," Nature Iraq, March 30, 2014, www.natureiraq.org/1/post/2014/03/updates-from-the-waterkeeper.html.

58. "ICEEAS 2016," Ishik University, May 24, 2016, www.ishik.edu.iq/conf/portfolio-item/iceeas-2016.

59. "The Kurdistan Region of Iraq," The World Bank; Nasih Othman, "Environmental Health Assessment in Sulaymaniyah City and Vicinity" (Kurdistan Institution for Strategic Studies and Scientific Research, 2017).

60. Save the Tigris and Iraqi Marshes Campaign, "Ilisu Dam and Legal Considerations in Iraq," February 22, 2014, www.iraqicivilsociety.org/wp-content/uploads/2014/04/ILISU-DAM-AND-LEGAL-CONSIDERATIONS-IN-IRAQ-Eng.pdf.

61. "Damaged Darbandikhan Dam Exacerbates Water Woes," *Rudaw*, June 6, 2018, www.rudaw.net/english/kurdistan/060620184.

62. Serkan Demirtaş, "Turkey, Iraq Vow to Advance Ties in All Fields Including Terror, Water Issues," *Hürriyet Daily News*, January 21, 2018, www.hurriyetdailynews.com/turkey-iraq-vow-to-advance-ties-in-all-fields-including-terror-water-issues-126060.

63. Kamal Chomani and Toon Bijnens, "The Impact of the Daryan Dam on the Kurdistan Region of Iraq," Save the Tigris and Iraqi Marshes

Campaign, October 2016, www.iraqicivilsociety.org/wp-content/uploads/2016/10/Daryan-Dam-Report.pdf.

64. Tinti, "Water Resources Management in the Kurdistan Region of Iraq," 10.

65. "Iraq Water Crisis: Little Zab River Shrinks by 70%," *Rudaw*, June 9, 2018, www.rudaw.net/english/kurdistan/090620182.

66. "Iraq-Complex Emergency" *Fact Sheet* no. 7, May 11, 2018, www.usaid.gov/sites/default/files/documents/1866/iraq_ce_fs07_05–11–2018.pdf.

67. Peter Schwartzstein, Interview, November 24, 2017.

68. Peter Schwartzstein, "The Dangerous State of Iraq's Rivers," *Foreign Affairs*, April 7, 2017, www.foreignaffairs.com/articles/iraq/2017–04–07/dangerous-state-iraqs-rivers.

69. "Sharp Drop in Groundwater Reserves Worries KRG," *Rudaw*, February 20, 2018, www.rudaw.net/english/kurdistan/190220183.

70. "Sharp Drop in Groundwater Reserves Worries KRG."

71. Hoerling, M., J. Eischeid, J. Perlwitz, X. Quan, T. Zhang, and P. Pegion, 2012: On the Increased Frequency of Mediterranean Drought. *J. Climate*, 25, 2146–2161, https://doi.org/10.1175/JCLI-D-11–00296.1

72. Nadhir Al-Ansari, "Hydro-Politics of the Tigris and Euphrates Basins," *Engineering* 8, no. 3 (2016): 140–72.

73. Al-Ansari, "Hydro-Politics of the Tigris and Euphrates Basins."

74. Colin P. Kelley et al., "Climate Change in the Fertile Crescent and Implications of the Recent Syrian Drought," *Proceedings of the National Academy of Sciences* 112, no. 11 (2015): 3241–46.

75. R. K. Pachauri, Leo Mayer, and Intergovernmental Panel on Climate Change, eds., *Climate Change 2014: Synthesis Report* (Geneva, Switzerland: Intergovernmental Panel on Climate Change, 2015).

76. E. Bou-Zeid and M. El-Fadel, "Climate Change and Water Resources in Lebanon and the Middle East," *Journal of Water Resources Planning and Management* 128, no. 5 (2002): 347.

77. Betsy Otto, "Aqueduct Water Risk Atlas," World Resources Institute, October 2013, www.wri.org/resources/maps/aqueduct-water-risk-atlas.

78. Rossella Messina, "Impact of Climate Change on Water Resources: A

New Modelling Study for the Arab Region," *Fanack Water*, October 31, 2017, https://water.fanack.com/impact-of-climate-change-on-water-resources.

79. Schwartzstein, interview.

80. Neda A. Zawahri, "Adapting to Climatic Variability along International River Basins in the Middle East," in *Water Security in the Middle East: Essays in Scientific and Social Cooperation*, ed. Jean Cahan (Anthem Press, 2017), 150.

81. Deniz Bozkurt and Omer Lutfi Sen, "Climate Change Impacts in the Euphrates–Tigris Basin Based on Different Model and Scenario Simulations," *Journal of Hydrology* 480 (February 2013): 149–61.

82. Conor Gaffey, "The Iran-Iraq Earthquake May Soon Be the Deadliest of 2017," *Yahoo! News*, November 13, 2017, https://uk.news.yahoo.com/iran-iraq-earthquake-may-soon-131344784.html.

83. "Iran-Iraq Earthquake: More than 300 Die in Heavy Tremor," *Al Jazeera*, November 13, 2017, www.aljazeera.com/news/2017/11/northern-iraq-rocked-72-magnitude-earthquake-171112184114150.html.

84. "World Bank and Ministry of Water Resources Evaluate Darbandikhan and Dokan Dams Following Iraq Quake," International Bank for Reconstruction and Development, World Bank, November 27, 2017, https://reliefweb.int/sites/reliefweb.int/files/resources/WB%20EN.pdf.

85. "Damaged Darbandikhan Dam Exacerbates Water Woes."

86. Dexter Filkins, "A Bigger Problem Than ISIS?," *The New Yorker*, December 26, 2016, www.newyorker.com/magazine/2017/01/02/a-bigger-problem-than-isis.

87. Tinti, "Water Resources Management in the Kurdistan Region of Iraq," 1–10.

88. Ibid.

89. Robert A. Hager, "The Euphrates Basin: In Search of a Legal Regime Note," *Georgetown International Environmental Law Review* 3, no. 1 (1990): 215.

90. "Global Water Security" Intelligence Community Assessment, Office of the Director of National Intelligence, February 2012, www.dni.gov/files/documents/Special%20Report_ICA%20Global%20Water%20Security.pdf.

91. David B. Ottaway, "Iraq's Kurdistan Takes a Giant Step toward Independence," *Viewpoints*, no. 46 (December 2013), www.wilsoncenter.org/sites/default/files/iraq_kurdistan_takes_giant_step_toward_independence.pdf.

5. GROUNDWATER RESOURCES: SUPPLY, USE AND SECURITY IMPLICATIONS IN THE MIDDLE EAST AND NORTH AFRICA

1. We define MENA as the region generally including the territory of Algeria, Bahrain, Egypt, Iran, Iraq, Israel, Jordan, Kuwait, Lebanon, Morocco, Oman, Palestine, Qatar, Saudi Arabia, Syria, Tunisia, Turkey, United Arab Emirates, and Yemen.

2. Tony J. A. Allan, "Rural Economic Transitions: Groundwater Use in the Middle East and its Environmental Consequences," in *The Agricultural Groundwater Revolution: Opportunities and Threats to Development*, eds. Mark Giordano and K.G. Villholth (Cambridge: CABI, 2007).

3. Marcel Kuper et al., "Liberation or Anarchy? The Janus Nature of Groundwater Use on North Africa's New Irrigation Frontiers," in *Integrated Groundwater Management*, eds. Anthony J. Jakeman et al. (Cham: Springer, 2016).

4. Elie Elhadj, "Camels Don't Fly, Deserts Don't Bloom: An Assessment of Saudi Arabia's Experiment in Desert Agriculture," *Occasional paper* 48, no. 6 (2004); Martin Keulertz et al., "The Water-Energy-Food Nexus in Arid Regions," in *The Oxford Handbook of Water Politics and Policy*, eds. Ken Conca and Erika Weinthal (Oxford: Oxford University Press, 2018).

5. Keulertz et al., "The Water-Energy-Food Nexus," 183.

6. Khalil Lezzaik and Adam Milewski, "A Quantitative Assessment of Groundwater Resources in the Middle East and North Africa," *Hydrogeology Journal* 26, no. 1 (2018).

7. Allan, "Rural Economic Transitions: Groundwater Use in the Middle East and its Environmental Consequences."

8. Wada, Yoshihide, L. P. H. Van Beek, and Marc F. P. Bierkens, "Nonsustainable Groundwater Sustaining Irrigation: A Global Assessment," *Water Resources Research* 48, no. 6 (2012).

9. The Gravity Recovery and Climate Experiment (GRACE) is a joint satellite mission between the United States National Aeronautics and Space Administration (NASA) and the German Aerospace Center (DLR). The mission is comprised of two satellites that launched in 2002 and orbit the Earth in tandem. Inter-satellite measurements are taken and correlate to the Earth's gravitational field. The satellites complete a full cycle around the Earth every month, allowing for a monthly assessment of mass change on Earth. Water, having large mass that does change on a monthly basis (as compared to a static mountain), was identified as one of the main earth system processes that can be monitored by GRACE.

10. Benjamin F. Zaitchik, Matthew Rodell, and Rolf H. Reichle, "Assimilation of GRACE Terrestrial Water Storage Data into a Land Surface Model: Results for the Mississippi River Basin," *Journal of Hydrometeorology* 9, no. 3 (2008).

11. Scott Moore and Joshua B. Fisher, "Challenges and Opportunities in GRACE-Based Groundwater Storage Assessment and Management: An Example from Yemen," *Water Resources Management* 26, no. 6 (2012): 1425.

12. Clifford I. Voss and Safaa M. Soliman, "The Transboundary Nonrenewable Nubian Aquifer System of Chad, Egypt, Libya and Sudan: Classical Groundwater Questions and Parsimonious Hydrogeologic Analysis and Modeling," *Hydrogeology Journal* 22, no. 2 (2014): 441–68.

13. Alexandra S. Richey, et al., "Quantifying Renewable Groundwater Stress with GRACE," *Water Resources Research* 51, no. 7 (2015): 5217–38.

14. Khalil Lezzaik, Adam Milewski, and Jeffrey Mullen, "The Groundwater Risk Index: Development and Application in the Middle East and North Africa Region," *Science of the Total Environment* 628 (2018): 1149–64.

15. M. Moench, "Groundwater and Poverty: Exploring the Connections," in *Intensive Use of Groundwater: Challenges and Opportunities*, eds. M. Ramon Llamas and E. Custodio (Florida: CRC Press, 2003); Qiuqiong Huang et al., "Irrigation, Agricultural Performance and Poverty Reduction in China," *Food Policy* 31, no. 1 (2006): 30–52; Tushaar Shah, "The Groundwater Economy of South Asia: An

Assessment of Size, Significance and Socio-Ecological Impacts," in *The Agricultural Groundwater Revolution: Opportunities and Threats to Development*, eds. Mark Giordano and Karen G. Villholth (Cambridge: CABI, 2007), 7–36.

16. Allan, "Rural Economic Transitions."

17. Küper et al., "Liberation or Anarchy?"

18. Rabah Arezki and Markus Brückner, "Food Prices and Political Instability," International Monetary Fund *Working Paper* 11/62 (2011), www.imf.org/external/pubs/ft/wp/2011/wp1162.pdf.

19. Philip C. Abbott, "Export Restrictions as Stabilization Responses to Food Crisis," *American Journal of Agricultural Economics* 94, no. 2 (2011): 428–34.

20. Ameen Kim and Hans van der Beek, "A Holistic Assessment of the Water-for-Agriculture Dilemma in the Kingdom of Saudi Arabia," *CIRS Occasional Paper* no. 19 (Doha: Center for International and Regional Studies, Georgetown University in Qatar), 4.

21. Mahdi Motagh et al., "Land Subsidence in Iran Caused by Widespread Water Reservoir Overexploitation," *Geophysical Research Letters* 35, no. 16 (2008).

22. F. El Youti, et al., "Salinization Processes in the Unconfined Aquifer of Bou-Areg (NE Morocco): A Geostatistical, Geochemical, and Tomographic Study," *Applied Geochemistry* 24, no. 1 (2009): 16–31.

23. A. R. Kacimov, et al., "Control of Sea-Water Intrusion by Salt-Water Pumping: Coast of Oman," *Hydrogeology Journal* 17, no. 3 (2009): 541–558.

24. Boulos Abou Zakhem and Rania Hafez, "Environmental Isotope Study of Seawater Intrusion in the Coastal Aquifer (Syria)," Environmental Geology 51, no. 8 (2007): 1329–39.

25. Robert D. Hayton, "The Law of International Aquifers," *Natural Resources Journal* 22, no. 1 (1982): 71–93; Albert E. Utton, "The Development of International Groundwater Law," *Natural Resources Journal* 22, no. 1 (1982): 95.

26. Giordano et al., 2013; Gabriel Eckstein, *The International Law of Transboundary Groundwater Resources*. Mark Giordano and Tushaar Shah, "From IWRM Back to Integrated Water Resources Management,"

International Journal of Water Resources Development 30, no. 3 (2014): 364–376; Gabriel Eckstein, *The International Law of Transboundary Groundwater Resources* (London: Routledge, 2017).

27. "Inventory of Shared Water Resources in Western Asia," United Nations Economic and Social Commission for Western Asia, Bundesanstalt für Geowissenschaften und Rohstoffe, 2013, www.unescwa.org/sites/www.unescwa.org/files/publications/files/e_escwa_sdpd_13_inventory_e.pdf.

28. Ibid.

29. Yoshihide Wada and Lena Heinrich, "Assessment of Transboundary Aquifers of the World-Vulnerability Arising from Human Water Use," *Environmental Research Letters* 8, no. 2 (2013).

30. "Inventory of Shared Water Resources in Western Asia."

31. Eran Feitelson and Marwan Haddad, eds. *Management of Shared Groundwater Resources: The Israeli-Palestinian Case with an International Perspective*, vol. 18 (Berlin: Springer Science & Business Media, 2012). Georges F. Comair et al., "Water Resources Management in the Jordan River Basin," *Water and Environment Journal* 27, no. 4 (2013): 495–504.

32. Clifford I. Voss and Safaa M. Soliman, "The Transboundary Non-renewable Nubian Aquifer System of Chad, Egypt, Libya and Sudan: Classical Groundwater Questions and Parsimonious Hydrogeologic Analysis and Modeling," *Hydrogeology Journal* 22, no. 2 (2014): 441–68.

33. "Inventory of Shared Water Resources in Western Asia."

34. Ibid.

34. Ibid.

36. Ahmed Mohamed and Karem Abdelmohsen, "Quantifying Modern Recharge and Depletion Rates of the Nubian Aquifer in Egypt," *Surveys in Geophysics* (2018): 1–23.

37. Stone, Richard, "Can Iran and Afghanistan cooperate to bring an oasis back from the dead,?" *Science, February 21, 2018* doi:10.1126/science.aat3862

38. Kibaroglu, Aysegul, and Waltina Scheumann. "Euphrates-Tigris rivers system: Political rapprochement and transboundary water cooper-

ation." *Turkey's water policy*. Springer, Berlin, Heidelberg, 2011. 277–299.

39. Katalyn A. Voss et al., "Groundwater Depletion in the Middle East from GRACE with Implications for Transboundary Water Management in the Tigris-Euphrates-Western Iran Region," *Water Resources Research* 49, no. 2 (2013): 904–14.

40. Ibid.

41. Gholamreza Joodaki, John Wahr, and Sean Swenson, "Estimating the Human Contribution to Groundwater Depletion in the Middle East, from GRACE Data, Land Surface Models, and Well Observations," *Water Resources Research* 50, no. 3 (2014): 2679–92.

42. Nengfang Chao et al., "Retrieving Groundwater Depletion and Drought in the Tigris-Euphrates Basin Between 2003 and 2015," *Groundwater* 56, no. 5: (2017): 770–82.

43. Colin P. Kelley et al., "Climate Change in the Fertile Crescent and Implications of the Recent Syrian Drought," in *Proceedings of the National Academy of Sciences* 112, no. 11 (2015), 3241–3246, doi:10.1073/pnas.1421533112.

44. William Blomquist and Helen M. Ingram, "Boundaries Seen and Unseen: Resolving Transboundary Groundwater Problems," *Water International* 28, no. 2 (2003): 162–9.; Gabriel E. Eckstein, "Protecting a Hidden Treasure: the UN International Law Commission and the International Law of Transboundary Ground Water Resources," *Sustainable Development Law & Policy* 5, no. 1 (2005): 5; Manuel Ramón Llamas and Pedro Martínez-Santos, "Intensive Groundwater Use: Silent Revolution and Potential Source of Social Conflicts," *Journal of Water Resources Planning and Management* 131, no. 5 (2005); Donal Daly, "Groundwater—The 'Hidden Resource,'" in *Biology and Environment: Proceedings of the Royal Irish Academy* 109, no. 3 (2009): 221–36; Shammy Shaminder Puri and Wilhelm Struckmeier, "Aquifer Resources in a Transboundary Context: A Hidden Resource?—Enabling the Practitioner to 'See it and Bank it' for Good Use," in *Transboundary Water Management*, ed. Anton Earle (London: Routledge, 2010), 73–90.

45. Moore and Fisher, "Challenges and Opportunities in GRACE-Based Groundwater Storage."
46. Voss et al., "Groundwater Depletion in the Middle East," 904–14.
47. Joodaki, Wahr, and Swenson, "Estimating the Human Contribution to Groundwater Depletion in the Middle East," 2679–92.
48. Suyog Chaudhari, *Modeling and Remote Sensing of Water Storage Change in Lake Urmia Basin, Iran* (PhD diss., Michigan State University, 2017); Othman Abdurrahman Fallatah et al., "Quantifying Temporal Variations in Water Resources of a Vulnerable Middle Eastern Transboundary Aquifer System," *Hydrological Processes* 31, no. 23 (2017): 4081–91.; E. Forootan et al., "Large-scale Total Water Storage and Water Flux Changes over the Arid And Semiarid Parts of the Middle East from GRACE and Reanalysis Products," *Surveys in Geophysics* 38, no. 3 (2017): 591–615; Jacques Hinderer et al., "Ground-Satellite Comparisons of Time Variable Gravity: Results, Issues and On-Going Projects for the Null Test in Arid Regions," in *International Symposium on Earth and Environmental Sciences for Future Generations*, eds. Jeffrey T. Freymueller and Laura Sánchez (Berlin: Springer, 2015); M. Khaki et al., "Determining Water Storage Depletion within Iran," 1–18; Jan Kostelecky, Jaroslav Klokocnik, and Ales Bezdek, "Variations of Geoid Undulations from Satellite Data of GRACE for Israel and Surrounding Countries," in *EGU General Assembly Conference Abstracts* 19 (2017): 5576; Khalil Lezzaik, Adam Milewski, and Jeffrey Mullen, "The Groundwater Risk Index: Development and Application in the Middle East and North Africa Region," *Science of The Total Environment* 628 (2018): 1149–64; Ahmed Mohamed et al., "Aquifer Recharge, Depletion, and Connectivity: Inferences from GRACE, Land Surface Models, and Geochemical and Geophysical Data," *GSA Bulletin* 129, nos. 5–6 (2017): 534–46.; Faramarz Nilfouroushan, Mohammad Bagherbandi, and Nureldin Gido, "Ground Subsidence and Groundwater Depletion in Iran: Integrated Approach using InSAR and Satellite Gravimetry," in *Proceedings of the Fringe* (2017); Mohammad Shamsudduha et al., "Recent Changes in Terrestrial Water Storage in the Upper Nile Basin: An Evaluation of Commonly Used Gridded GRACE Products," *Hydrology and Earth System Sciences* 21, no. 9

(2017): 4533–49; K. H. Zahran, "Estimation of Lake Nasser Water Storage Using Satellite Altimeter and Gravity Data," 79th EAGE Conference and Exhibition, 2017; Ahmed and Abdelmohsen, "Quantifying Modern Recharge and Depletion Rates;" Youssed Wehbe et al., "Consistency of Precipitation Products over the Arabian Peninsula and Interactions with Soil Moisture and Water Storage," *Hydrological Sciences Journal* 63, no. 3 (2018): 408–25.

49. Moore and Fisher, "Challenges and Opportunities in GRACE-Based Groundwater Storage."

50. E.g. in the MENA see Taha Taher et al., "Local Groundwater Governance in Yemen: Building on Traditions and Enabling Communities to Craft New Rules," *Hydrogeology Journal* 20, no. 6 (2012): 1177–88, on Yemen before the current conflict.

51. Yacov Tsur and Theodore Graham-Tomasi, "The Buffer Value of Groundwater with Stochastic Surface Water Supplies," *Journal of Environmental Economics and Management* 21, no. 3 (1991): 201–24.

52. Joodaki, Wahr, and Swenson, "Estimating the Human Contribution to Groundwater Depletion in the Middle East," 2679–92.

53. Brian Wright and Carlo Cafiero, "Grain Reserves and Food Security in the Middle East and North Africa," *Food Security* 3, no. 1 (2011), 61–76.

54. Zahra Babar and Suzi Mirgani, eds. *Food Security in the Middle East* (New York: Oxford University Press/Hurst, 2014).

55. Aaron T. Wolf, Shira B. Yoffe, and Mark Giordano, "International Waters: Identifying Basins at Risk," *Water Policy* 5, no. 1 (2003): 29–60.

56. Bart Hilhorst, "Water Management in the Nile Basin: A Fragmented but Effective Cooperative Regime," *CIRS Occasional Paper* no. 17 (Doha: Center for International and Regional Studies, Georgetown University in Qatar, 2016).

57. "Inventory of Shared Water Resources in Western Asia."

58. Elena Lopez-Gunn and W. Todd Jarvis, "Groundwater Governance and the Law of the Hidden Sea," *Water Policy* 11, no. 6 (2009): 742–62.

59. E.g. Marc F. Müller et al., "How Jordan and Saudi Arabia are avoiding a Tragedy of the Commons over Shared Groundwater," *Water Resources Research* 53, no. 7 (2017): 5451–68.

6. COMMUNITY-BASED WATER PRACTICES IN YEMEN

1. I thank the participants at the workshops in Doha, held by the Center for International and Regional Studies (CIRS) at Georgetown University in Qatar, for their useful comments and, in particular, for helping me to take a broader perspective on the issues of water conflicts in the region. I retain responsibility for both interpretation and any errors remaining in the text.

2. No data have been provided on this at the national level since the early years of this decade.

3. Taha Taher, Bryan Bruns, Omar Bamaga, Adel al Weshali, Frank van Steenbergen 'Local Groundwater governance in Yemen: building on traditions and enabling communities to craft new rules', in *Hydrogeology Journal*, 2012, 20, p. 1177; Qahtan Yehya al Asbahi, 'Water Resources Information in Yemen', in *IWG-Env International Work Session on Water Statistics, Vienna*, June 20–22 2005, p. 1.

4. Christopher Ward, *The Water Crisis in Yemen* book launch at St. Antony's College, Oxford, June 4, 2015.

5. I have addressed these aspects in greater detail in Hamid Pouran and Hassan Hakimian, eds., *Environmental Challenges in the MENA Region: The Long Road from Conflict to Cooperation* (Chicago: Gingko, 2018; forthcoming); and "Climate Change and Security: Major Challenges for Yemen's Future" in *Climate Hazard Crises in Asian Societies and Environments*, ed. Troy Sternberg (Abingdon: Routledge, 2017), 103–19.

6. Christopher Ward, *The Water Crisis in Yemen: Managing Extreme Water Scarcity in the Middle East* (London: IB Tauris, 2015), 309.

7. For a discussion of the evolution of state policies in water management, see Helen Lackner, "Water Scarcity: Why Doesn't it Get the Attention it Deserves?" in *Why Yemen Matters: A Society in Transition*, ed. Helen Lackner (London: Saqi, 2014), 161–182.

8. Republic of Yemen, Law 33, 2002.

9. "National Water Sector Strategy and Investment Program (NWSSIP)," Republic of Yemen, Ministry of Water and Environment (December 2004), 15, http://extwprlegs1.fao.org/docs/pdf/yem147103.pdf

10. Ward is the author of the main externally financed documents on water

management in Yemen between the early 1990s and the current crisis. He was a World Bank staff member for much of the period.

11. Ward, *The Water Crisis in Yemen*, 363 (italics removed).

12. Gerhard Lichtenthaeler, "Customary Conflict Resolution in Times of Extreme Water Stress: A Case Study of a Document from the Northern Highlands of Yemen," in *Why Yemen Matters*, ed. Helen Lackner, 183–96; Chris D. Handley, *Water Stress: Some Symptoms and Causes: A Case Study of Ta'iz, Yemen* (Aldershot: Ashgate, 2001). Handley focuses on the case of Ta'iz, Yemen's most extreme example of the difficulties involved in rural-urban transfers.

13. "National Water Sector Strategy and Investment Program," 20.

14. *Sana'a Declaration on Yemeni Partnership for Water Management* (Recommendations of the National Conference on Water Resources Management and Development, Sana'a, January 15–17, 2011), in *Management and Development of Water Resources in Yemen*, eds. Christopher Ward, Naif Abu-Lohom, and Suhair Atef (Sana'a: Sheba Center for Strategic Studies, 2011), 240–4.

15. Christopher Ward et al., "Yemen's Water Sector Reform Program—A Poverty and Social Impact Analysis (PSIA)," Republic of Yemen, Ministry of Water and Environment, Ministry of Agriculture and Irrigation (October 2007), ix, http://siteresources.worldbank.org/INTSOCIALDEV/Resources/Yemen-Water-FINAL-English.pdf.

16. Ibid.

17. Ibid.

18. Qahtan Yehya al Asbahi, 'Water Resources Information in Yemen', pp 42–58

19. A critique of development policies can also be found in Martha Mundy, Amin al-Hakimi, and Frédéric Pelat, "Neither Security nor Sovereignty: The Political Economy of Food in Yemen," in *Food Security in the Middle East*, eds. Zahra Babar and Suzi Mirgani (Oxford: Oxford University Press, 2014), 135–57.

20. In the Yemeni context, farms of more than 10 hectares qualify for the term "large," and in these areas some farms were close to 100 hectares. The only agricultural census undertaken has a single category of 5 hectares and more which includes only 7 percent of all landholders, while

58 percent have less than 1/2 hectare. Moreover, these include the very marginal, mostly pasture lands of the desert borders, where holdings of more than 5 hectares are by no means indicators of wealth. Ministry of Agriculture and Irrigation, Agricultural Census (Sana'a, 2003).

21. Local experts have argued that "traditional" soil spate structures are both more sustainable and financially viable than the modern "cement" structures introduced by the different projects.

22. Ward, *Water Crisis*, 317.

23. Laura Bonzanigo and Cecilia Borgia, "Tracing Evolutions of Water Control in Wadi Siham, Yemen," (MSc thesis, Wageningen University, 2009), particularly 49, 54, 63.

24. The Imamate period ended in 1962 with the republican revolution in Sana'a.

25. Water shaykhs are local senior individuals, mostly with long experience of water management, whose authority is recognised by farmers and who allocate the distribution of water on separate spate sites. Village *aqils* are state appointed community level authorities.

26. Bonzanigo and Borgia, "Tracing Evolutions of Water Control in Wadi Siham," 60.

27. Ward et al., *Yemen's Water Sector Reform Program*, 28.

28. By "democratic" here we mean simply "one person, one vote."

29. A point worthy of note: the immediate impact of increased diesel prices this century has initially been demand for electric pumps, followed—when the electricity crises expanded—by demand for solar operated pumps.

30. It may be worthy of note that these are areas where jihadis are currently particularly active.

31. "Groundwater and Soil Conservation Project: Additional Financing," The World Bank, *PID report* 43664, July 1, 2008, http://documents. worldbank.org/curated/en/112711468181773323/PID0Appraisal0stage 0FINAL0312512008.doc.

32. A landrace is a domesticated, locally adapted, traditional variety of a species of plant that has developed over time through adaptation to its natural and cultural environment of agriculture and pastoralism, and due to isolation from other populations of the species.

33. See "Independent Evaluation Group," The World Bank, *Report* ICTT14793, August, 2015.

34. See "Towards a Water Strategy: An Agenda for Action," The World Bank, *Report* 15718, August, 1997, annex 11; Christopher Ward and Nasser Al-Aulaqi, "Yemen: Issues in Decentralized Water Management, a Wadi/MENA Research Study" (IDRC/IFAD, 2008), chapter 4; among other documents.

35. Prior to 2001, the institution was known as General Authority for Rural Electricity and Water Supply (GAREWS).

36. "National Water Sector Strategy and Investment Program," ix.

37. Ibid.

38. Ward et al., *Yemen's Water Sector Reform Program*, 45.

39. Ibid, 46.

40. Ibid.

41. Ahmed Alderwish, *Study of Inventory for Existing Rural Water Supply Projects and Sanitation* (Ministry of Water and Environment, General Authority of Rural Water Supply Projects, Final Report, February, 2013). The Arabic and English versions provide slightly different information and their organization is also different, but overall they are sufficiently similar. Quotes here are based on the English version.

42. Alderwish, *Study of Inventory*, 21.

43. See Martine Valo, *Sécheresse, surexploitation: le monde a soif*, [Drought, overexploitation: the world is thirsty] *Le Monde*, 19 Février, 2018, www.lemonde.fr/planete/article/2018/02/17/secheresse-surexploitation-le-monde-a-soif_5258325_3244.html.

44. Given that Ta'iz is one of the most active military fronts in the current war, and has been largely destroyed, it is important to note that all statements here concerning Ta'iz refer to the prewar situation. For more details on this crisis, see Helen Lackner, *Yemen in Crisis: Autocracy, Neo-Liberalism and the Disintegration of a State* (London: Saqi, 2017), 221–3.

7. WEAPONIZING WATER IN THE MIDDLE EAST: "LESSONS LEARNED" FROM IS

1. See for instance Sarah Shapiro and Gabrielle Hobson, "Weaponization

of Water," Story Maps, 2017, http://waterandconflict.web.unc.edu/weaponization-of-water.

2. Tobias von Lossow, "Wasser als Waffe: Der IS an Euphrat und Tigris. Die Systematische Instrumentalisierung von Wasser birgt Zielkonflikte für den IS," *SWP-Aktuell* 94 (2015).

3. Von Lossow, "Wasser als Waffe: Der IS an Euphrat und Tigris"; Tobias von Lossow, "Der Kampf um die Dämme: Die Kontrolle des Wassers in Syrien und im Irak," *Zeitschrift Für Friedens-und Konfliktforschung (ZeFKo)* 5, no. 1 (2016a): 96–103; Tobias von Lossow, "The Rebirth of Water as a Weapon: IS in Syria and Iraq," *The International Spectator* 51, no. 3 (2016): 82–99; Marcus D. King, "The Weaponization of Water in Syria and Iraq," *The Washington Quarterly* 38, no. 4 (2016): 153–69; Ibrahim Mazlum, "ISIS as an Actor Controlling Water Resources in Syria and Iraq," in *Violent Non-state Actors and the Syrian Civil War— The ISIS and YPG Cases*, eds. Özden Zeynep Oktav and Emel Parlar DalAli Murat Kurşun (Springer, 2018), 109–25.

4. See for example ICRC, "Urban Services during Protracted Armed Conflict: A Call for a Better Approach to Assisting Affected People," ICRC Geneva, 2015; Jeannie Sowers, Erika Weinthal, and Neda Zawahri, "Targeting Environmental Infrastructures, International Law, and Civilians in the New Middle Eastern Wars," *Security Dialogue* 48, no. 5 (2017): 410–30.

5. See for example John Herrman, "Everything Can be 'Weaponized,' What Should we Fear?" *The New York Times Magazine*, March 14, 2017, www.nytimes.com/2017/03/14/magazine/if-everything-can-be-weaponized-what-should-we-fear.html; von Lossow, "The Rebirth of Water as a Weapon"; von Lossow, "Wasser als Waffe: Der IS an Euphrat und Tigris."

6. See in this context also Jan Selby, "The Geopolitics of Water in the Middle East: Fantasies and Realities," *Third World Quaterly* 26, no. 2 (2005): 329–49; Muhammad M. Rahaman, "Water wars in the 21st Century: Speculation or Reality?" *International Journal of Sustainable Society* 4, no. 1/2 (2012): 3–10; Peter H. Gleick, "Water and Conflict: Fresh Water Resources and International Security," *International Security* 8, no. 1 (1993): 97–112; Peter H. Gleick, "Water and Terrorism," *Water*

Policy 8, no. 6 (2006): 481–503; Peter H. Gleick, "Water, Drought, Climate Change, and Conflict in Syria," *Weather, Climate and Society* 6, no. 3 (2014): 331–40.

7. Von Lossow, "The Rebirth of Water as a Weapon."

8. Von Lossow, "Wasser als Waffe: Der IS an Euphrat und Tigris."

9. Rebecca Collard, "Iraq's Battleground Dams are Key to Saving the Country from ISIS," *Time*, September 8, 2014, http://time.com/3303403/strikes-against-isis-in-iraq-dams; von Lossow, "Der Kampf um die Dämme," 96–7.

10. Alex Milner, "Mosul Dam: Why the Battle for Water Matters in Iraq," *BBC*, August 18, 2014, www.bbc.com/news/world-middle-east-28772478; Collard, "Iraq's Battleground Dams."

11. Ellen Francis, "U.S.-Backed Syria Militias Say Tabqa, Dam Captured from Islamic State," *Reuters*, May 10, 2017, www.reuters.com/article/us-mideast-crisis-syria-tabqa-idUSKBN1862E4; "U.S.-backed Syrian Forces Seize Dam West of Raqqa from Islamic State: SDF," *Reuters*, June 4, 2017, www.reuters.com/article/us-mideast-crisis-syria-raqqa-idUSKBN18V0EX.

12. Von Lossow, "The Rebirth of Water as a Weapon," 87.

13. Erin Cunningham, "For Islamic State, Water is a Weapon," *The Washington Post*, October 8, 2014; for more details see also von Lossow, "The Rebirth of Water as a Weapon," 85.

14. Nadia Massih, "ISIS Gains Highlight 'Aggressive' Use of Water as Weapon of War," *The Daily Star Lebanon*, July 21, 2014, www.daily-star.com.lb/News/Middle-East/2014/Jul-21/264554-isis-gains-highlight-aggressive-use-of-water-as-weapon-of-war.ashx; for more detail on the motives, see von Lossow, "The Rebirth of Water as a Weapon," 85.

15. The typology outlined in this paragraph is a brief excerpt according to von Lossow, "The Rebirth of Water as a Weapon," 85; von Lossow, "Wasser als Waffe: Der IS an Euphrat und Tigris."

16. von Lossow, "Wasser als Waffe: Der IS an Euphrat und Tigris."

17. von Lossow, "Der Kampf um die Dämme."

18. "Environmental Issues in Areas Retaken From ISIL: Mosul, Iraq," UN Environment, Rapid Scoping Mission, July–August 2017, http://wed-

ocs.unep.org/bitstream/handle/20.500.11822/22434/environmental_issues_Isil_Iraq.pdf.

19. "ISIS Captures Iraqi Dam, Floods Areas," *Al-Akhbar*, April 11, 2014, https://english.al-akhbar.com/node/19385; Mohanad H. Ali, "ISIS' Path of Destruction Drains Iraq and Syria's Water Supplies," *Al Arabiya*, June 21, 2014, http://english.alarabiya.net/en/perspective/analysis/2014/06/21/ISIS-path-of-destruction-drains-Iraq-and-Syria-s-water-supplies.html#.

20. Debora MacKenzie, "Extremists in Iraq Now Control the Country's Rivers," *New Scientist*, June 12, 2014, www.newscientist.com/article/dn25722-extremists-in-iraq-now-control-the-countrys-rivers; Cameron Harrington and Schuyler Null, "What Can Iraq's Fight over the Mosul Dam Tell Us about Water Security?" NewSecurityBeat Wilson Center, August 20, 2014, www.newsecuritybeat.org/2014/08/iraqs-fight-mosul-dam-water-security.

21. Birgit Svensson, "Flood Disaster in Iraq: Water as an Instrument of War," *Qantara.de*, June 13, 2014, https://en.qantara.de/content/flood-disaster-in-iraq-water-as-an-instrument-of-war.

22. Von Lossow, "The Rebirth of Water as a Weapon."

23. See The Islamic State, "The Flood," *Dabiq* 2, 2014, https://clarion-project.org/docs/isis-isil-islamic-state-magazine-Issue-2-the-flood.pdf

24. As for example at Tabqa dam or at Fallujah dam.

25. See for example; Nafeez Ahmed, "War crime: Nation Deliberately Destroyed Libya's Water Infrastructure," *Ecologist*, May 14, 2015, www.theecologist.org/News/news_analysis/2869234/war_crime_nato_deliberately_ destroyed_libyas_water_infrastructure.html; or Amnesty International "Lebanon: Deliberate Destruction or 'Collateral Damage'? Israeli Attacks on Civilian Infrastructure," August 22, 2006, www.amnesty.org/en/documents/MDE18/007/2006/en.

26. von Lossow, "The Rebirth of Water as a Weapon."

27. See for example Hans Petter Wollebæk Toset, Nils Petter Gleditsch, and Håvard Hegre, "Shared Rivers and Interstate Conflict," *Political Geography* 19, no. 8 (2000): 971–96; Selby, "The Geopolitics of Water in the Middle East," 329–49; Gleick, "Water and Terrorism," 481–503; Tobias von Lossow, "The Multiple Crisis: Perspectives on Water

Scarcity in the Euphrates and Tigris Basin," *Orient* 58, no. 1 (2017): 45–53.

28. Aysegul Kibaroglu, "Facing Water Challenges in the Middle East," Middle East Institute *Policy Paper* 8 (September 2016).

29. Francesca De Châtel, "The Role of Drought and Climate Change in the Syrian Uprising: Untangling the Triggers of the Revolution," *Middle Eastern Studies* 50, no. 4 (2014): 521–35; Gleick, "Water, Drought, Climate Change"; Harrington and Null, "What Can Iraq's Fight over the Mosul Dam Tell Us."

30. De Châtel, "The Role of Drought and Climate Change," 521–35.

31. Cunningham, "For Islamic State, Water is a Weapon."

32. Ali, "ISIS' Path of Destruction"; von Lossow, "The Rebirth of Water as a Weapon."

33. Gleick, "Water and Conflict."

34. Von Lossow, "The Rebirth of Water as a Weapon."

35. Danya Chudacoff, "'Water War' Threatens Syria Lifeline," *Al Jazeera*, July 7, 2014, www.aljazeera.com/news/middleeast/2014/07/water-war-syria-euphrates-2014757640320663.html.

36. Von Lossow, "The Rebirth of Water as a Weapon."

37. For an in-depth analysis see Peter Schwartzstein, "Climate Change and Water Woes Drove ISIS Recruiting in Iraq," *National Geographic*, November 14, 2017, https://news.nationalgeographic.com/2017/11/climate-change-drought-drove-isis-terrorist-recruiting-iraq.

38. Von Lossow, "The Rebirth of Water as a Weapon."

39. Von Lossow, "Wasser als Waffe: Der IS an Euphrat und Tigris."

40. "Environmental Issues in Areas Retaken From ISIL," UN Environment.

41. In case of IS the lines between classic state actors, non-state actors and terrorist groups are rather blurred; this phenomenon also applies to most conflict parties in Syria and Iraq.

42. Thalif Deen, "U.N. Decries Water as Weapon of War in Military Conflicts," *Inter Press Service*, May 19, 2014, www.ipsnews.net/2014/05/u-n-decries-water-as-weapon-of-war-in-military-conflicts; Laura Puts, "Water on the International Security Agenda—Does Water Scarcity Encourage the Use of Water as Weapon or Target of War?" *Humanitäres Völkerrecht* 27, no. 1 (2014): 36–44.

43. "Islamic State Militants use Water as Weapon in Western Iraq," *Reuters*, June 3, 2015, www.reuters.com/article/us-mideast-crisis-iraq-water-idUSKBN0OJ1TN20150603.

44. Hamza Mustafa, "Haditha Dam under Threat from ISIS, Warns Official," *Asharq Al-Awsat*, August 19, 2014, https://eng-archive.aawsat.com/hamzamustafa/news-middle-east/haditha-dam-under-threat-from-isis-warns-official.

45. Svensson, "Flood Disaster in Iraq"; MacKenzie, "Extremists in Iraq Now Control the Country's Rivers."

46. Hamza Mustafa, "Iraqi Government Forces say ISIS Water Supply Sabotage Foiled," *Asharq Al-Awsat*, April 9, 2014, https://eng-archive.aawsat.com/hamzamustafa/news-middle-east/iraqi-government-forces-say-isis-water-supply-sabotage-foiled; Alissa J. Rubin and Rod Nordland, "Sunni Militants Advance toward Large Iraqi Dam," *The New York Times*, June 25, 2014, www.nytimes.com/2014/06/26/world/middleeast/isis-iraq.html.

47. Tobias von Lossow, "Wenn der Damm bricht," *Zeit Online*, April 1, 2017, www.zeit.de/politik/ausland/2017–03/islamischer-staat-rakka-tabka-staudamm-euphrat.

48. Francis, "U.S.-backed Syria Militias say Tabqa Dam Captured from Islamic State."

49. Tobias von Lossow, "More than Infrastructures: Water Challenges in Iraq," Clingendael & PSI *Policy Brief*, July 2018, www.planetarysecurityinitiative.org/sites/default/files/2018–07/PSI_VonLossow_2018_More%20than%20infrastructures%20water%20challenges%20in%20Iraq.pdf.

50. In particular Geneva Protocol I, Art. 54 (2): "It is prohibited to attack, destroy, remove or render useless objects indispensable to the survival of the civilian population, such as foodstuffs, agricultural areas for the production of foodstuffs, crops, livestock, drinking water installations and supplies and irrigation works, for the specific purpose of denying them for their sustenance value to the civilian population or to the adverse Party, whatever the motive, whether in order to starve out civilians, to cause them to move away, or for any other motive."

51. Von Lossow, "The Rebirth of Water as a Weapon"; examples from

WWI by the Belgians when flooding the Yser plain or during WWII by the British related to Operation Chastise, see Guido Demerre and Johan Termote, "The Flooding of the Yser Plain," *De Grote Rede (VLIZ)* 36 (2013): 47–52; Marc A. Olinger, "Airpower and the Targeting of a Nation's Energy Infrastructure," in *Airpower and the Environment: The Ecological Implications of Modern Air Warfare,* ed. Joel Hayward (Alabama: Air University Press, 2013), 48–9.

52. Sowers, Weinthal, and Zawahiri, "Targeting Environmental Infrastructures."

53. Waltina Scheumann, "Water and Electricity—Weapons in the Syrian Conflict," *The Current Column,* June 30, 2014, www.die-gdi.de/uploads/media/German_Development_Institute_Scheumann_30.06.2014.pdf; Deen, "U.N. Decries Water as Weapon of War."

54. See for instance "Syria/Russia: Airstrikes, Siege Killing Civilians," Human Rights Watch, December 22, 2017, www.hrw.org/news/2017/12/22/syria/russia-airstrikes-siege-killing-civilians.

8. IN PURSUIT OF SECURITY AND INFLUENCE: THE UAE AND THE RED SEA

1. Alfred Thayer Mahan, *The Interest of America in Sea Power, Present and Future* (Hamburg, Germany: tredition GmbH, 2012), 54.

2. Alliances, foreign policy objectives, and leaders' idiosyncrasies are in constant change in the Middle East, including the UAE. Hence, the Emirati foreign policy objectives analyzed in this chapter, and based on visible trends in the immediate past and the present, may change if unforeseen short-term developments take place. However, the framework used to understand foreign policy change in the UAE and new tools of Emirati foreign policy remains relevant despite possible changes in these objectives, alliances, and idiosyncrasies.

3. K. J. Holsti, *Why Nations Realign: Foreign Policy Restructuring in the Postwar World* (London & Boston: Allen & Unwin, 1982), 8; Robert Gilpin, *War and Change in World Politics* (Cambridge: Cambridge University Press, 1981), 4–6.

4. Stanley Hoffmann, "What Should We Do in the World?" *Atlantic*

Monthly, October 1989, www.theatlantic.com/past/docs/politics/foreign/hoffman.htm.

5. Kjell Goldmann, *Change and Stability in Foreign Policy: The Problems and Possibilities of Détente* (Princeton: Princeton University Press, 1988).

6. David Skidmore, "Explaining State Responses to International Change: The Structural Sources of Foreign Policy Rigidity and Change," in *Foreign Policy Restructuring: How Governments Respond to Global Change*, eds. J. A. Rosati et al. (Columbia: University of South Carolina Press, 1994), 43–64.

7. Walter Carlsnaes, "The Agency-Structure Problem in Foreign Policy Analysis," *International Studies Quarterly* 36, no. 3 (1992): 245–70; J. A. Rosati, "Cycles in Foreign Policy Restructuring: The Politics of Continuity and Change in US Foreign Policy," in *Foreign Policy Restructuring: How Governments Respond to Global Change*, ed. J. A. Rosati et al. (Columbia: University of South Carolina Press, 1994), 221–61.

8. Jakob Gustavsson, "How Should We Study Foreign Policy Change?" *Cooperation and Conflict* 34, no. 1 (1999): 73–95; Charles Hermann, "Changing Course: When Governments Choose to Redirect Foreign Policy," *International Studies Quarterly* 34, no. 1 (1990): 3–21.

9. Crises are defined as sudden and dramatic changes in the environment that are threatening, urgent, and whose fate is uncertain. In his model, Gustavsson used the term "crisis," which corresponds to Hermann's use of the term "external shocks," which he defines as "large events in terms of visibility and immediate impact on the recipient. They cannot be ignored, and they can trigger major foreign policy change." See Hermann, "Changing Course," 12.

10. Hermann, "Changing Course," 5. Rosati uses a quite similar typology, suggesting four ordinal levels of change—"intensification," "refinement," "reform," and "restructuring"—to identify small, minor, moderate and major changes in the scope and goals of foreign policy. See Rosati, "Cycles in Foreign Policy Restructuring," 236.

11. Mehran Kamrava, *Qatar: Small State, Big Politics* (New York: Cornell University Press, 2013), 104.

12. Khalid Almezaini, *The UAE and Foreign Policy: Foreign Aid, Identities*

and Interests (Abingdon: Routledge, 2012), 38. Abu Musa, Lesser Tunb and Greater Tunb are three islands over which Iran and the rulers of both Sharjah and Ras Al-Khaima, and the UAE later on, have been at dispute. For more information on this dispute, refer to: Richard Schofield, "Borders and territoriality in the Gulf and the Arabian Peninsula During the Twentieth Century," in *Territorial Foundations of the Gulf States*, ed. Richard Schofield (London: University College London Press, 1994), 1–77.

13. Abdul-Monem Al-Mashat, "Politics of Constructive Engagement: The Foreign Policy of the United Arab Emirates," in *The Foreign Policies of Arab States: The Challenge of Globalization*, eds. Bahgat Korany and Ali Al-Din Hilal (Cairo: American University in Cairo Press, 2010), 465.

14. For more information on Sheikh Khalifa bin Zayed and Sheikh Muhammed bin Zayed, see Christopher Davidson, "After Shaikh Zayed: The Politics of Succession in Abu Dhabi and the UAE," *Middle East Policy* 13, no. 1 (2006): 42–60.

15. When Arab youth were asked in a 2014 survey about which country "they would most like their own country to emulate," the UAE was ranked first, see Rashed Lekhraibani, Emilie Rutledge, and Ingo Forstenlechner, "Securing a Dynamic and Open Economy: The UAE's Quest for Stability," *Middle East Policy* 22, no. 2 (Spring 2015): 121.

16. Karen Young, "The Emerging Interventionists of the GCC," *LSE Middle East Centre Paper Series* 02, December 2013, 16.

17. "United Arab Emirates," The World Bank, https://data.worldbank. org/country/united-arab-emirates?view=chart; and "Report for Selected Countries and Subjects," International Monetary Fund, www.imf.org/ external/pubs/ft/weo/2017/01/weodata/weorept.aspx?pr.x=55&pr.y=1 5&sy=2016&ey=2020&scsm=1&ssd=1&sort=country&ds=.&br=1& c=466&s=NGDPD%2CNGDPDPC%2CPPPGDP%2CPPPPC&grp =0&a=.

18. "World Development Indicators 2017," The World Bank, 2017, https:// openknowledge.worldbank.org/handle/10986/26447

19. "The Gulf's 'Little Sparta': The Ambitious United Arab Emirates," *The Economist*, April 6, 2017, www.economist.com/news/middle-east- and-africa/21720319-driven-energetic-crown-price-uae-build- ing-bases-far-beyond-its

20. Anthony H. Cordesman, Bryan Gold, and Garrett Berntsen, *The Gulf Military Balance: The Conventional and Asymmetric Dimensions* (Washington, D.C.: Center for Strategic and International Studies, 2014), 40.

21. Ola Salem, "UAE Cabinet Introduces Mandatory Military Service for Emirati Males," *The National*, January 19, 2014, www.thenational.ae/uae/government/uae-cabinet-introduces-mandatory-military-service-for-emirati-males-1.685784

22. To read more on Machiavelli's views on mercenaries and auxiliaries, please refer to: Nicolo Machiavelli, *The Prince*, trans. W. K. Marriot, ed. Anthony Uyl (Woodstock, Ontario: Devoted Publishing, 2016), 31.

23. Alissa Fromkin, "Part Two: The UAE Military against Islamism," *International Affairs Review*, February 20, 2015, www.iar-gwu.org/content/part-two-uae-military-against-islamism

24. Murhaf Jouejati, E-mail interview by authors, April 18, 2017.

25. "2016 Defense Markets Report Regional and Country Case Study," U.S. Department of Commerce, International Trade Administration, 2016, 1–2, www.trade.gov/topmarkets/pdf/Defense_Middle_East.pdf

26. Ibish, *The UAE's Evolving National Security Strategy*, 20.

27. Young, "The Emerging Interventionists of the GCC," 19.

28. "2016 Defense Markets Report Regional and Country Case Study," 2.

29. "About Abu Dhabi Ship Building," Abu Dhabi Ship Building, www.adsb.ae/the-company/about-abu-dhabi-ship-building.

30. Frank Slijper, *Under the Radar: The United Arab Emirates, Arms Transfer and Regional Conflict*, ed. Susan Clark, Report no. PAX/2017/10 (Netherlands: PAX, September 2017), www.paxforpeace.nl/media/files/pax-report-under-the-radar—arms-trade.pdf

31. Hermann, "Changing Course," 12.

32. Ingo Forstenlechner, Emilie Rutledge, and Rashed Salem Alnuaimi, "The UAE, the Arab Spring and Different Types of Dissent," *Middle East Policy* 19, no. 4 (2012): 55.

33. Nour Malas, "UAE Citizens Petition Rulers for Elected Parliament," *The Wall Street Journal*, March 9, 2011, www.wsj.com/articles/SB10001424052748704132204576190012553500944.

34. Ibid.

35. Yousef Khalifah Al-Yousef, "The United Arab Emirates at a Crossroads," *Contemporary Arab Affairs* 6, no. 4 (2013): 572.

36. Kristian Ulrichsen, *The United Arab Emirates: Power, Politics, and Policymaking* (New York & Abingdon: Routledge, 2017), 192.

37. Christopher Davidson, *After the Sheikhs: The Coming Collapse of Gulf Monarchies* (London: Hurst, 2012), 130.

38. Ian Black, "Emirati Nerves Rattled by Islamists' Rise," *The Guardian*, October 12, 2012, www.theguardian.com/world/on-the-middle-east/2012/oct/12/uae-muslimbrotherhood-egypt-arabspring.

39. Rajiv Chandrasekaran, "In the UAE, the United States Has a Quiet, Potent Ally Nicknamed 'Little Sparta,'" *The Washington Post*, November 9, 2014, www.washingtonpost.com/world/national-security/in-the-uae-the-united-states-has-a-quiet-potent-ally-nicknamed-little-sparta/2014/11/08/3fc6a50c-643a-11e4–836c-83bc4f26eb67_story.html?utm_term=.b304b585e82b.

40. "Abu Dhabi Turns Attention to Potential Ticking Time-Bomb in Northern Emirates," *Gulf States News*, August 5, 2011, https://archive.crossborderinformation.com/Article/Abu+Dhabi+turns+attention+to+potential+ticking+time-bomb+in+the+Northern+Emirates.aspx?date=20110805.

41. The security crackdown included arresting dissidents and revoking their citizenship. In the past few years, the UAE has revoked the citizenship of some 200 nationals, most of them Islamists, see Nael Shama, "Stripping Away Identity: The Dangers of a Repressive New Nationality Law in Egypt," *POMED*, December 2017, http://pomed.org/wp-content/uploads/2017/12/Shama_FINAL_171205.pdf.

42. Emma Soubrier, "Evolving Foreign and Security Policies: A Comparative Study of Qatar and the United Arab Emirates," in *The Small Gulf States: Foreign and Security Policies before and after the Arab Spring*, eds. Khalid Almezaini and Jean-Marc Rickli (London and New York: Routledge, 2017), 123.

43. Yoel Guzansky, "The Foreign-Policy Tools of Small Powers: Strategic Hedging in the Persian Gulf," *Middle East Policy* 22, no. 1 (2015): 113.

44. Quoted in Leah Sherwood, "Risk Diversification and the United Arab

Emirates' Foreign Policy," in *The Small Gulf States: Foreign and Security Policies before and after the Arab Spring*, eds. Khalid Almezaini and Jean-Marc Rickli (London and New York: Routledge, 2017), 157.

45. Caline Malek, "Anwar Gargash: Six Pillars that Support Security in the UAE," *The National*, March 31, 2014, www.thenational.ae/uae/government/anwar-gargash-six-pillars-that-support-security-in-the-uae-1.592418.

46. Kenneth Katzman, "The United Arab Emirates (UAE): Issues for U.S. Policy," *Congressional Research Service*, May 23, 2011, http://usuae-business.org/wp-content/uploads/2012/06/CRS-The_United_Arab_Emirates_UAE_Issues_for_US_-Policy.pdf

47. Chandrasekaran, "In the UAE, the United States Has a Quiet, Potent Ally"; Ulrichsen, *The United Arab Emirates*, 143.

48. Ulrichsen, *The United Arab Emirates*, 146.

49. Jean-Marc Rickli, "The Political Rationale and Implications of the United Arab Emirates," in *Political Rationale and International Consequences of the War in Libya*, eds. Dag Henriksen and Ann Karin Larssen (Oxford: Oxford University Press, 2016), 147.

50. Riham Bahi, "Iran, the GCC and the Implications of the Nuclear Deal: Rivalry versus Engagement," *The International Spectator* 52, no. 2 (2017): 97.

51. Jeffrey Goldberg, "The Obama Doctrine," *The Atlantic*, April 2016. www.theatlantic.com/magazine/archive/2016/04/the-obama-doctrine/471525

52. Abdulaziz Sager, "Whither GCC-US Relations?" *Arab News*, March 29, 2013, www.arabnews.com/news/446395. Emphasis added.

53. Robert O. Keohane, "The Big Influence of Small Allies," *Foreign Policy*, no. 2 (1971): 165.

54. Ibid., 165–6.

55. For more discussion on the political, economic, and military orders in the US power elite, refer to: C. Wright Mills, *The Power Elite* (New York: Oxford Press, 1999), 7.

56. Anoushiravan Ehteshami and Emma Murphy, *International Politics of the Red Sea* (London and New York: Routledge, 2013), 1–3.

57. Fahd Al Rasheed, "Red Sea—Artery of Global Trade," *Arab News*, February 12, 2016, www.arabnews.com/columns/news/879221

58. Ibid; "Homepage," Red Sea Gateway Terminal, www.rsgt.com

59. Lejla Villar and Mason Hamilton, "Three Important Oil Trade Chokepoints are Located around the Arabian Peninsula," Today in Energy, U.S. Energy Information Administration (EIA), August 4, 2017, www.eia.gov/todayinenergy/detail.php?id=32352

60. "World Population Prospects: The 2015 Revision," Department of Economic and Social Affairs, United Nations, 2015, https://esa.un.org/unpd/wpp/publications/files/key_findings_wpp_2015.pdf; Villar and Hamilton, "Three Important Oil Trade Chokepoints."

61. Christian Henderson, "The UAE's Nexus State: Logistics, Transport and Foreign Policy," Middle East Centre Blog, September 26, 2015, http://blogs.lse.ac.uk/mec/2015/11/26/the-uaes-nexus-state-logistics-transport-and-foreign-policy.

62. For more information about the destinations of the UAE's exports and imports, see Alexander Simoes, "United Arab Emirates," The Observatory of Economic Complexity, https://atlas.media.mit.edu/en/profile/country/are.

63. "The Gulf's 'Little Sparta.'"

64. Hussein Ibish, "The UAE's Evolving National Security Strategy," The Arab Gulf States Institute in Washington, Issue Paper no. 4, April 2017, 20, https://agsiw.org/wp-content/uploads/2017/04/UAE-Security_ONLINE.pdf.

65. Ulrichsen, The United Arab Emirates, 151.

66. Islam Hassan, "The UAE: A Small State with Regional Middle Power Aspirations," in Middle Power Politics in the Middle East, ed. Adham Saouli (New York: Oxford University Press).

67. The Islamic State of Iraq and al-Sham (ISIS) is a Salafi jihadist militant group designated as a terrorist organization by the United Nations and many countries. The group proclaimed itself a worldwide caliphate claiming religious, political and military authority over all Muslims worldwide.

68. "Seeking Tranquility around the Red Sea," Stratfor Worldview, January 3, 2017, https://worldview.stratfor.com/article/seeking-tranquility-around-red-sea; "United Arab Emirates: Shifting Foreign and Domestic Policies May Increase Risk of Attacks," Protection Vessels International,

March 23, 2015, www.pviltd.com/news-insight/news/article/united-arab-emirates-shifting-foreign-and-domestic-policies-may-increase-risk-of-attacks.html

69. "Abdullah bin Zayed: International Efforts Reduced Piracy Attacks over the Last Two Years to Zero," *Emirates News Agency*, October 30, 2014, http://wam.ae/en/details/1395271638616

70. Ola Salem, "UAE Military Intervention in Yemen was 'Inevitable,'" *The National*, March 26, 2015, www.thenational.ae/uae/uae-military-intervention-in-yemen-was-inevitable-1.82859

71. David Goldman, "Types of Weapons Used by Al-Shabaab in Kismayo, Intelligence on Battery Positions," *Strategic Intelligence Service*, July 25, 2012, https://intelligencebriefs.com/types-of-weapons-used-by-al-shabaab-in-kismayo-intelligence-on-battery-positions.

72. See Islam Hassan, "The UAE: A Small State with Regional Middle Power Aspirations."

73. In February 2019, the Djibouti government unilaterally terminated DP World's lease for the operation of the Doraleh Container Terminal (DCT). The government-controlled company Port de Djibouti SA (PDSA) took over DCT's operations. In response, DP World sued the Djibouti Government in the High Court of England & Wales to regain control of its assets. On August 31, 2019, the court issued an injunction against PDSA, ordering that the Djibouti government must not act as though its joint venture with DP World had been terminated, must not remove any DP World board members, and must not use the London-based Standard Chartered Bank to transfer funds to Djibouti. However, Djibouti broadly ignored the ruling, and it has proceeded to cooperate with China Merchants Port Holdings (CM Port) on port-related development projects. (https://www.maritime-executive.com/article/djibouti-ordered-to-pay-dp-world-530m-in-port-dispute)

74. Francis Matthew, "Expanding Naval Presence in the Red Sea," *Gulf News*, March 1, 2017, http://gulfnews.com/opinion/editorials/expanding-naval-presence-in-the-red-sea-1.1986734.

75. Tahani Karrar, "DP World Unveils Plan to Improve Jeddah Port," *Arabian Business*, October 26, 2017, www.arabianbusiness.com/industries/transport/382125-dp-world-unveils-plan-to-improve-jeddah-port

76. "History," DP World Sokhna, www.dpworldsokhna.com/History.htm

77. DP World evolved out of the merger between Dubai Ports International and Dubai Ports Authority in 2005, both state-owned entities. Through a holding company, Sheikh Mohammed bin Rashid Al Maktoum, the ruler of Dubai and the UAE's Prime Minister, had full control over DP World. In 2007, the company was listed in NASDAQ Dubai, and 20 percent of the company's shares were offered to the public. Despite this, the government of Dubai remains the majority shareholder of the company.

78. "History," DP World Sokhna.

79. "Suez Canal Economic Zone Authority and DP World Sign Agreement for Development of Economic Zone in Sokhna, Egypt," *MENA Herald*, November 7, 2017, www.menaherald.com/en/business/transport-logis-tics/suez-canal-economic-zone-authority-and-dp-world-sign-agree-ment.

80. "DP World to Develop Suez Canal Economic Zone," *Port Technology*, August 10, 2017, www.porttechnology.org/news/dp_world_to_develop_suez_canal_economic_zone.

81. "Djibouti—Doraleh," DP World, www.dpworld.com/en/what-we-do/our-locations/Middle-East-Africa/djibouti-doraleh.

82. Ibid.

83. "Berbera—Somaliland," DP World, www.dpworld.com/what-we-do/our-locations/Middle-East-Africa/berbera-somaliland

84. Ibid.; Matina Stevis and Asa Fitch, "Dubai's DP World Agrees to Manage Port in Somaliland for 30 Years," *Dow Jones*, www.dowjones.com/scoops/dubais-dp-world-agrees-to-manage-port-in-somaliland-for-30-years

85. P&O, previously known as the Peninsular and Oriental Steam Navigation Company, was a British shipping and logistics company. In 2006, Thunder FZE, a subsidiary owned by DPW, took over the company. Currently, DPW operates three of P&O branded businesses: P&O Ferries, P&O Maritime and P&O Heritage.

86. Abdi Latif Dahir, "The UAE is Expanding its Influence in the Horn of Africa by Funding Ports and Military Bases," *Quartz Africa*, April 11, 2017, https://qz.com/955585/in-somalia-and-eritrea-the-united-

arab-emirates-is-expanding-its-influence-by-building-ports-and-funding-military-bases

87. Peter Salisbury, "Sad Decline of Aden's Once-Thriving Port," *Financial Times*, March 6, 2013, www.ft.com/content/e64e90fe-8644-11e2-ad73-00144feabdc0

88. Mohammed Mukhashaf, "Saudi-Backed Yemen Forces Take Aden Port from Houthis: Residents," *Reuters*, July 15, 2015, www.reuters.com/article/us-yemen-security-aden/saudi-backed-yemen-forces-take-aden-port-from-houthis-residents-idUSKCN0PP16I20150715

89. "The Gulf's 'Little Sparta.'"

90. Ibid.

91. "Yemen Govt Forces Push toward Hodeidah Port," *Arab News*, December 10, 2017, www.arabnews.com/node/1206916/middle-east

92. Paola Tamma, "Has the UAE Colonised Yemen's Socotra Island Paradise?" *The New Arab*, May 17, 2017, www.alaraby.co.uk/english/indepth/2017/5/17/has-the-uae-colonised-yemens-socotra-island-paradise

93. "Saudi Arabia—Jeddah," DP World, www.dpworld.com/what-we-do/our-locations/Middle-East-Africa/saudi-arabia-jeddah

94. NEOM is a 10,230-square-mile transnational city and economic zone planned to be constructed in Tabuk, Saudi Arabia, close to the border region of Saudi Arabia, Jordan, and Egypt as part of the Saudi Vision 2030.

95. "Cyprus—Limassol," DP World, www.dpworld.com/what-we-do/our-locations/Middle-East-Africa/cyprus-limassol; "UAE Strengthens Military Presence in Egypt," Middle East Monitor, February 13, 2018, https://www.middleeastmonitor.com/20180213-uae-strengthens-military-presence-in-egypt/

9. CONCLUSION: CHANGING REGIONAL OUTLOOK AND PATHWAYS TO PEACE

1. Ravnborg, H. M.; Bustamante, R.; Cissé, A.; Cold-Ravnkilde, S.M.; Cossio, V.; Djiré, M.; Funder, M.; Gómez, L.I.; Paz, T.; Le, P.; Mweemba, C.; Nyambe, I.; Huong, P.; Rivas, R.; Yen, N.T.B.; Skielboe,

T. (2012). "The challenges of local water governance: The extent, nature and intensity of local water-related conflict and cooperation". Water Policy (2011) 14 (2): 336–357. 1 April 2012. https://doi.org/10.2166/wp. 2011.097, and PBL (2018): *Linking water security threats to conflict*, The Hague, August.

2. See, e.g., P.H. Gleick, "Water and Conflict: Fresh Water Resources and International Security, International Security, 18(1) (1993)

INDEX

INDEX

INDEX

INDEX

INDEX

INDEX

INDEX

INDEX

INDEX

INDEX

INDEX

INDEX

INDEX